THE PARADOXES OF NATIONALISM

SUNY series in National Identities

Thomas M. Wilson, editor

THE PARADOXES OF NATIONALISM

The French Revolution and Its Meaning for Contemporary Nation Building

Chimène I. Keitner

State University of New York Press

Published by
State University of New York Press, Albany

Printed in the United States of America

For information, address State University of New York Press,
194 Washington Avenue, Suite 305, Albany, NY 12210-2384

Production by Judith Block
Marketing by Michael Campochiaro

Library of Congress Cataloging-in-Publication Data

Keitner, Chimène I.
The paradoxes of nationalism : the French Revolution and its meaning for contemporary nation building / Chimène I. Keitner.
p. cm. — (SUNY series in national identities)
Includes bibliographical references and index.
ISBN 978-0-7914-6957-6 (hardcover : alk. paper)
ISBN 978-0-7914-6958-3 (pbk. : alk. paper)
1. France—History—Revolution, 1789–1799—Influence.
2. Nationalism—France—History. 3. Nation-building. I. Title. II. Series.

DC148.K45 2007
320.1—dc22

2006012822

10 9 8 7 6 5 4 3 2 1

For Idan

"*La Nation consentie, voulue par elle-même*" (The Nation consented to, self-willed) *was France's contribution to history.*

—Eric Hobsbawm, quoting
historian Ernest Lavisse

I love all men; I particularly love all free men; but I love the free men of France better than all other men in the universe.

—François Robert to the National
Convention, April 26, 1793

Contents

Acknowledgments

I am grateful to numerous colleagues and friends who offered input and support at various stages of this project, especially Andrew Hurrell, Adam Roberts, James Mayall, Jennifer M. Welsh, Elena Jurado, Jan-Werner Müller, Linda B. Miller, Jenia Iontcheva Turner, and the two anonymous reviewers for State University of New York Press. I also benefited greatly from conversations with Erica Benner, Mark Philp, and Karma Nabulsi, and from presenting my work at meetings of the International Studies Association, the British International Studies Association, the Association for the Study of Ethnicity and Nationalism, and the Yale Law School Human Rights Workshop. I am grateful to the Rhodes Trust for funding my research in Oxford and Paris. My sincere thanks to Michael Rinella, Judith Block, Michael Campochiaro, and the editorial staff at State University of New York Press. Finally, my love and thanks to my family for their unfailing support.

Prologue

Paris, June 1789

A monarchy on the brink of bankruptcy. Short on options, Louis XVI convokes the Estates-General, a meeting of delegates from all over France, for the first time since 1614. As in 1614, delegates are summoned from France's three "estates": the nobility, the clergy, and the so-called Third Estate, which encompasses almost everyone else. Perhaps not surprisingly, many of the Third Estate's delegates are lawyers.

The deputies from the Third Estate are not as accommodating as they apparently had been in 1614. They want a voice in the proceedings commensurate with the size of their constituent base, which vastly outnumbers the nobility and the clergy combined. On June 17, after long debates, they adopt a resolution naming themselves the National Assembly and establishing the principle of national consent as a prerequisite for government action.[1]

Not all of the deputies' concerns are so lofty. One delegate, Doctor Joseph Ignace Guillotin, draws the Assembly's attention to a more basic issue, ventilation: "The heavy and pestilential air emanating from the body of more than three thousand individuals packed into the room will inevitably produce a mortal effect on all the deputies!"[2] (Though perhaps not as mortal as the invention later named for the doctor.) Dr. Guillotin is put in charge of finding and configuring a proper meeting space. Even the most basic nation-building tasks require logistical support.

In their resolution of June 17, the deputies from the Third Estate recognized and entrenched the political power of nationhood—a theoretical gesture with important practical implications. French—and, ultimately, world—politics would never be quite the same again.

The struggle for self-government has animated, and continues to animate, some of history's most intractable conflicts. This book focuses on one "self"—the nation—that has emerged and endured as a platform for political and territorial claims. The principle of national self-determination has often been honored in the breach, for example, as a basis for redrawing boundaries in the wake of the two world wars. Even so, the idea that human beings with shared understandings and traditions can be divided into territorial groupings called nations, and that nations are most strongly entitled and best equipped to govern their own states, continues to provide one of the most powerful arguments for reconfiguring political and territorial boundaries, from Gaza and the West Bank, to (now independent) East Timor, to the Basque Country, to Kashmir, to Kurdistan. Each nation's quest for self-determination is steeped in complexities linked to its own unique historical, religious, cultural, and linguistic context, but all seek to derive legitimacy from—and to implement—a basic proposition: to each nation, its own state.

National self-determination, though notoriously problematic, represents a core, constitutive principle of international politics. It holds that every "nation," a unified community of people with a desire and capacity for self-governance, is entitled to exclusive control of its own territorial state.[3] Its corollary is the nation-state principle: the idea that nations and states are or should be congruent. The nation-state principle is centrally, if ambiguously, embedded in the international legal order.[4] It gives rise to powerful, informal sets of understandings that can both legitimize and delegitimize states, depending on how the component groups of a state's population define their national identity. A state with a unified national population can seek to derive strength from such unity, for example, in times of war. Thus, it is often in wartime that leaders deploy the most nationalistic and even "jingoistic" political ideology and rhetoric. Similarly, the lack of a unified national identity can be exploited by groups seeking to overturn the political and territorial status quo, as illustrated by various "separatist" movements around the globe.

The continued resonance of national self-determination as a political principle and rallying point for political and territorial claims has been and remains evident in separatist or "sovereigntist" movements, which seek to carve out control of part of an existing state (as in Québec or Kosovo). It can also manifest itself in "irredentist" movements, which seek to unify a national population that is claimed to exist within multiple states (such as German and Italian unification movements in the nineteenth and twentieth centuries). Some movements are difficult to classify; for example, the creation of a Kurdish state would have both separatist and irredentist features. They also confront the inevitable challenge of conflicting national definitions: Is being Québecois a national identity, or is it a provincial identity within the national identity of Canada? These questions are complex and often defy objective or straightforward answers.

This book is one contribution to the cumulative endeavor of deepening our understanding of national self-determination and its implications as a basis for international political order. While the substance of the first four chapters is largely historical, this is not a work of history. I spend more time examining French Revolutionary history than would most international relations theorists, and less time than would (and have) historians of the period. This is because I use the exegesis of key Revolutionary texts and events to ground the development of a theoretical framework for identifying and examining some of the persistent problems of nationalism and "nation-building" in the modern world. The purpose of the work is thus both theoretical and pragmatic: to interpret and distill past phenomena in an effort to better identify, and hopefully avoid, some of the pitfalls associated with building and legitimizing nation-states.

Examining the Nation-State Principle

Before turning to the French Revolution, it is worth canvassing some salient aspects of the nation-state model. This model prescribes that each self-identified nation should have exclusive control of a single, uninational state. Any arrangement short of sovereign statehood is, by definition, suboptimal. This is because a belief in the primacy of the nation (as opposed to any other form of human association) leads logically to the goal of political independence as a sovereign nation-state, allowing the nation most fully to regulate its own internal affairs, and to institutionalize its separate existence vis-à-vis other nation-states. In practice, power-sharing alternatives within existing multinational states will be more or less appealing depending on demographic patterns (the geographical distribution and concentration of national groups) and economic factors (the economic viability of separate national units). In theory, however, the nation-state model holds out sovereign statehood as the ultimate form of political recognition and territorial control.[5]

Despite its apparent simplicity in theory, the nation-state model defies tidy implementation. Most states in the world today are not, strictly speaking, nation-states. The tenacity of the nation-state idea, despite the widespread incongruity between theory and practice, makes this idea particularly intriguing and worthy of investigation.[6] In practice, multinational states and transnational processes are pervasive, and the international community remains reluctant to uphold new claims to separate statehood, except when presented with a fait accompli. Yet the myth of a general right of national self-determination persists, and has even been upheld as a peremptory norm of international law.[7] As long as the nation-state idea informs the perceptions, assumptions, expectations, and attitudes of actual and would-be international actors (whether or not it is widely corroborated by the geopolitical status quo), it will continue to shape the limits of our international political imagination, providing grounds for competing claims to power and compromising the attractiveness of alternative, non-state options for self-identified nations seeking greater internal control and external recognition.

The persistent fiction of a world of nation-states and its embedded assumptions also affect how we discuss politics and international relations. In scholarly literature, both political theory and international relations (IR) theory tend to take for granted that we live in a world of nation-states. The frequent failure properly to interrogate this assumption represents a serious oversight.[8] The tendency to use the terms "nation" and "state" interchangeably encapsulates a common understanding, or rather *mis*understanding, of the foundations of existing states in the contemporary international system.[9] Although the dominant understanding of this system is essentially state-based, nations and states are by no means universally congruent, and disputes over political and territorial control remain a central source of international conflict. With the widespread rejection of conquest and colonialism as legitimate grounds for maintaining political and territorial control, state leaders have had to turn elsewhere to legitimate their authority and foster compliance and stability.

The idea of national self-determination affirms the value of self-government (presumably, though not necessarily, democratic), and the particular political relevance of the nation, as opposed to any other form of human association. Many other political configurations could be, and have been, envisaged, from city-states to multinational empires. The doctrine of national self-determination encapsulates a commitment to national self-government concretized in the rule of "one nation, one state." As a corollary, it posits sovereign nation-states as the units whose patterns of interaction constitute "international" relations (even though, increasingly, the rights of individuals have been deemed a matter of inclusive international concern).

In theory, the nation-state principle provides a standard for resolving disputes over political and territorial arrangements: nations and states should be congruent. In this formulation, congruence is not simply a matter of convenience. Sovereignty and inviolability, the hallmarks of nation-statehood, are justified based on two central criteria: (1) effectiveness, and (2) legitimacy. A nation-state is presumed to be *effective* at maintaining order and a monopoly on the use of force within its borders; it is presumed to be *legitimate*, because it can credibly embody a self-identified and self-determining nation.

From a nation-statist perspective, the state by itself has virtually no independent constitutive power: it relies for its content and its justification on the existence and continued support of a self-determining nation. The state provides the vehicle through which the nation exercises sovereignty and enshrines its own independent status vis-à-vis other nations in the international system. The state is the shell; the nation, the substance. The content (the nation) justifies and dictates the form (the state), providing an ethical basis for the attributes of sovereignty and inviolability. These attributes, in turn, can be justified most convincingly by the idea (or the illusion) of states as the embodiments of groups of individuals distinguished by a particular shared conception of the good, rather than by arbitrary territorial divisions created and maintained by force.[10] Nations can therefore be seen as giving nation-states an ethical content, providing "bottom-up" legitimating criteria for what is sometimes referred to as the "Westphalian" model of an international system of sovereign states.

In constituting and demarcating domestic political space, the nation-state principle also defines and configures the international system. In a nation-statist system, the domestic and international spheres are envisaged as distinct and governed by different rules and expectations. The nation-state is assumed to be based on a "thicker" and more substantive consensus among its members rooted in their shared national identity, whereas international institutions derive their legitimacy from procedural agreements that encompass the wide range of diverse and potentially contradictory self-understandings of their component nation-states.

In a nation-statist perspective, the top-down idea of statehood without the bottom-up support of nationhood would be insufficient to justify ethically the core prerogatives of sovereignty and inviolability.[11] In other words, states need nations just as much as nations need states. Of course, historically, states have often preceded nations, with administrative centralization and linguistic homogenization creating the conditions for forging a common political and even cultural identity. But strict nation-statists tend to assume (or to "imagine") that nations exist independently of their corresponding states, making the idea of the nation a more powerful legitimating platform. As nationalist political leaders have discovered, the ability to appeal to the idea of a nation, however historically questionable it may be, is a prerequisite for invoking national self-determination as a basis for adjudicating amongst rival political and territorial claims.

On a rhetorical level, states invoke the attributes of sovereignty and inviolability to defend themselves from internal and external political and territorial challenges. On the ethical level, these prerogatives (at least in a nation-statist framework) seem to rely on the assumption that existing states represent and embody self-determining nations. This leads to the puzzling result that states may rely for their legitimacy on a principle that can also be invoked to undermine that legitimacy, and to challenge their political and territorial integrity. It would seem that states are strongest when they can viably assert a unified national identity, and most vulnerable when they can be challenged by one or more substate groups whose members have stronger and denser ties of identification and loyalty with other members of the same substate group than they do with the larger state. This tension between an existing state's ability to invoke the nation-state idea to legitimate its existence, and substate groups' ability to invoke the same idea to challenge existing states, lies at the heart of the contemporary international system.

If nations are to legitimize (or delegitimize) states, the question arises: how to identify nations? Debates about the criteria for nationhood are never-ending, but Alfred Cobban's suggestion that "[t]he best we can say is that any territorial community, the members of which are conscious of themselves *as* members of a community, and wish to maintain the identity of their community, is a nation" offers a reasonable starting point.[12] Nations are generally imagined as nonpolitical in nature; states are the political and territorial structures that nations inhabit or seek to create. Whether one subscribes to a view of nations as preexisting entities in the world, or to a more historically evolutionist narrative of nation-formation, the idea that human beings are divided into relatively coherent and cohesive groupings based on shared languages, practices, beliefs, experiences, characteristics, memories, and aspirations,[13] and that these groupings are not necessarily congruent with—and can be identified separately from—existing state institutions, underlies the commitment to reflecting these divisions as closely as possible in global political and territorial arrangements.

The puzzle of how individuals could share national bonds prior to the experience of living together may force recourse to a kind of political "creationism," in which nations are imagined as preexisting entities separate from state institutions. This somewhat ahistorical idea of preexisting solidarity remains the foundation of arguments for the ethical primacy of nationhood, and for creating congruence between nations and states where this does not already exist.[14] Although assimilation historically might underlie many culturally unified nation-states, national identity is rarely, if ever, acknowledged as an artifice or a deliberate creation. This is largely because the idea of a preexisting nation plays an important justificatory role in the nation-state model (as opposed to the state-nation, or the multinational state). While attempting to determine the conceptual relationship between the nation and the state might seem like the riddle of the chicken and the egg, the ability to imagine the nation as separate from the state becomes central when the nation is upheld as an independent standard for the legitimacy of the state. Nationalist arguments based on the idea of a preexisting, internally cohesive nation may become particularly salient when they seek to challenge, rather than reinforce, the political and territorial boundaries of an existing state.

Different nationalist arguments may appeal to different kinds of allegedly preexisting bonds among members of a nation: those that may be acquired, and those that are innate. This leads to a perceived distinction between "civic" nationalism, which is portrayed as liberal, inclusive, and moderate, and "ethnic" nationalism, which is portrayed as illiberal, exclusionary, and extremist. Chapter five examines this distinction and its implications in greater detail. At this juncture, it is sufficient to note this perceived distinction between what can perhaps more accurately be termed "voluntarist" and "nonvoluntarist" models. Voluntarist nations are especially interesting because they seem to offer grounds for social cohesion, territorial delineation, and political mobilization that are maximally inclusive and minimally predetermined. For this reason, a persistent question throughout this book is: can voluntarist nations fulfill this "liberal" promise?

It is difficult to imagine how voluntarist nations could fit into the framework established by the nation-state principle: the idea that there are preexisting nations that merit having their own territorial states. On a conceptual level, the question of what criteria one could point to as evidence of the existence of a voluntarist nation separate from an existing state remains unresolved, suggesting a difficulty with this category itself. It seems much more straightforward to conceive of an ethnic or nonvoluntarist nation as existing prior to or separate from a given state. For example, during the 1998–99 crisis in Kosovo, the Kosovar Albanians could be thought of as an entity distinguishable from the Serbs, even though they were politically and territorially part of Serbia. Thinking of the Kosovar Albanians as a distinct group might have been facilitated by the existence of the Kosovar Liberation Army and Kosovar political leaders, even if these did not speak with a monolithic voice. But the ability to conceive of the Kosovar Albanians as forming a cohesive entity did and does not depend on these organizational or administrative trappings.

This mental exercise of separating a nation from its institutions becomes more difficult when the predominant characteristics that define the nation's members are not readily apparent. Ethnicity itself may be largely a matter of subjective definition or invention, but it still seems more concretely ascertainable than other membership criteria or characteristics. For example, I, a Caucasian, would be unable to self-identify as ethnically Japanese. In this sense, I could not belong to the Japanese nation if this were defined nonpolitically as based on shared ethnic traits (even if, depending on citizenship policies, I could become a member of the Japanese state). If membership in a nation cannot be chosen, that nation may be characterized as nonvoluntarist.

Voluntarist nations, by contrast, may be more porous, because their membership criteria ostensibly involve characteristics that are willed or acquired, rather than innate. Language is often upheld as a voluntarist criterion since languages may be learned, even though native speakers are generally distinguishable from those who acquire a language later in life. However, the qualitative distinction between voluntarist and nonvoluntarist membership criteria is not clear-cut: I, a French speaker, could perhaps claim to be a self-identified member of the Québec nation even though I was born in Ontario and grew up in an anglophone household, but it is less certain that all self-identified Québec nationalists would automatically accept me as a member of the Québec nation, whether or not I supported their political cause.

National cohesiveness need not be based on characteristics that are perceived as innate, such as race or ethnicity. It does, however, need to be based on some perceived or actual shared understandings and characteristics among members that distinguish them from nonmembers. These shared understandings and characteristics provide the basis for a common identity, sense of commitment, and willingness to comply with rules established by members of the nation or its chosen leaders. These requirements can be referred to as cohesion, commitment, and compliance. Without cohesion, commitment, and compliance, there is little hope that a self-identified group will be able to establish effective and legitimate internal political institutions, let alone claim the external prerogatives of sovereignty and inviolability in the face of potentially competing claims. The question for proponents of voluntarist nationalism is:

in a voluntarist nation, where do cohesion, commitment, and compliance come from? Could a voluntarist nation ever challenge an existing state?

One can always seek to create cohesion, commitment, and compliance in existing states. This is, in fact, how many well-established states have been formed.[15] This "state-nation" idea, however, is intrinsically conservative, since it seeks to reinforce the effectiveness and legitimacy of existing states. The nation-state idea, by contrast, can be revolutionary, since it enables nations to challenge the political composition and territorial boundaries of existing states.

Mindful of this revolutionary potential, states in the international community have embraced the liberationist rhetoric of self-determination, but they have not accepted the destabilizing implications of implementing the nation-state model in favor of substate groups demanding political independence. The "principle of equal rights and self-determination of peoples" is enshrined in Article 1, paragraph 2, and Article 55 of the United Nations Charter; General Assembly Resolution 1514 on the Granting of Independence to Colonial Countries and Peoples (1960); General Assembly Resolution 2625 on the Principles of International Law Concerning Friendly Relations and Cooperation Among States (1970); and the 1966 International Covenants on Human Rights.[16] The practical implications of the nation-statist imperative in an international system comprised of multiethnic and multinational states are threatening, to say the least. It is therefore not surprising that championing self-determination has largely meant displacing colonial leaders, rather than redrawing colonial boundaries. The international rhetoric of self-determination has not been accompanied by support for self-determination movements that seek to modify state borders, and not just displace colonial rule.

Perhaps the closest flirtation with a widespread implementation of the nation-state idea came in the wake of the First World War. In 1919–20, a number of arguments were made in support of nation-states over empires: the idea that large empires are exploitative and undemocratic, the hope that national self-determination would reduce the incidence of conflict, and the general feeling that "small is beautiful."[17] Unfortunately for its advocates, this nation-based conception was virtually impossible to implement in practical terms, as U.S. President Woodrow Wilson's Secretary of State Robert Lansing foresaw, and his colleagues realized, during the Paris peace negotiations.[18]

Setting aside the interests of colonial powers that kept them from advocating the uniform application of this principle in postwar territorial and political arrangements, even negotiators devoted to the idea of national self-determination would have been hard pressed to ascertain exactly what that commitment entailed. Definitional problems abounded. The lack of agreed-upon criteria for nationhood makes top-down solutions difficult. Plebiscites can be problematic, particularly if national boundaries are contested to begin with: how to decide who is entitled to have an authoritative say in determining the political status of a given territory or population? A given territory is not necessarily a nation;[19] self-identified members of a single nation do not necessarily inhabit the same territory; and resettlement policies may fundamentally alter the demographic balance in a region, creating tensions between historical claims and the situation on the ground.

It is also far from clear that implementing the nation-state principle, were this possible, would promote international stability. From an international order perspective, the argument for national self-determination tends to assume that nation-states will, by definition, be territorially satiated, and thus coexist more peacefully than states built on other principles. By contrast, multinational states would face threats of rebellion and secession, and nations straddling state borders might pursue policies of consolidation based on irredentist aspirations. However, the contestability of national boundaries means that national self-determination does not, in fact, avoid these problems.[20] To the contrary, in a world *not* composed of nation-states, the clash between the principles of national self-determination and existing state sovereignty might turn out to be "a recipe for international disorder" by inciting more disputes than it resolves.[21] On a basic level, the principle of national self-determination begs the question "What are nations?," thus failing to specify the circumstances under which particular groups can legitimately challenge state borders: that is, when they can justifiably violate the very principles of state sovereignty and inviolability that make statehood attractive in the first place.

Notwithstanding these difficulties, Common Article 1 of the 1966 Covenants affirms: "All peoples have the right of self-determination. By virtue of this right they freely determine their political status and freely pursue their economic, social, and cultural development."[22] It seems difficult to imagine how a group could "freely determine [its] political status" without the possibility of independent statehood, but this is precisely the option that existing states have sought to preclude, both within and alongside the United Nations framework. In his 1992 *Agenda for Peace*, UN Secretary-General Boutros Boutros-Gali identified this tension without, however, resolving it:

> The sovereignty, territorial integrity and independence of States within the established international system, and the principle of self-determination for peoples, both of great value and importance, must not be permitted to work against each other in the period ahead. Respect for democratic principles at all levels of social existence is crucial: in communities, within States and within the community of States. Our constant duty should be to maintain the integrity of each while finding a balanced design for all.[23]

Consistent with this admonition, the international community's general refusal to endorse outright Kosovar separatism in the winter of 1998–99, while at the same time condemning Serb aggression towards ethnic Albanians in the region, stemmed in no small part from a fear of establishing a precedent of support or even passive legitimation of separatist movements. The resistance to self-determination as a basis for dismantling existing states sits uncomfortably with the affirmation of a right of self-determination of peoples, pointing to a tension at the heart of the contemporary international system.

Closely tied to the idea of a right to national self-determination—and counterbalancing its disruptive potential—is a pervasive fiction that the states in the international system are (or approximate) nation-states: that is, that they should be treated as unitary and, to a large extent, self-enclosed. Paradoxically, an increasing emphasis on human rights and rights to national self-determination also makes the international community more likely to intervene in this self-enclosed space and to legitimate, at least tacitly, certain nation-based political and territorial claims, for example, in the form of election monitoring in places such as East Timor. Even nonmilitary intervention can highlight tensions between the claims of nations and those of existing states. Finding a "balanced design," in Secretary-General Boutros-Gali's words, is a laudable goal, but it remains elusive.

Chapters one through four use the story of the French Revolution to examine these contested concepts, and to explore the uses and abuses of the nation-state idea. Their goal is both theoretical and pragmatic: theoretical, in the sense that discussions of the nation-state idea and national self-determination in political theory and international relations can benefit from a historically informed conceptual analysis; and pragmatic, because the idea of a right to national self-determination continues to animate political and territorial claims and challenges today. Each chapter focuses on a "paradox" in the nation-state idea. The notion of a paradox is intended to evoke the tensions and trade-offs involved in imagining and building nation-states.

The French Revolutionaries did not succeed in endowing their own version of the nation with lasting and exclusive legitimacy, but they did help to enshrine nationhood as a central platform for articulating and contesting claims to political power and territorial control.[24] A deeper understanding of the challenges faced by the French Revolutionaries, and of their responses to these challenges, can help us develop tools to grapple with national self-determination claims in the present, and to evaluate alternative forms of political association for the future. Chapter five explores the tension between voluntarist and nonvoluntarist nationalism in more detail, and chapter six suggests some ways in which these analytical tools can be applied by discussing the contemporary situation in Iraq in terms of the tensions that flow from the nation-state ideal.

Exploring the French Revolution

Chapters one through four focus on a critical stage in the development of the principle of national self-determination: the years of the French Revolution, during which the idea of the nation was fused with that of self-government. Other historical periods and events have also clearly had an impact on ideas of international legitimacy and the configuration of international order, including the Magna Carta, the American Revolution, the Congress of Vienna, and the First World War. Nevertheless, historians and international relations scholars routinely cite the French Revolution as the origin of nationalism and the source of national self-determination. Despite this almost habitual invocation, scholars have by and large failed to explore the implications of this conceptual and historical connection.[25] This book aims, in part, to remedy that omission, and to apply the insights gained from this analysis to contemporary political dilemmas.

In examining the interplay between French Revolutionary rhetoric and nationalist political theory, I draw on three main categories of sources: philosophical, political, and literary texts from the French Revolutionary period; historical works on the French Revolution; and studies of nationalism from the perspectives of international relations, political theory, and international law. While the bodies of secondary literature on the French Revolution and on national self-determination are each enormous, relatively few works explicitly conjoin the two subjects in an attempt to dig more deeply into the assumptions behind and the implications of national self-determination as an international political standard. Tracing the emergence of the French notion of the nation during the Revolutionary period can provide insights into the main virtues and defects of national self-determination as a basis for domestic and international order, both as these were seen at the time and in their subsequent manifestations.

The key aspect of the French Revolution, from the perspective of this analysis, is the emergence of the nation as a political actor—the holder of sovereignty and the touchstone for political legitimacy. The assumption that there exists a natural connection among nationhood, political legitimacy, and popular emancipation—attributable largely to the French Revolution and its surrounding mythology—has contributed to a widespread presumption in favor of nation-states over other political models, such as empires. We live—or at least *think* we live—in a world of nation-states.

I do not assert that there is some Platonic, unchanging meaning of the term "nation," nor that the French Revolutionary use of this term can be equated in all respects with its use by later self-determination movements. Rather, I contend that the deployment of the concept of nationhood by French Revolutionary thinkers and politicians provides a rich laboratory for exploring this concept and testing its ethical and logical limits. Although political terms do not travel through time unchanged, early formulations of the entitlements of nationhood reveal central, enduring tensions in this political ideal. In particular, the idea of a voluntarist nation, often conflated with that of a democratic state, merits critical scrutiny. From this perspective, this study also contributes to the ongoing exploration of the uneasy relationship between liberalism and nationalism in political theory and international relations.

My approach follows the tradition of historically informed international relations scholarship associated with the English School, viewing international relations as a product of the interaction between doctrines and practice.[26] The configuration of international political life is itself a historical product, forged by processes of construction and interaction that have been underpinned by and also generative of its conceptual justifications. This tends to make strictly empirical or strictly theoretical investigations of principles such as national self-determination somewhat incomplete.[27]

This analysis takes it for granted that ideas matter. In the international arena, international norms provide actors with justifications that shape their political options: they do not prescribe actions, but they do shape the ways in which they can be legitimated. The perceived importance of public opinion (what in eighteenth-century France was called "*le que dira-t-on*") can either fuel or temper nationalist political platforms, depending on the target audience. By concretizing sets of intersubjective understandings, justifications offered by international actors can have a cumulative effect in reinforcing and pushing forward the development of broader international standards and codes of conduct.[28]

This book, in both its subject matter and its methodology, focuses on the link between principles and practice in international law and politics. Concepts such as national self-determination create expectations and establish legitimating criteria, shaping the way in which international actors articulate and justify political and territorial claims.[29] Just as today the political possibility of secession depends on the acceptance of national self-determination as a legitimate political goal (one recognized informally in shared sets of understandings or formally in international law), so were the political paths available to the French Revolutionaries informed, if not determined, by certain conceptual limits. The transformation of political vocabulary at the time of the French Revolution provides a key entry point to studying the construction of a certain way of thinking about the nation and its entitlements.[30] What Alexis de Tocqueville somewhat derisively termed the "abstract, literary politics" of the Revolution actually represented the core of a new legitimating political discourse.[31] Distinctions between the nation and the state, debates over the proper form of political representation, definitions of citizenship and nationality, and foreign policy dilemmas involving questions of nationhood and sovereignty were central to the French Revolutionary project, and remain basic tensions in building nation-states today.

The French Revolution met with fierce opposition by political elites in the rest of Europe precisely because it was perceived as exporting a new standard of political legitimacy directly at odds with prevailing monarchical and dynastic principles.[32] This uneasiness was not unique to the Revolutionary context. Over a century later, U.S. President Woodrow Wilson realized the unintended consequences of his rhetorical support for national self-determination when representatives of nationalities he had never heard of flocked to him as a champion for their separatist aspirations at the close of the First World War, indicating the potency of ideas in fueling concrete political claims.[33] Russian Revolutionary leader Vladimir Lenin found national self-determination a particularly useful platform for fomenting rebellion against the "imperial yoke" of the czarist regime, further assisting the development of this political ideal.[34] The power of national self-determination as a platform for challenging oppressive and colonial rule during the 1960s and 1970s, and during the breakup of the Soviet Union in the 1990s, illustrates the broad appeal of this principle in validating the political and territorial aspirations of nations seeking control of their own states.

Some contend that, because nationalism is multipurpose, it does not have the status of a distinct ideology.[35] Although the rhetoric of nationhood historically has been appropriated by groups and individuals from various points along the political spectrum, the emphasis on the primacy of the nation as the basis for the configuration of international political life constitutes a core political premise meriting exploration. The flexibility of the nation as a political platform makes it more, not less, compelling as a focus for inquiry. However ill-defined the nation was or has remained, and however ambiguous or contested its international legal status, the enduring practice of using a nation's existence and/or oppression to legitimate claims to political and territorial independence warrants continued analysis. In addition to being of historical and theoretical interest, a conceptual analysis of the nation-state principle can provide additional tools for understanding contemporary political dilemmas. Chapter six seeks to illustrate this through a preliminary examination of the U.S. government's attempt to export democracy to Iraq.

The first four chapters of this book maintain a historical and theoretical focus. They address four core "paradoxes" in nationalist justifications, both at the time of the French Revolution and in subsequent arguments. I label these paradoxes conception, constitution, composition, and confrontation. The four paradoxes, presented chronologically, identify specific tensions in the use of the nation as a political platform during the French Revolution that remain problematic in the present day. These paradoxes are especially relevant to evaluating the viability of a civic or voluntarist model of nationhood, often upheld as a benign or even positive form of nationalism and identified with the French Revolution (despite clear limitations on the inclusiveness of the Revolutionary project, particularly with respect to women).

The first paradox involves the issue of *conception*. Evident in a close reading of the eighteenth-century Encyclopedists and of Jean-Jacques Rousseau, the paradox of conception challenges the idea that voluntarist, preexisting entities can be identified as inherently appropriate and legitimate bases for delineating states. It seems difficult, if not impossible, to conceive of a nation based on ties that are nonessentialist, voluntarist, and inclusive, without reference to the state's territorial and institutional framework. This poses a problem for the theory of national self-determination because, in order for the nation to embody a separate and independent legitimating platform, one must be able to conceive of the nation without reference to its corresponding state, whether or not the nation is actually "preexisting" in a chronological sense.

The idea of the nation as distinguishable from the state may depend on a historical fiction, but it is a crucial conceptual premise of national self-determination arguments. Once the conceptual distinction between nation and state collapses, the principle of national self-determination becomes redundant, if not incoherent. For example, the ability to conceive of a Québec nation separate from a Canadian state, or a Kosovar nation separate from a Serb state, enables political leaders in Québec and Kosovo to mobilize their respective populations and to seek political independence based on the principle of national self-determination. Were these self-identified nations not ethnically or linguistically distinct, mobilizing around the idea of national self-determination would be more difficult, both in theory and in practice. A conception of the Québec nation that included more than just native French-speakers or people born or raised in Québec would be closer to a voluntarist model, if an appeal could be made to a nonlinguistic and nongenealogical definition of Québec nationhood.[36]

While the problem of constituting a nation out of nothing may also be a perennial one for democratic and republican theorists, its implications are particularly critical for nationalists who rely on the idea of "preexisting" nations to justify their political claims. Especially in the case of nations formed by the will of their members to live together, rather than by ethnic or allegedly "objective" criteria, the problem of how to differentiate between institutions that are emblematic of preexisting voluntarist nations and ones that are constitutive of them may prove insurmountable. For example, can the population of the United States be conceived of separately as a self-determining nation, or is it rather the classic example of a state-nation, in which political institutions have forged cohesion, commitment, and compliance among members of the population? The latter account seems more plausible. This points to a more general difficulty: the circularity of voluntarist definitions of nationhood that appeal to institutions as evidence of supposedly pre-institutional bonds. For example, it would be difficult for Californians to self-identify as a separate nation without referring to the fact that they all vote in California elections, or that they are all bound by California laws. The sheer "will to be Californian" would seem insufficient to identify members of this would-be nation, and to differentiate between authentic and nonauthentic national spokespersons. This leads to the second paradox.

The paradox of *constitution* follows from the observation that national self-determination forces reliance on those who claim to speak in the nation's name, meaning that some recourse to existing political power structures is inevitable in advancing nation-based claims.[37] Predictably, this fosters the abuse of nationalist platforms by political power seekers, a phenomenon difficult to reconcile with the "liberal" advocacy of national self-determination as an emancipatory ideal. Of course, it would be naïve to suggest that anybody could claim to speak on behalf of a nation, or that elections and representative bodies cannot mitigate these risks. But the exaltation of the nation has often been accompanied by the subordination of the actual wishes of the individuals within it, a problem compounded by gauging the legitimacy of authority by reference to preexisting social units, instead of judging state institutions on their own merits. The phenomenon of postcolonial dictatorships is all too familiar: although many African states, for example, are not truly national, certain postcolonial leaders have learned to use the language of self-determination to deter external interference while suppressing internal dissent.[38]

In the decades leading up to the French Revolution, the importance of national spokespersons became evident as the French *parlements* (aristocratic, sovereign law courts) claimed power for themselves as the representatives of the French people, and ultimately of the French nation. In so doing, the *parlements* played a key role in promoting the idea of the nation as an autonomous and self-legitimating entity. The Abbé Sieyès built on and furthered this development by arguing for the creation of a nonaristocratic National Assembly. His rhetoric helped to foster the perception of a close and even necessary connection between an affirmation of the nation as the source of political authority, and the liberal ideal of self-government. However, the former by no means guarantees the latter, and can often acutely undermine it, as leaders may play the nationalist card to the detriment of the people they claim to represent.

If the nation is to have some kind of autonomous existence as a basis of identification and legitimacy, it needs to be more than just a rhetorical fiction: self-definition is a prerequisite for self-determination. The paradox of *composition* addresses the issue of how a nation, especially one that exists separate from the state, could enjoy a high enough degree of external distinctiveness and internal cohesion to substantiate its political claims. In the liberal argument for civic nationalism, how could a civic nation be held together if not by either internal ethnic ties (because these are nonvoluntarist) or external political institutions? The allegedly separate and distinct existence of any nation in self-determination arguments forces recourse to some suggestion of preexisting ties, even though this may involve accepting the foundations of solidarity in a nonvoluntarist nation that a voluntarist model seeks to contradict. In the Kosovo example, how can one provide an account of national membership that does not rely on ethnicity? If one cannot, what does this say about the viability of relying on voluntarist nations to ensure cohesion, commitment, and compliance? What would hold a voluntarist nation together, if not the coercive power of the state?

The correlation between the strength of intra-group ties and their perceived innateness tends to push even voluntarist national self-definitions closer and closer to a nonvoluntarist model. Particular voluntarist definitions of nationhood are thus also susceptible to manipulation for exclusionary political ends. As chapter five explores in more detail, simply defining a nation as "civic" rather than "ethnic" does not solve the problem of how to promote internal cohesion, commitment, and compliance while avoiding exclusion, discrimination, and xenophobia.

The paradox of composition focuses on the kind of internal policies needed to forge a strong sense of national unity and identity. Particularly in times of perceived national vulnerability, such as the early stages of nation-building or times of internal political dissent or external geopolitical conflict, building unity often comes at the expense of inclusiveness. In the French Revolutionary context, the paradox of composition is illustrated by a study of attempts to forge a civic culture, including proposed measures for ensuring linguistic uniformity advocated by the Abbé Grégoire and Bertrand de Barère. Today, for example, there remains a constant dialogue in Israel about how the state can be both "democratic" and "Jewish"; in the United States, questions about the appropriateness of bilingual public education persist; in France, attempts by Muslim girls to wear the veil in public schools are perceived as a threat to the secular French national identity. As a political model, the nation-state is assumed to possess a high degree of internal homogeneity and coherence. Fostering this can be both useful and dangerous.

The fourth and final paradox, *confrontation*, captures a corresponding tension in the global arena, as the ideal of cosmopolitanism and the project of national consolidation generate conflicting pressures. While the Enlightenment values thought to accompany voluntarist nationalism might hold that all individuals are morally equal, the nationalist principle pushes against this vision, establishing a particularist standard of obligation that distinguishes between members and nonmembers, and that prioritizes members. The possible ways of circumventing this problem do not offer satisfying solutions. If one simply regards a world of nation-states as one stage in the movement towards a "global village," this begs the question of how a moral division of nations, and thus of their members, can be justified in the interim. If one upholds the existence of distinct nations as the best means of organizing international political life, one faces the difficulty of maintaining that national divisions, however arbitrary, are nevertheless morally significant: that is, that they should be the basis for creating and legitimizing political arrangements that govern distributive justice, welfare provision, and the definition of reciprocal rights and obligations.

Viewed from within a given nation-state, it is difficult to maintain that one's own national model is simultaneously superior for members and morally equivalent to other distinct, and potentially contradictory, national models. For this reason, nationalism tends to be the inverse of cosmopolitanism, and can even assume imperialist and racist overtones as nationalists (especially revolutionary nationalists) seek to protect and even to impose their own particular visions. In this sense, as chapter six explores, the French Revolution's attempt to export the French ideal of self-government has remarkable echoes in the United States's military operation in Iraq, named "Operation Iraqi Freedom." In the case of a voluntarist nation, one specific national model may be exported under a pretense of universal validity, as the temptation of "Revolutionary Messianism" fosters imperialist projects couched in emancipatory terms.

The paradox of confrontation highlights the potential contradiction involved in affirming one's identity as both "person" and "citizen," especially when crisis situations force action based on loyalty to members of one's own nation, rather than to humanity as a whole. This dilemma was compounded in the French Revolutionary era by France's self-image as the "universal nation," but it is arguably contained within ideas about national self-determination more generally, even in the absence of belligerent or expansionist undertones of a particular nationalist movement. Even though the French Revolutionaries were challenged externally by a monarchical alliance and superseded internally by Napoleon, reactions against the French Revolution in invaded territories often involved appropriating, rather than rejecting, nationalist ideas, contributing to the development and entrenchment of the nation-state principle as an international political standard.

National self-determination draws on a particular *conception* of the relationship between nation and state: the idea of the nation as a separate and even preexisting entity whose internal cohesion both facilitates the operation of and confers moral value on its corresponding state. A preexisting nation can be upheld as the standard for a state's legitimacy based on that state's *constitution* (political structures) and *composition* (membership). These criteria establish the entitlement of nation-states to *confront* each other as equal members of international society.

Chapters five and six draw on the preceding historical material to consider the following questions:

1. What are the existing attempts to develop an intellectually coherent understanding of the principle of national self-determination? How have they succeeded or failed?
2. How has the evolution and entrenchment of the concept of nationhood as part of a discourse of political emancipation contributed to current understandings of its legitimacy as a basis for political and territorial claims, and with what effects?
3. Are the contradictions highlighted by this analysis irreconcilable (in theory and/or in practice) and, if so, what does this say about the idea of national self-determination more generally, and about the utility—or danger—of the persistent fiction of a world of nation-states?

It is difficult to consider questions relating to the formation of identity-based political communities without engaging in a certain degree of speculation about the psychological and social drives that shape human interactions. That said, the primary goal of the analysis contained in the following chapters is to foster greater conceptual clarity and coherence in discussions about the relationship between nations and states. This conceptual framework can, in turn, serve as an analytical structure for future explorations of the psychological, empirical, and other dimensions of this relationship.

The French Revolution played a crucial, although clearly not exclusive, role in concretizing and propagating national self-determination as an international political standard. The frequent invocation of the French Revolution as the birthplace of the modern nation-state justifies examining the Revolution as a source of relevant insights for ongoing debates about the relationship between nations and states in a state-based international order. Adam Roberts has observed that "[t]he disjunction between 'nation' and 'state' has been among the major causes of practically every war this century."[39] As long as political ideas—both those enshrined in international instruments and those existing in the penumbra of the formal international legal order—shape political choices, the terms in which we conceive of and legitimate the configuration of international society will require continued attention and analysis, particularly when ideas and practice are as fraught with tension as they are with respect to the principle of national self-determination. Twenty-first century experiments in "nation-building" can learn from the experiences of the eighteenth century. Not surprisingly, these experiences instruct that nothing is as simple as it appears.

Chapter 1

Conception

How to Imagine a Preexisting, Voluntarist Nation

Introduction

The paradox of conception flows from the need to be able to imagine the nation in order to articulate nation-based arguments and build nation-based states. This need is paradoxical because national identity is often, and even usually, forged by state and other administrative institutions. However, a logically coherent account of national self-determination ends up having to imagine nations as existing separately from, and prior to, states. In this sense, the paradox of conception forms the very basis of the nation-state principle: that is, the idea that nations are sufficiently independent of state institutions to serve as separate and authoritative guides to political and territorial legitimacy.

During the eighteenth century in France, the concept of the nation provided political challengers with a source of legitimacy that they could uphold as separate from the monarch—the cornerstone of the logic behind nationalist claims. The largely unprecedented consolidation of authority under Louis XIV prompted the Parisian and provincial *parlements*, aristocratic law courts, to guard their prerogatives jealously, and even to seek to extend them in a series of public power struggles with the king, as explored in chapter two. The resulting debates confirmed and entrenched the resonance of the idea of the nation as a basis for political claims.

Political actors seeking greater influence within and beyond existing institutions first had to challenge the self-referential and self-justifying quality of monarchical rule. They did this by developing and relying on the idea of the nation in a partially self-conscious and largely need-driven series of rhetorical challenges to the exclusive authority of the king. Early references to the "nation" evoked two related ideas: first, an embryonic notion of the French population as a rights-bearing (if passive) constituency, and second, a more abstract vision of the nation as a transcendent source of political authority and legitimacy that the king could no longer claim exclusively to embody or to represent. These ideas foreshadowed later French Revolutionary rhetoric and resonate in nation-based rhetoric today.

Two bodies of thought illustrate the contours of this evolving concept of the nation: definitions of the nation and its correlates in serious and in satirical works (section 1.1), and contractarian ideas about the basis of legitimate political authority (section 1.2). Both of these strands of argument were intertwined with concrete power struggles. Tracing them separately allows a focus on the paradox of conception: the difficulty of conceiving of a pre-political entity without reference to institutions, especially if that entity is envisaged as voluntarist. While this ambiguity could have rendered nationalist claims more precarious and less convenient, it in fact contributed to the expediency and popularity of the nation as a political platform, as chapter two explores in more detail.

1.1 Conceptions of the Nation in Eighteenth-Century Polemical Dictionaries

Dictionary definitions, while not always reliable indicators of popular understandings, nevertheless provide an illustrative starting point for analyzing eighteenth-century French ideas of nationhood.[1] This is especially true of Revolutionary dictionaries, which offer a rich body of political commentary. Many of these dictionaries have been preserved in the microfiche collection of the French National Archives in Paris. The following discussion is based on a systematic, though not exhaustive, review of these dictionaries, which provide rich illustrations of the evolution of political concepts during the pre-Revolutionary and Revolutionary period.

Upheaval in political concepts and vocabulary during the mid- to late-eighteenth century presaged and accompanied the transformation of political institutions. The popularity of the satirical dictionary as a vehicle for political debate underscores the connection between linguistic and political instability and change. The change in everyday language was palpable. Contemporaries observed:

> on ne parle plus que des *droits et des intérêts de la Nation* [we now speak of nothing else but the *rights and interests of the Nation*];[2] never have the words "nation" and "state" been as frequently used as they are today. . . . These two terms were never uttered under Louis XIV; even the idea of them was lacking. We have never been so aware as we are today of the rights of the nation and of liberty.[3]

This chapter explores the development of the concept of the nation and its implications for the foundations of political legitimacy in France.

Although providing a coherent chronological account of the evolution of the term "nation" is complicated by the concurrent use of conflicting and imprecise definitions (a problem that persists to the present day), general and important changes can be traced. The early, absolutist definition of the nation associated with the reign of Louis XIV was fairly straightforward. The word was relatively rarely used, since it was considered basically synonymous with both the monarch and the state: "The Crown, the State and the Nation were but three words for the same thing."[4] The king was both the sovereign lawmaking power and the embodiment of the kingdom as a whole. The medieval slogan "*[S]i veut le roy, si veut la loy*" (what the king desires, so commands the law) equated the king's will with the law of the land.[5] This did not imply that the king could arbitrarily impose his personal will: rather, it affirmed that the law, understood as a transcendent principle of social order, would by definition be in harmony with and express itself through the will of the monarch.[6] As Nannerl Keohane suggests, "absolutist theory makes the state constitutive of social order and unity in a very direct way. . . . The ordering authority of the king literally holds the nation together."[7] The symbolic identity between king and nation meant that there was little need to identify any additional constitutive or cohesive principle for the French polity, other than the king himself.

Political power struggles between the king and the *parlements* contributed to the increasing conceptual independence of the nation, an entity distinct from both the king and the state. This process was gradual. When Denis Diderot and Jean le Rond d'Alembert's *Encyclopédie, ou Dictionnaire raisonné des sciences, des arts et des métiers, par une Société de Gens de lettres*, a massive reference work and chronicle of Enlightenment ideas, was compiled in the 1750s and 1760s, the idea of the nation as distinct from the state had not yet emerged fully.[8] According to the *Encyclopédie*, the state is not merely an administrative structure, but rather "une société d'hommes vivant ensemble sous un gouvernement quelconque, heureux ou malheureux" (a society of men living together under whichever government, happy or unhappy).[9] The state seems indistinguishable from the nation, a not-yet-popularized "mot collectif dont on fait usage pour exprimer une quantité considérable de peuple, qui habite une certaine étendue de pays, renfermée dans de certaines limites, & qui obéit au même gouvernement" (collective word used to denote a large quantity of people that inhabits a particular stretch of land, enclosed within certain limits, & that obeys the same government).[10] Each nation possesses certain characteristic traits, giving each one the potential to serve as a more central and resonant identity platform (a feature that would take on increasing importance as the century progressed). But the nation is still defined in the *Encyclopédie* by the territorial and administrative unity created by the state ("& that obeys the same government"), preventing it from playing an independent legitimating role.

While the term "nation" first referred to essentially the same thing as the state, it was gradually appropriated to designate a group of people independent of its governmental structures. The difference between the 1694 and 1740 versions of the *Dictionnaire de l'Académie française* is instructive on this point. The 1694 version lists "nation" under the entry for *Naître* (to be born), defining it as "un terme collectif. Tous les habitants d'un même Etat, d'un même pays, qui vivent sous les mêmes lois, et usent de la même langue" (a collective term. All the inhabitants of one and the same State, one and the same country, who live under the same laws, and use the same language).[11] By 1740, "nation" has its own entry, with an added qualification:

> Se dit aussi des habitants d'un même pays, encore qu'ils ne vivent sous les mêmes lois, et qu'ils soient sujets à différents princes. Ainsi quoique l'Italie soit partagée en divers Etats et en divers gouvernements, on ne laisse pas de dire la *nation italienne*. [Also used to speak of the inhabitants of one and the same land, even if they do not live under the same laws, and are subjects of different princes. So even though Italy is divided into different States and into various governments, we do not stop saying the *Italian nation*.][12]

The use of the word "pays" in the 1694 definition as a synonym for the state, and its use in the 1740 definition to mean a territorially defined population *without* the administrative element, illustrates the shifting nature of these terms. The close connection between *naître* and *nation* emphasizes the familial bonds at the heart of the concept of nationhood, bonds that even voluntarist conceptions seek to create through an actual or hypothetical act of collective will.

This 1740 definition preceded the *Encyclopédie*'s more state-based definition of the nation, and it focused more on informal usage than on political terminology. Such gradual shifts in vocabulary accompanied and underpinned shifts in political understandings. It is also not entirely clear whether the key principle of national differentiation in this 1740 definition is territory (Italy) or culture (Italian). Either way, this 1740 definition suggests that states and nations are not inherently congruent, and that something other than existing governmental structures could be used to delineate national boundaries. This conceptual separation creates the potential for the principle of national self-determination to serve as a basis for establishing—and challenging—the political authority and boundaries of states.

Almost two centuries later, French legal scholar Léon Duguit described the relationship between nation and state in a nation-statist framework in his 1921 *Traité de droit constitutionnel*:

> La nation est le titulaire originaire de la souveraineté. La nation est une personne, avec tous les attributs de la personnalité, la conscience et la volonté. La personne *nation* est, en réalité, distincte de l'État; elle lui est antérieure; l'État ne peut exister que là où il y a une nation; et la nation peut subsister même quand l'État n'existe plus ou n'existe pas encore. [The nation is the original holder and source of sovereignty. The nation is a person, with all the attributes of personality, conscience, and will. The person *nation* is, in reality, distinct from the State; it is anterior to it (the State); the State cannot exist except where there is a nation; and the nation can subsist even when the State no longer exists or does not yet exist.][13]

This definition illustrates the implications of conceiving of the nation as prior to and independent of the state. Instead of the nation relying on the state, the state relies on the nation—even if the nation is not clearly defined and serves a more abstract, rather than empirical, legitimating function. During the eighteenth century, the emergence of a new political vocabulary both signaled and fueled the transformation of ideas about the legitimate foundations of states, with the implications seen in Duguit's 1921 definition.

Popular definitions of the nation from the French Revolutionary period, identified in dictionaries found in the microfiche collection of the

National Archives, reveal that the nation could be seen as either benevolent or dangerous. Both sympathetic and critical definitions highlight the nation's centrality as a legitimating principle and a justification for political action. In 1789, the *Catéchisme national* was published under the auspices of the *Imprimerie des bons Citoyens* (Good Citizens' Publishing House). Pamphlet literature in the form of catechisms was common, serving the same purposes of clarification and political commentary as the polemical dictionaries. The 1789 *Catéchisme national* included the following dialogue:

> D. Comment appelle-t-on une société qui s'est donné un chef, & soumise à des loix?
> R. On l'appelle nation, peuple. Ainsi on dit, la *nation françoise*, le *peuple françois*.
> D. Qu'est-ce donc qu'une nation?
> R. Une nation est une société d'hommes libres qui vivent sous un même chef, ou plusieurs chefs qu'ils se sont donnés volontairement, pour ne faire qu'un seul & même corps dont l'ame [*sic*] sont les loix par lesquelles ils prétendent être gouvernés.
> [Q. What does one call a society that has given itself a leader, and submitted itself to laws?
> A. One calls it nation, people. So we say, the *French nation*, the *French people*.
> Q. What then is a nation?
> A. A nation is a society of free men who live under the same leader or several leaders that they have voluntarily given themselves, so as to form but one and the same body whose spirit is the laws by which they say they are governed.][14]

This dialogue is noteworthy as an example of the definition and propagation of new political terms in a self-consciously religious idiom. Although the nation here can be recognized by its political unity ("who live under the same leader"), this unity is based on a preexisting, nonpolitical grouping (the "society" referenced above logically must exist before it can choose leaders and submit itself to laws). In this account, social cohesion and unity do not depend on the prior existence of a common government. This catechism emphasizes freedom, the voluntary selection of leaders, and the "submission" to laws rather than to leaders, illustrating a voluntarist and contingent relationship between governor and governed. The greater the emphasis on voluntary choice, the greater the political leverage that could be exercised in the name of the nation to challenge existing political arrangements.

The Revolutionary idea of the nation was thus associated with new political expectations and a new self-conception, which it both fueled and symbolized. A contemporary definition of this term by journalist Pierre-Nicolas Chantreau highlights the connection between language, self-conception, and self-creation:

> [C]ertes, avant le 17 juillet 1789, il n'y avoit jamais eu de Parisien qui se fût avisé de crier *vive la nation* en voyant passer les grands carrosses à huit chevaux, qui venoient de temps en temps de Versailles pour aller à Notre-Dame ou au palais. Mais . . . les langues se modifient et prennent le caractere [*sic*] des peuples; ainsi *nation* a signifié tout parmi nous, dès l'instant que nous avons été réellement une nation. [Certainly, before 17 July 1789, there had never been any Parisian bold enough to cry *long live the nation* upon seeing the great eight-horse carriages go by, that came from time to time from Versailles to go to Notre-Dame or to the palace. But . . . languages change and take on the character of peoples; so *nation* signified everything among us, from the instant that we had really become a nation.][15]

At this early stage in the Revolution, the cry "long live the nation" at the passage of the king heralded him as an agent of the nation, rather than its competitor or even adversary. The nation was emerging as a new source of allegiance and identity, challenging the absolutist model. Chantreau's definition goes on to note the obsolescence of expressions such as "good of the state," "state interest," and "to serve the state," an observation that would have made Cardinal Richelieu, Louis XIII's chief minister and infamous exponent of the doctrine of *raison d'état*, turn in his grave.

The process of consolidating the self-image of the French people as a nation was reflected in and enhanced by the use of the adjective "national." Chantreau's dictionary defines this word, wryly emphasizing its pervasiveness:

> adjectif qui qualifie tout ce qui appartient à la nation; or, tout appartient à la nation, donc tout est national. Aussi depuis la révolution notre maniere [*sic*] d'être physique et morale est devenue entiérement [*sic*] nationale; notre costume, depuis la cocarde jusqu'aux boucles, et [*sic*] national; rien ne paroit sur la toilette de nos dames [qui] ne soit national; chapeau national, ceinture nationale, jusqu'au rouge est national. Notre façon de penser, Dieu sait comme elle est nationale! et nos écrits sont comme nos pensées. [adjective that qualifies all that belongs to the nation; moreover, everything belongs to the nation, so everything is national. Also since the revolution our physical and

> moral way of being has become entirely national; our attire, from the cockade down to the buckles, is national; nothing appears in our ladies' dress that is not national; national hat, national belt, all the way to their rouge is national. Our way of thinking, Lord knows how national it is! and our written works are like our thoughts.][16]

This statement illustrates just how all-encompassing the Revolutionary idea of the nation could become. (Corroborating Chantreau's impression, the permanent exhibit on the French Revolution at the Musée Carnavalet, Paris, displays everything from dinnerware painted with Revolutionary mottoes to trunks with locks sculpted in the shape of the Bastille.) Even in personal matters such as a person's way of being, thinking, and dressing, the concept of the nation was omnipresent. Chantreau's commentary testifies to the role of language and symbols in forging a national consciousness that can manifest itself even in the mundane activities of daily life.

Despite widespread agreement on the importance of this changing vocabulary, some commentators voiced skepticism about the viability of the nation as a guide for creating political institutions. One anonymous dictionary author devotes several pages to the concept of the nation, but seems equivocal about its political utility. He (or she) explicitly affirms the contractarian account of the origins of society and government: individuals in the state of nature join together in order to protect themselves and to enjoy freedom as members of a common community. But he questions how a person could at once have a private will and be part of a unified body, insisting that this could only work within a very small group of people and that, as soon as a leader began to act out of private rather than public interest, the association would dissolve back into the state of nature.[17] Through such critiques, pamphleteers pinpointed the more problematic aspects of Rousseauean and Revolutionary thought.

Skepticism could engender outright cynicism and even protest. A 1792 dictionary by André-Quentin Buée was incisive in its critique of the concept of *Souveraineté de la Nation* (National Sovereignty):

> La volonté d'un individu réel est une et indivisible. Quand je verrai une telle volonté exister, non pas métaphysiquement, mais réellement, mais physiquement dans cette masse qu'on appelle *la nation françoise*, alors je reconnoîtrai en elle une souveraineté réelle. . . . [M]es amis, n'ayez pas peur; vous aurez long-tems [*sic*] votre roi, si vous le conservez jusqu'à ce qu'on voie vingt-cinq millions de têtes sous un même bonnet. [The will of a real individual is one and indi-

> visible. When I see such a will exist, not metaphysically, but really, but physically in this mass that is called *the French nation*, then I will recognize a real sovereignty in it. . . . My friends, fear not; you will have your king for a long time yet, if you keep him until we see twenty-five million heads fit under the same cap.][18]

This critique highlights the appeal of the monarchical conception of governmental legitimacy, namely, the ability to equate the monarch's will with the will of the nation. The problem of a "divisible" will arises when a "real individual" can no longer be thought of as embodying sovereign authority. Discerning a national will capable of providing a basis for political decision making remains a perennial problem for nonauthoritarian regimes. For Buée, the ability to identify a national will capable of fitting "under the same cap" required an unrealistic degree of uniformity among the "mass" of individuals comprising the would-be French nation. This raises a central—and unresolved—question: How much uniformity is required to ensure cohesion, commitment, and compliance in a nation-state? For Buée, the answer was clearly: more uniformity than existed in eighteenth-century France.

Despite Buée's (and others') incredulity, the nation did in time replace the king, first conceptually and then constitutionally. In September 1789, a new slogan—"*la Nation, la Loi, le Roi*"—captured this transition, and enshrined the primacy of the nation as a principle of cohesion, object of allegiance, and source of legitimate authority. An earlier slogan had used the term "*une foi*" (one faith) instead of "*la Nation.*" Eventually, the idea of the nation became the new social cement, and the focus of a "secular religion."[19]

Even the king's own statements indicate a consciousness of the evolving distinction between the monarch and the nation, and the political implications of this development. At the height of the absolute monarchy, the king was viewed as embodying three other "potential" entities: the state (territory plus administrative structure), the nation (the population conceived of in an abstract but administratively defined fashion), and the people (his actual subjects). A conceptual distinction between these categories was precluded by definition. Louis XIV was famous for allegedly declaring, *l'État, c'est moi* (I am the State); he further insisted: "la nation ne fait pas corps en France. Elle réside toute entière dans la personne du roi" (the nation has no body in France. It resides entirely in the king's person).[20] By 1766, Louis XV could not simply assert his authority as had his predecessor, but instead felt compelled to defend it:

> As if anyone could forget that the sovereign power resides in my person only . . . , that public order in its entirety emanates from me and that the rights and interests of the nation, which some dare to regard as a separate body from the monarch, are necessarily united with my rights and interests, and repose only in my hands.[21]

In insisting that the nation's interests were united with his and depended on him, Louis XV contributed to the very conceptual distinction that he was trying to negate.[22] His successor Louis XVI did the same, prefacing a declaration of October 4, 1789, with the words: "dans un moment où nous invitons la Nation à venir au secours de l'État" (at a moment when we are inviting the Nation to come to the rescue of the State).[23] Louis XIV's statement "I am the State" was meant to be an assertion of total power, but had Louis XVI uttered this same phrase during the Revolution, it would have been construed as overreaching. The nation could be invoked to bolster the state, but it could also be used to check it. This was the first step on the path to the nation becoming the state's very basis.

The process of conceptual disaggregation did not end with the distinction between nation and state. As explored in chapter two, the king was also separated from the state such that the representatives of the nation could control and eventually depose him.[24] The centrality of the nation implied the superfluity of the king:

> Par-delà les rois et les dynasties mêmes, . . . s'établit une permanence appelée le peuple ou la nation. Les rois et les dynasties peuvent disparaître; la nation demeure. . . . D'Holbach, dans *Le Système social* [1773], résume la pensée du siècle: ". . . Il est évident que ce ne sont pas les Rois qui font les nations, mais que c'est le consentement des nations qui fait les Rois. Une nation peut sans Roi être très bien gouvernée, mais un Roi ne peut ni exister, ni gouverner sans nation." [A permanent force called the people or the nation establishes itself over and above kings and even dynasties. . . . Kings and dynasties can disappear; the nation remains. . . . D'Holbach, in *The social system*, sums up the century's thought: ". . . It is evident that it is not Kings who make nations, but that it is the consent of nations that makes Kings. A nation can be very well governed without a King, but a King can neither exist, nor govern without a nation."][25]

This view was directly opposed to that of Jacob Nicolas Moreau, the king's historian, who insisted in 1789: "Sans le roi point de nation" (Without the king, no nation).[26] A dividing line arose between those who championed the primacy of the nation and those who continued to view the nation as subsumed by, and dependent on, the king.

The concept of the *patrie*, related to that of the nation, was also at stake in this semantic struggle. Historian Henri Hauser suggested in 1916 that the idea of the *patrie* "resulted from the dissociation of the idea of the king from the idea of the nation."[27] While the word *patrie* appeared in French in the mid-sixteenth century, and the word *patriote* a century later, they did not become central to political vocabulary until the pre-Revolutionary period.[28] The Abbé Gabriel-François Coyer published a treatise devoted to reviving the concept of *patrie* in 1755, in which he wrote: "J'interroge ce citoyen qui marche toujours armé: Quel est votre emploi? *Je sers le Roi*, me dit-il, pourquoi pas la *Patrie*? Le Roi lui-même est fait pour la servir" (I ask this citizen who always walks armed: "What is your occupation?" *I serve the King*, he tells me. "Why not the *Patrie*? The King himself was created to serve it").[29] For Coyer, as for many others, political experience and political language are closely connected. Coyer wrote: "Il s'agit donc ici de ressusciter l'idée pour rétablir le mot" (It is thus a question here of resuscitating the idea in order to reestablish the word).[30] For Coyer, the words "France," "State," and "Kingdom" were inadequate to express the idea of the *patrie* as a union constituted by a paternal bond between ruler and ruled. The *patrie* is characterized by social unity, "fellow-feeling," respect for the human race, freedom, and harmony. Only in a country with all the required characteristics does the term *patrie* have any meaning; indicating its absence from France was itself a form of political critique.

Above all, the *patrie* is antithetical to all forms of despotism, though not necessarily to monarchy. Jean de La Bruyère, author and tutor in the house of Louis II de Bourbon, prince de Condé, had already written in the late seventeenth century that "[i]l n'y a point de patrie dans le despotique; d'autres choses y suppléent: l'intérêt, la gloire, le service du prince" (there is no *patrie* in that which is despotic; other things take its place: interest, glory, service to the prince).[31] The remedy is not necessarily to eliminate the monarch, but simply to ensure good governance: "[faire] d'une cour, et même de tout un royaume, comme une seule famille, unie parfaitement sous un même chef, dont l'union et la bonne intelligence est redoutable au reste du monde" (to make of a court, and even of a whole kingdom, one single family, perfectly united under the same leader, whose union and good intelligence are formidable to the rest of the world).[32] The idea of *patrie* is connected to that of political unity: unlike nation, *patrie* does not appear to have taken on a nonpolitical meaning. However, it did acquire a Revolutionary charge derived from its emphasis on freedom. In his 1765 article on "*patrie*" in the *Encyclopédie*, the philosopher Louis, chevalier de Jaucourt, emphasized the impossibility of having a *patrie* under "the yoke of despotism," noting that a *patrie* is only possible in democracies where individuals put the public interest ahead of their own.[33] Support for the *patrie* became antimonarchical once the king himself became perceived as a threat to the freedom of the nation, with which he was no longer equated.

The widespread view of the *patrie* as inextricably linked to freedom did not go uncontested, highlighting the politicization of vocabulary and the partisan implications of competing definitions. André-Quentin Buée, the satirical lexicographer cited above, wrote of *patriotisme*:

> Les grammairiens disent, que *c'est le courage de sacrifier son intérêt particulier à sa patrie.*
> Les historiens qui se proposent d'écrire l'histoire de la révolution, disent, que c'est maintenant *le courage de sacrifier sa patrie à son intérêt particulier.*
> J'aime sincèrement ma patrie; ce qui le prouve, c'est que je n'ai pas encore un seul acte de patriotisme à me reprocher.
> [Grammarians say that (patriotism) is *the courage to sacrifice one's particular interest for one's* patrie.
> Historians who intend to write the history of the revolution say that it is now *the courage to sacrifice one's* patrie *for one's particular interest.*
> I sincerely love my *patrie*; the proof is that I do not yet have a single act of patriotism with which to reproach myself.][34]

Struggles over semantics also involved attempts to appropriate words for conflicting political purposes. The *patrie* might be antithetical to despotism but, for some, Revolutionary despotism was the worst form of tyranny.

By the time of the Revolution, the nation was poised to become the central platform for claims to political legitimacy and territorial control. This was reflected in the terms for crimes of treason. Historian Beatrice Hyslop, who undertook a major study of Revolutionary *cahiers de doléances* (booklets of grievances) in 1934, notes:

> The traditional term for treason was *lèse-majesté*. The changing psychology and sentiments were illustrated by the use of five other terms in the cahiers of 1789: *crime d'état*, *lèse-nation*, *lèse-patrie*, *lèse-liberté*, and *lèse-humanité*. . . . In all of these cases, treason was no

> longer action against the monarch, but against the rights and interests of the French people. For such cahiers, patriotism clearly was loyalty to the nation.[35]

In his 1792 dictionary, Buée laments: "L'amour des François pour leurs rois est devenu un crime de lèze-nation" (The love of the French for their kings has become a crime of treason against the nation).[36] The nation and the king were increasingly construed as antithetical. "Loyalty to the nation" became the litmus test for political and social acceptability, as explored further in the chapters on constitution and composition below.

Semantic debates such as those traced above confirmed the centrality of new and revived concepts such as "nation" and "*patrie*." The Revolutionary account of the relationship between king and nation, and its expression in political vocabulary, ultimately defined the criteria for political authority and allegiance in France. This, in turn, contributed to the development of a nation-based conception of the political and territorial legitimacy of states as members of international society.

1.2 Conceptions of the Nation in Social Contract Theories

Although monarchical authority was not challenged directly until late in the eighteenth century, Enlightenment thinkers drew a sharp distinction early on between absolute and arbitrary rule, only the first of which was deemed legitimate. Support for monarchy in general did not entail unconditional support for the king. This implied the existence of some alternative standard of action besides the king's own wishes, embodied in the idea of "fundamental laws" that circumscribed the operation of a monarchy guided by reason.[37] The fundamental laws formed part of a rudimentary contract circumscribing the actions of the king, the foundation for a conditional view of his political mandate.

The emerging distinction between the nation and the king created the possibility for the popular or national will to contradict that of the monarch. The development and popularization of contractualist theories reinforced this conceptual separation and enhanced the potential for conflict. The emphasis on governmental accountability implicit in contractual ideas required the identification of separate contracting parties. The king went from being the embodiment of the French territory and administration to a functionary charged with its preservation;[38] the people or nation emerged as the entity to which he was accountable. Contractualist theories propagated by the *parlements* in their struggle for power created the nation as a political actor with rights that could be opposed to those of the king.[39] This had the subsidiary effect of suggesting a further distinction between the king as a functionary and the state as a territorially specific administrative structure, introducing the possibility of a king-less state.

The appeal to a contract between rulers and ruled as the basis for legitimate government assumes the existence of a separate nation as a contracting party. Whether a particular contractarian doctrine invoked the "people," the "nation," or "society" in general, the core idea of a group of individuals existing—or at least conceivable—separate from its political institutions, and thus possessing the potential to challenge these institutions, was a crucial development in political thought. This section explores this implicit premise of social contract theory as a framework for articulating and justifying nation-based claims. The contractualist model of the state, in which a people chooses its government, seems maximally consistent with the voluntarist model of nationhood, in which individuals choose their national membership. The question of what factors can best ensure cohesion, commitment, and compliance in such a nation-state remains central to contemporary nation-building projects that are grounded, at least in theory, in conceptions of political authority that seek to maximize individual choice.

Hints of a possible contractual relationship between the king and the nation can be detected in French political rhetoric before the eighteenth century. For example, in 1527, the president of the *parlement* of Paris used a marriage metaphor to describe the relationship between the king and the realm, "predicat[ing] the duration of that fictive espousal upon the monarch's successful maintenance of French Public Law."[40] Such conditionality was also implicit in the notion of the king as charged with upholding France's fundamental laws. The contractual paradigm made this agreement explicit, creating the conditions for the king's potential forfeiture of public power.

Contractualist logic contributed to an emerging view of sovereignty as residing in the nation rather than the king, with the king only provisionally invested with the executive power and susceptible to censure for violations of the public trust. Bordeaux lawyer Guillaume-Joseph Saige explained in his 1788 *Catéchisme du citoyen*:

> Toute aliénation, permanente ou passagère, du pouvoir social se trouve également opposée aux droits de l'homme & à la nature du corps politique. . . . Il suit de ce raisonnement, que le pouvoir souverain est inséparable du corps du peuple; qu'il ne peut en sortir dans aucune circonstance; & que l'aliéner, c'est le détruire, violer le

> pacte social, & dissoudre le corps politique. [Any alienation, permanent or passing, of the social power is equally opposed to the rights of man and to the nature of the political body. . . . It follows from this reasoning that the sovereign power is inseparable from the body of the people; that it cannot depart from this body under any circumstances; and that to alienate it is to destroy it, to violate the social compact, and to dissolve the political body.][41]

Locating the sovereign power in the "body of the people" rather than the body of the king meant that the king could no longer claim to hold the nation together. The king was no longer constitutive of the nation, making his position more precarious.

The central innovation of the contractual paradigm was the notion of the nation itself as the source of the monarch's legitimacy, conferred through an original act of consent. This consent also entailed an ongoing right of the nation to monitor the government, if not to participate in it. The nation became a political subject, rather than just the object of laws.[42] The contractual paradigm per se did not ensure the self-sufficiency of the nation, but it did create a powerful metaphor for the conditional nature of the king's authority, introducing the potential for the nation to revoke the king's claim to legitimate control. Different contractual models attribute different degrees of independence to the nation as a conceptual category and potential political actor. They can be labeled the Hobbesian, Lockean, and Rousseauean versions, respectively.

Thomas Hobbes's 1651 *Leviathan* presented a model in which individuals come together and submit themselves to the sovereign in an act that simultaneously creates the state and the people.[43] In the Hobbesian version of the social contract, a strong state gives the people a basis for cohesion by providing structures that respond to a common need for security. Even after joining together, the people cannot be conceived of as existing independent of the state. The sovereign power might have a contractual basis, but the arrangement is largely one-sided: while the ruler's obligation to provide protection might make political authority conditional in the abstract, the drastic, destabilizing consequences of dissolving the sovereign strongly discourage revolutionary challenge. The people depends on the sovereign for its existence as a coherent whole: if the state were to crumble, individuals would lose their cohesive framework and would return to the state of nature. The Hobbesian account of the social contract provides a powerful disincentive for popular uprisings: indeed, this was Hobbes's intention, as he sought to avoid a repetition of the English Civil War.

Later in the seventeenth century, John Locke published *Two Treatises of Government*. The Lockean version of the social contract enables the people to remain unified separate from its governing structures by positing a two-step process: the formation of the people, followed by the institution of government.[44] In this conception, the people reserves the right to challenge and to transform state institutions if these do not fulfill their function. If the state succumbs, the people remains intact, since its cohesion no longer depends on governmental structures. This conceptual modification was a prerequisite for the reconceptualization of authority as inhering in the people rather than the king: as highlighted by the Hobbesian contract, the people could not easily challenge the king while it was still seen as depending on him for its very existence. On a theoretical level, this Lockean right of rebellion provided a justification for the American Revolution, based explicitly on alleged violations of governmental obligations by King George III. As stated in the 1776 American Declaration of Independence: "[T]o secure these [unalienable] rights, Governments are instituted among Men, deriving their just powers from the consent of the governed. . . . [W]henever any Form of Government becomes destructive of these ends, it is the Right of the People to alter or to abolish it, and to institute new Government." In this model, specific abuses of authority trigger a latent right inherent in the people to withdraw its consent and depose the offending official.

The French Revolution went farther than the American one, not only in its universalist ambitions, but also because it framed national self-determination as a fundamental right inhering in the nation, rather than a contingent prerogative created by persistent governmental abuse.[45] This distinction is of crucial importance in contemporary self-determination arguments, since it determines whether or not the demonstration of a violation is a prerequisite for exercising the right to national self-determination, often in the form of secession.[46] It also accounts in part for the focus of this study on the French, rather than the American, experience, as the French Revolutionaries articulated and sought to implement a more expansive version of the national self-determination principle.

In France, the influence of Jean-Jacques Rousseau was determinative in guiding the reconceptualization and reconstruction of legitimate political authority.[47] While Hobbes had been unable to conceive of a people without reference to a *pactum repraesentationis* that gave it unity and made it capable of acting on its will,[48] Rousseau envisaged the people as a pre-political entity that gave rise to governmental institutions.[49] For Rousseau, the state is nothing more than the concrete expression of the will of the people, which is assumed to be unified and coherent. Individuals do not renounce their freedom by creating society and the state: they retain it, and exercise it all the more effectively by channeling it into common institutions, guided by an omniscient Legislator, a sort of Enlightened *Leviathan.* Sovereignty, conceived of as indivisible and inalienable, inheres in the people, which must therefore also be conceived of as a unified and independent whole. Only an entity with its own internal principles of cohesion could challenge a monarch who had historically embodied the state's constitutive power. By giving the people a separate rhetorical existence, Rousseau provided a conceptual framework in which the people could and did become the ultimate political actor.

Rousseau's vision, however compelling, was far from unproblematic. Historically speaking, the ability to conceive of a French nation was very much a product of the administrative centralization and territorial consolidation achieved by French kings, partially validating Hobbes's skepticism about the possibility of a pre-institutional people. Four questions arise in the face of the Rousseauean idea of the people as a political actor that is, by nature, pre-political:

1. How can such an entity exist? (conception)
2. How can one identify it, if it does exist? (constitution)
3. How can it be held together, if not by political institutions? (composition)
4. What rules govern its interaction with other political units? (confrontation)

The doubts raised by these questions jeopardize the logical coherence and practical viability of relying on nonpolitical entities as the bases for constructing and legitimizing the component units of international society.

Rousseau defines his project in terms of the first question: discerning and describing "l'acte par lequel un peuple est un peuple" (the act by which a people is a people), which precedes "l'acte par lequel le peuple élit un roi" (the act by which the people elects a king).[50] His version of the social contract, which constitutes a society coextensive with the body politic, refers only to this first, fundamental agreement. In contrast to Hobbes's vision of an exchange of freedom for security, Rousseau imagines a form of protective association in which all members retain their freedom by obeying only self-given laws.[51] The initial associative act, requiring the total surrender of the self to the community,[52] "produit un corps moral et collectif . . . lequel reçoit de ce même acte son unité, son *moi* commun, sa vie et sa volonté" (produces a moral and collective body . . . which receives from this same act its unity, its common *me*, its life and its will).[53] As anti-individualist as this act appears, it remains in Rousseau's vision the "acte constitutive de la patrie à l'origine de toute liberté civile" (constitutive act of the *patrie* at the origin of all civil liberty).[54] In theory, guarantees of individual freedom are no longer dependent on the caprice or even on the commitment of the monarch, but emanate from the very configuration of civil and political life itself. However, it remains unclear what would motivate a people to engage in this bottom-up act of association to begin with. If pre-political sociability is a contradiction in terms (as it is for Rousseau), then finding a solution to the paradox of conception seems an impossible task.

The second question—how to identify a voluntarist, preexisting nation if one does exist—is, on the surface, equally puzzling. How can one point to evidence of an agreement to live under common institutions except by looking to those institutions themselves? Doing so would require begging the question of how a pre-political entity can exist as the constituent power *behind* political institutions, since one is forced from the beginning to take these institutions and their boundaries as given. This problem is compounded by the fact that conceiving of the nation as a pre- or nonpolitical entity becomes more important when there are challenges to existing political and territorial boundaries. In contrast to Hobbes, Rousseau is adamant that sovereignty cannot be represented: political decisions are the direct emanation of a people's will, derived from its particular nature.[55] But while Rousseau envisions state institutions as emblematic, rather than constitutive, of a people, this distinction is conceptually difficult to maintain.[56] This problem of circularity plagues attempts to identify nations without looking to their institutional manifestations. It is exacerbated in the case of a voluntarist nation whose self-definition precludes reference to innate characteristics as a basis for national identification, political constitution, and territorial delineation.

Rousseau relies on the notion of "national character" as the marker of a voluntarily constituted people. This idea offers a potential solution to the paradox of conception, and it foreshadows Rousseau's answer to the paradox of composition—the question of how a voluntarist nation can be conceived of as internally, as opposed to externally, cohesive. However, once again, the difference between internal and external cohesion is undermined by a problematic circularity, since national character is largely a product of institutions: once the people create the state, the state cannot help but define the people.[57] The possibility of nation-building by the state becomes increasingly important as theory is put into practice, as Rousseau discovered in his later attempts to devise constitutions for Poland and Corsica.

In the *Social Contract*, Rousseau insists that despotism can never provide the kind of internal cohesion needed to hold a people together: "c'est, si l'on veut, une agrégation, mais non pas une association: il n'y a ni bien public, ni corps politique" (it is, if you wish, an aggregation, but not an association: there is neither public good, nor body politic).[58] This echoes the view in the *Encyclopédie* that a *patrie* cannot exist under despotism. The Hobbesian model is inadequate because it does not provide the people with a strong, independent existence. But Rousseau ends up needing something more than pure voluntarism and its implied revocability to serve as an adequate replacement for insecurity or compulsion as the basis of social cohesion. He asserts that there exist fundamentally harmonious "real" interests among individuals in society despite their divergent "apparent" interests, which enables him in theory to maintain a unitary vision of the sovereign people without recourse to coercion. In practice, the French search for solidarity in the name of Rousseauean ideals would ultimately entail a campaign against divergence, blurring the line between natural community and enforced conformity. Instead of institutionalizing diversity and individual freedom, the doctrine of popular sovereignty ended up buttressing a monolithic and even exclusionary conception of nationhood.

The circularity of Rousseau's answers to the first and second questions of how a nonpolitical entity can exist and be identified (conception and constitution), and the difficulty of holding a people together without relying on institutions (composition), create the need to posit even stronger pre-institutional ties among members. The difficulty of reconciling voluntarism with the idea of "automatic" or preexisting bonds among individuals, already present in the Rousseauean model, took on increasing importance as the theory of popular sovereignty was put into practice during the Revolution. These conceptual and concrete problems challenge the strict dichotomy between voluntarist and nonvoluntarist definitions of national membership, and call into question the "liberal" credentials of contractarian ideas intended to promote inclusiveness and individual freedom. The paradox of conception highlights the risks involved in basing political legitimacy exclusively on the idea of a separate, nonpolitical nation, even one united by supposedly voluntarist ties.

The French Revolution was torn between individualist and collectivist principles and priorities. The emphasis in Revolutionary rhetoric on the nation, rather than on "civil society" or some other less holistic image, reinforced the collectivist strand in Revolutionary thought. The primacy of the nation entailed the subordination and even the suppression of alternative associations and allegiances. Associative ties at the subnational level constitute the very fabric of civil society, but they were considered parasitic on the exclusive allegiance demanded by the Revolutionary nation. The mobilizing power of the nation was enhanced by its conceptual independence from the state. Civil society, by contrast, remained largely political in nature.[59] This made civil society much weaker than the nation as a platform for political opposition; unlike the nation, "civil society" did not become entrenched in the Revolutionary lexicon (although Emmanuel-Joseph Sieyès's conception of the Third Estate, discussed in chapter two, can be viewed as a description of what we would call "civil society," showing the influence of Scottish philosopher and economist Adam Smith).

For Adam Smith, "[t]he state provided a rule-bound framework within which people could live and work, exchange and contract. . . . But it had no other responsibility; it could not lay down the parameters of a good life, or define the collective good, or represent the collective will, or prescribe roles for the people."[60] The French Revolutionary model, by contrast, upheld the nation-state as the highest realization of the collective good, the expression and embodiment of the collective national will: "Robespierre, asked what constitution he wanted, replied 'That of Lycurgus'" (invoking a Spartan, rather than an Athenian, model).[61] The Revolutionary nation was initially envisaged as a check on the state, but its potency as a political platform fueled a process whereby the nation came to define the state itself. The Revolutionaries created a secular religion of nationhood based on liberty, but they inculcated a civic culture that was highly intolerant of divergence and dissent.[62]

Invoking German sociologist Ferdinand Tönnies's distinction between *Gesellschaft* (society) and *Gemeinschaft* (community), Ernest Gellner observes of nationalism in general: "Rooted in an emerging *Gesellschaft*, it preached *Gemeinschaft*."[63] This observation is particularly relevant in the context of the French Revolution. The political ideas of civil society and of the sovereign nation both stemmed from an emancipatory impulse, but they parted company in their tendencies (individualist vs. collectivist) and in their primary political functions (private vs. public mobilization). Riding the crest of the conceptual innovations described above, the French Revolutionaries chose the path of the unitary nation-state.

Conclusion

This chapter has canvassed the paradox of conception: how to imagine a nonpolitical, voluntarist nation as the basis for the political and territorial legitimacy of a state. During the eighteenth century, this dilemma was situated within a particular set of concerns, namely, how to develop principles of governmental accountability against the historical backdrop of monarchical absolutism. A combination of political ambition (on the part of French aristocrats seeking to maintain and to enhance their power) and Enlightenment rationality (on the part of thinkers seeking to articulate principled justifications for submission to political authority) fueled the conceptual separation of king, state, and nation, a first step towards establishing a sovereign nation in the place of a sovereign king.

This development was both favorable and foreboding. It was favorable in that it opened the door to a more broadly participatory form of government, based on principles of governmental accountability and popular consent. It was foreboding in that, in order to provide a counterweight to an absolutist monarch (in addition to the competing identities and allegiances demanded by various corporate bodies or *corps*, such as provinces, guilds, village communes, and the Church[64]), the people was envisaged as essentially unitary, with potentially repressive results. Even in the absence of a discourse of ethnic homogeneity more commonly associated with illiberal models of nationhood, the idea of the nation in pre-Revolutionary France contained the potential, and even the propensity, to become an exclusionary platform for claims to political power.

The next three chapters continue to trace the evolution of the French Revolutionary nation in an effort to gain a deeper understanding of the theoretical and practical issues at stake in the articulation of nation-based claims to political power and territorial control. This historical analysis provides a framework for exploring ongoing contradictions and dilemmas involved in national self-determination, a project begun in chapters five and six.

Chapter 2

Constitution

How to Give the Nation a Political Voice

Introduction

In addition to emerging political theories, concrete power struggles within France served as a catalyst for an increasing emphasis on the idea of the nation, a development with crucial conceptual and institutional implications. In co-opting and operationalizing the contractualist requirement of popular consent to bolster their own importance, the *parlements* (French sovereign law courts), among other actors, helped enshrine the effectiveness of claims to political power made in the name of the nation, a rhetorical entity abstract enough to be manipulated but concrete enough to be compelling.[1] Not surprisingly, the deliberate use of the nation by the *parlements* as a vehicle for their own political ambitions had the unintended effect of opening the door for other self-styled national spokespeople to override even the *parlements*' claims.[2]

The paradox of constitution focuses on the need to rely on those who speak on behalf of the nation in order to validate and to effectuate the nation's political claims, including the claim to statehood. This leads to a certain circularity, as "the ability to support a claim to statehood is partly *constitutive* of our notion of a nation."[3] In theory, the Revolutionary nation became a political actor; in practice, politics became a competition between individuals and groups claiming to speak on the nation's behalf. Political discourse became a sort of reverse ventriloquism whereby rhetoricians (notably lawyers acting as delegates for the Third Estate) asserted that they were speaking in the nation's name and even with the nation's voice: conflicting claims led successive leaders to be denounced as "inauthentic" and replaced with often equally precarious pretenders.[4] The paradox of constitution highlights the susceptibility of nationalist platforms to appropriation by different political groups claiming to represent and even to incarnate the nation. In France, Revolutionary leaders ultimately came to uphold the nation as the constitutive basis of the state and the sole source of legitimate political authority. In large part, speaking for the nation meant controlling the state.

This chapter looks at how nation-based claims to political power were made, first by the *parlements* (section 2.1), and then by a National Assembly (section 2.2) supported in part by the arguments of the Abbé Sieyès (section 2.3). It focuses on the early stages of the Revolution, when the abstract idea of the nation became a concrete political tool. The theoretical potential of the nation as a political platform was actualized by practical imperatives: the *parlements* made strategic use of the nation to bolster their position vis-à-vis the king in the administrative hierarchy; the members of the National Assembly used the nation as a platform to combat their exclusion from political decision making; and the Abbé Sieyès argued for a shift in the balance of political power toward the numerically superior and economically vital Third Estate. The process of constitution entrenched the nation as a central legitimating platform without necessarily promoting the interests of the individuals within it, or contributing to political stability.

The nation might have been conceptualized as a pre-political association, but it was only by adopting concrete institutions that it could translate theoretical power into effective political sway. This is where the paradox of constitution complicates the paradox of conception. The practical imperative of creating political institutions in order to effectuate the nation's claims means that those who succeed in speaking for the nation will become the authors of the national will. In addition, because the unity of national identity and purpose is often expressed in—if not created by—state institutions such as the National Assembly, the nation and the state become even more difficult to distinguish. This lack of clarity can further undermine the potency of nationhood as a legitimating platform: as the paradox of conception indicates, it is difficult to adjudicate between rival territorial and political claims based on a standard (the nation) that is not identifiable separate from the entity it is meant to legitimate or challenge (the state). The paradox of constitution adds to this dilemma, because it enhances the presumptive legitimacy of nation-based claims without providing a guide for ascertaining the credibility of demands apart from the convictions of those who make them.

The challenge of building nation-based political institutions makes nationalist arguments vulnerable to competing claims and pressures. The rise of the nation as a political platform in the early stages of the French Revolution illustrates this problem of competing claims and its implications. In any nation-building project, practical constraints can shape emerging political ideals, often with predictable results. In the Revolutionary context, these constraints pushed a voluntarist ideal of nationhood towards a more exclusionary model, as explored more fully in chapter three. This chapter suggests how and why the nation became politically important in the first place, foreshadowing the dangers nationalist rhetoric can entail. While the potential for abusing nationalist platforms does not necessarily diminish the ethical value and importance of nationhood, it does suggest a need for caution in accepting and supporting nation-based arguments for political and territorial control.

2.1 The Entrenchment of the Nation in French Political Rhetoric

The emergence of the nation as a political platform was fueled by parliamentary remonstrances, petitions submitted by the *parlements* to the king. Under Louis XIV, remonstrances were a mere formality, presented after royally enacted laws had already been registered. At Louis XIV's death in 1715, the regent Philippe d'Orléans allowed the remonstrances to be given before registration, inadvertently making them a vehicle for competing claims to political power.[5] Although they were meant to be secret, certain remonstrances were leaked and published, leading to public debate when the monarch felt compelled to respond.[6]

The remonstrances were not always combative: in some respects, they actually served the king and his ministers by creating the impression of an institutionalized check upon the monarchy. But the relationship between the king and the *parlements* was tense, leading to successive crises—most notably in 1771, when the royal chancellor sparked public outrage by exiling the Paris *parlement*.[7] Such hostility could make the *parlements* bolder, rather than more conciliatory, as they used their remonstrances to claim political standing, often at the king's expense.[8] In their campaign to ensure their own continued viability, the *parlements* developed and popularized new political concepts, providing a catalyst for the reconceptualization of political legitimacy as based on the nation rather than the king.

The remonstrances offer a privileged window into the nature and development of theories about governmental legitimacy, since they were not only reflective but also partly constitutive of a new political discourse. Parliamentary arguments operated largely within a contractual vision of the relationship between government and governed, showing the strong influence of the eighteenth-century *philosophes*.[9] For example, the *Encyclopédie* defined "Sovereigns" as "ceux à qui la volonté des peuples a conféré le pouvoir nécessaire pour gouverner la société" (those to whom the peoples' will has conferred the power necessary for governing society).[10] The *parlements* found the contractarian idea of a separate, preexisting basis of legitimacy particularly expedient in power struggles with the king, and used this abstract notion to support their concrete political claims.

The remonstrances had three important effects from the perspective of this analysis. First, they emphasized the distinction between king and state: they extrapolated from the idea of "fundamental laws" as checks on the arbitrary exercise of monarchical power to suggest the conditional nature of the king's legitimacy, separate from the stable existence of the French state per se. Second, they reinforced the idea of a people with its own rights and interests that had to be protected (by the *parlements*) against unjustified encroachment. Third, they enshrined the concept of the nation as a particularly strong and compelling way to represent the French population as spatially unified and temporally continuous: they created a practice of making political claims in the nation's name. These three developments formed important stages in the emergence of the nation as the basis of the state's legitimacy and a central platform for claims to political power.

The first effect of the debates between the king and *parlements* was to weaken the monolithic conception of government by suggesting a separation between the king and the state.[11] In the seventeenth century, the notion of the state had little independence in France.[12] The idea of *raison d'état* as a potential justification for the king's actions suggested an emerging separation between the king and the state (with the state representing something distinct from the personal interests of the ruler), but it remained largely the king's prerogative to discern and define state interests. A shift in emphasis was foreshadowed in 1664, when Louis XIV's finance minister Nicolas Fouquet was condemned for treason to the state, rather than the king.[13] By 1750, the *Encyclopédie* showed evidence of a more drastic reconceptualization:

> Ce n'est pas l'état qui appartient au prince, c'est le prince qui appartient à l'état. . . . En un mot, la couronne, le gouvernement, & l'*autorité* publique, sont des biens dont le corps de la nation est propriétaire, & dont les princes sont les usufruitiers, les ministres & les dépositaires. [It is not the state that belongs to the prince, it is the prince who belongs to the state. . . . In a word, the crown, the government, and public *authority*, are goods of which the body of the nation is the proprietor, and of which princes are the usufructuaries, the ministers and the depositaries.][14]

According to this definition, institutions of public authority were entrusted to the prince by the nation: they did not belong to him and were not uniquely subject to his discretion. This carried the revolutionary implication that the nation could challenge the legitimacy of the monarch without jeopardizing the state itself, making the king's position conditional at best, precarious at worst. The *parlements* capitalized on this tripartite conception (king, state, nation), enhancing their own importance by claiming to uphold the interest of the nation in their dealings with the king.

Both the *parlements* and the king upheld the good of the nation as a standard for governing the kingdom. However, they disagreed about how to discern and defend the nation's interest, and about whether or not this interest was separate from that of the monarch. The conditional nature of the monarchy was based on the idea of a contract between the nation and the king. This contract was reflected in the kingdom's fundamental laws, which constrained the exercise of royal power.[15] This foundational agreement established a critical distinction between absolute and arbitrary rule, only the former of which was legitimate.[16] The *parlements* presented themselves as the historical guardians of the fundamental laws, based on the notion, expressed by the *philosophe* Abbé Mably, that "[a]ucune autorité légitime n'est fondée que sur un contrat raisonnable, et il faut veiller à ce que les rois ne le remettent en cause par de menus empiètements" (no legitimate authority can be founded except upon a reasonable contract, and it is necessary to keep watch to make sure that kings do not jeopardize this through piecemeal encroachments).[17] The power-hungry *parlements* justified their own existence by invoking the spectre of a power-hungry king, whom only parliamentary vigilance could prevent from usurping the rights of the nation. Paradoxically, this arrangement also reinforced the king's legitimacy by providing reassurance that he could not surreptitiously abuse his position.

The *parlements* rarely if ever accompanied their insistence on the centrality of the fundamental laws with an explicit attempt to define them. The Parisian *Cour des Aides* was particularly blunt on this issue: "Il existe en France, comme dans toutes les Monarchies, quelques droits inviolables qui appartiennent à la Nation. Nous n'aurons pas la témérité de discuter jusqu'où ils s'étendent; mais en un mot il en existe" (There exist in France, as in all Monarchies, some inviolable rights that belong to the Nation. We shall not be so bold as to discuss how far they extend; but in a word, some exist).[18] Besides Salic law (first compiled in the sixth century under the Frankish king Clovis I), only custom could be upheld as evidence of these laws in operation, as they were not contained in any written code. The idea of fundamental laws was more important than their content. The *parlements*' self-proclaimed role as the guardian of these laws let the *parlements* claim to legitimize the king (by institutionalizing a potential check on him) while protecting the nation (by monitoring the king's use of the power delegated to him by the nation).

The *parlements* played an important role in developing the terms of new political arguments, and especially in entrenching the centrality of the nation itself. This process had limited motives but far-reaching consequences. The *parlements*' logic was simple: the fundamental laws could only provide a viable platform for parliamentary claims to political power if public opinion sided consistently with the *parlements*' interpretation of their role.[19] The *parlements* recognized that they could best ensure their own survival by articulating their claims on behalf of the people upon whom they depended for political support. This recognition led to their strategic emphasis on popular consent, an idea that would prove central to subsequent arguments for political reform.

The *parlements*' position did not enjoy universal support and enthusiasm. Pamphlets including the sarcastically titled *Remontrances d'un citoyen aux Parlemens* [*sic*] *de France* (Remonstrances of a Citizen to the *Parlements* of France) accused the *parlements* of wanting to turn the French monarch into an English-style king, and reaffirmed the legitimacy of the French king's absolute power as "une de ces vérités évidentes, connues des plus grands idiots" (one of these self-evident truths, known to the biggest idiots).[20] Even some who subscribed to a broadly contractual model of governmental authority proved hesitant to criticize the king, supporting the *parlements* as a reinforcement of monarchical legitimacy rather than a challenge to it. Jean Denis Lanjuinais, lawyer and professor of ecclesiastical law at the University of Rennes, wrote in a 1788 pamphlet:

> Un Roi est un Magistrat, mais le premier, le plus nécessaire des Magistrats, surtout dans un Empire étendu comme la France; c'est le chef de famille sans lequel il n'y aurait qu'un amas désordonné de peuplades incohérentes; le Roi est le moteur suprême, le dépositaire de la puissance exécutrice; il donne aux lois que la Nation a consenties le sceau de l'autorité publique, il est l'appui essentiel du peuple, la pierre fondamentale de notre édifice social. [A King is a Magistrate, but the first, the most necessary of Magistrates, especially in a vast Empire such as France; he is the head of the family without which there would be nothing but a disorganized heap of incoherent clans; the King is the supreme motor, the depositary of the executive power; he gives the seal of public authority to the laws to which the Nation has consented; he is the essential support of the people, the cornerstone of our social edifice.][21]

Sympathy for a nation-based political discourse was not incompatible with support for the monarch (Lanjuinais, a delegate to the Estates-General from the Third Estate, later opposed the trial of Louis XVI). Revolutionary politicians denounced the aristocratic *parlements* long before they turned against the king.

The second effect of the parliamentary remonstrances was to reinforce the emerging conception of "the people" as a check on, and even the source of, political authority. This gave the people itself a more concrete, separate, and independent existence, and undermined the absolutist vision of the king as the sole embodiment of the nation.[22] The *parlements* accomplished this transformation by invoking a largely mythic tradition of required consent to legislation derived from the ninth-century Edict of Pistes, propagated by king of the West Franks (and later Holy Roman Emperor) Charles the Bald: *Lex consensu populi fit et constitutione Regis* (Law is made by the consent of the people and the decree of the king).[23] The *parlements* asserted that it was their responsibility and prerogative, acting on behalf of the people, to ensure that new legislation was not only in accordance with the fundamental laws, but also in the broader public interest. The *parlements*' arguments, intended to enhance and to entrench their own power, were increasingly phrased with reference to the people, elevating the people itself in the kingdom's political hierarchy.

The third and ultimate effect of the remonstrances was to place the people, increasingly referred to as the nation, at the heart of political discourse.[24] The *parlements* soon found that the role of mere guardian of the fundamental laws was not sufficiently compelling to ensure their own survival: there had to be some reason *why* these laws were worth defending, some entity so crucial that its rights and interests merited protection even against the king's own claims. The idea of the nation called to mind both the actual and historical populations of France, evoking a sense of temporal and spatial continuity and even transcendence. The infrequent use of the word "nation" during the early eighteenth century and its prior lack of emotional resonance made it the ideal semantic vessel for those seeking to re-establish the legitimacy of political institutions on new conceptual foundations.[25] According to parliamentary rhetoric, only those who upheld the rights of the nation could stake a legitimate claim to political power. In this fashion, the nation provided a crucial platform for the *parlements*' claims, as long as they could ensure a monopoly on its use. Predictably, this strategy proved dangerous by paving the way for the appropriation of the *parlements*' arguments by other political contenders also claiming to speak on the nation's behalf.

The more the *parlements* felt their own existence was threatened, the more they emphasized the importance of the nation and their unique role in protecting it, again demonstrating the importance of practical imperatives in shaping political principles:

> [C]e droit ne pourrait pas être perdu pour la Nation; il est imprescriptible, inaliénable. Attaquer ce principe, c'est trahir non seulement la Nation, mais les rois mêmes; c'est renverser la constitution du Royaume, c'est détruire le fondement de l'autorité du Monarque. [This right could not be lost for the Nation; it is imprescriptible, inalienable. To attack this principle is to betray not only the Nation, but kings themselves; it is to overturn the constitution of the Kingdom, it is to destroy the foundation of the authority of the Monarch.][26]

This argument invokes the inviolable rights of the nation and connects these to the king's legitimacy. The *parlements* did not seek to depose the king, only to exert greater influence over legislation and local affairs. It is therefore not surprising that they presented themselves as indispensable to the king's political survival, while at the same time staking out their own political territory. Although clever, the *parlements*' dual strategy (upholding both the nation and the king) proved difficult to sustain, and their emphasis on the rights of the nation eventually overrode their claims to bolster the king. If the king were not at least potentially threatening to the rights of the nation, there would be no need for the *parlements*:[27] the nation had to trump the king as a parliamentary priority. From mere guardians of the social contract, the *parlements* came to portray themselves as defenders of the nation itself.

The revolutionary implications of the *parlements'* assertions became manifest in claims that the fundamental laws could not be altered without the nation's formal consent. Such claims advanced an even bolder interpretation of the conditional nature of the king's mandate.[28] According to this vision, if the king did not fulfill his end of the bargain, the nation was no longer bound to him and the contract joining them was nullified. The introduction of an exit option marked a fundamental break with traditional conceptions of absolute monarchical authority and undivided popular loyalty.[29] This idea of "[l]a monarchie créée par le peuple, donc, dépendante du peuple" (the monarchy created by the people, therefore, dependent on the people),[30] the natural outgrowth of a contractual conception of the relationship between government and governed, set the stage for the sovereignty of the nation to replace that of the king.[31]

The *parlements'* arguments did not simply entrench the nation's importance: they also reinforced the nation's unity, notably through their propagation of the so-called *théorie des classes*. The *théorie des classes* both expressed the conception of a unified *parlement* and concretized the idea of a unitary nation.[32] Although the *parlements* were distinct law courts with separate jurisdictions, they often presented themselves as a unified body in order to augment their institutional clout: "La Cour métropolitaine et toutes ses colonies sont les diverses classes d'un seul et unique *Parlement*, les divers membres d'un seul et unique Corps, animés du même esprit, nourris des mêmes principes, occupés du même objet" (The metropolitan Court and all its colonies are the different classes of one single and unique *Parlement*, the different members of a single and unique Body, animated by the same spirit, nourished by the same principles, working for the same goal).[33] This statement plays on the double meaning of "members" and "body" as both figurative (parts of an associative whole) and literal (limbs of a physical body). In so doing, it appropriates a metaphor traditionally used to represent the king, namely, the king as the head to which the parts of the kingdom are integrally attached and upon which they depend. The use of the word "esprit" further co-opts this image, as *esprit* can mean both "spirit" and, more literally, "mind": in an extreme reading of this passage, the Parisian court is in fact symbolically appropriating the king's position as the "head" of the entire realm.

Having entrenched the nation as the basis for their own political claims, the *parlements* conceptualized their importance to the nation in three distinct but related ways. They presented themselves as a medium of communication between the king and the nation, as an organ of the nation, and as the nation's representative—a subtle but important difference that allowed the *parlements* to speak for the nation and to formulate the national will, rather than just acting as a passive intermediary. The movement from one conception to another was neither linear nor entirely self-conscious, although it was self-serving. This progression played a crucial role in strengthening the idea of the nation as an independent legitimating platform for political claims.

In the first relationship, the *parlements* mediated between the interests of the king and those of the nation. Increasingly, they portrayed these interests as competing instead of identical.[34] The king sought to counter the disruptive impact of this idea by asserting that his subjects were bound by the "liens indissolubles de l'obéissance" (indissoluble ties of obedience) and "le devoir inviolable de leur fidélité" (the inviolable duty of their loyalty).[35] But the *parlements* could and did turn the king's own arguments against him, using his claim to be bound to the nation by indissoluble ties to reinforce their own importance as the vehicles for and protectors of this special relationship.[36]

Not limiting themselves to an intermediary role, the *parlements* also claimed to be an organ of the nation itself. The word "organ" has a double meaning, since it is both a "medium of communication . . . which serves as the mouthpiece of a movement" and a "self-contained part of an organism having a special vital function."[37] The dual connotations of this term reinforced its utility for the *parlements* in their transition from an essentially passive to a more active role. In 1780s France, an *organe* was also a periodical publication considered to be the expression and the interpreter of opinions held by a particular group or set of interests.[38] By claiming to be the *organe* of the nation, the *parlements* empowered themselves not only to act on behalf of the nation's interest, but also to define this interest as they saw fit.[39] The political force of the *parlements*' claim was enhanced by the emerging idea of the nation as a unified body capable of possessing a will—an idea bolstered by this very claim in a circular process typical of this period.

The idea of required consent to laws, and its connection to a broader claim for a share in the exercise of sovereignty, prompted the *parlements* to go beyond their self-image as an "organ" and claim to be the nation's representative.[40] The *parlements* presented themselves as a stand-in for the Estates-General, an assembly of delegates from all parts of France not convened since 1614. The self-appointed role of representative, although powerful, carried the risk that parliamentary power could be circumscribed if a more authentically "national" assembly were (re)constituted.[41] In 1788, the Parisian lawyer Jacques Godard wrote that "[l]e *Parlement* est devenu Nation" (the *Parlement* has become the Nation).[42] Unfortunately for the *parlements*, their claim to represent the nation would be eclipsed by a body with an even stronger claim—the National Assembly.

The parliamentary remonstrances developed and entrenched a set of political concepts that, when taken to their logical conclusion, posited popular and ultimately national sovereignty as the source of monarchical power. What began as a legitimation of the monarch's authority—the presence of intermediary bodies as the guardians of fundamental laws—became the most serious challenge to it. The *parlements* may have used the remonstrances as a self-serving political tool but, especially after the reforms of 1771, they began couching their demands in contractualist terms that included the doctrinal primacy of the nation and an emphasis on the importance of national consent. These concepts became disengaged from parliamentary rhetoric and entered popular political discourse, laying the foundations for a radical reconceptualization of the nature and origins of legitimate political authority. The ultimate consequences of this transformation soon exceeded the *parlements*' control.

2.2 The Creation of a National Assembly

Emphasizing the rights of the nation served the *parlements* for as long as they could claim to be the nation's most authentic "organ." In the absence of an Estates-General, and assuming that the nation was indeed separate from the king, the *parlements* enjoyed this privileged status largely by default. The Estates-General, last convened in 1614, was a formal gathering of local representatives from each of France's three estates: the clergy (the First Estate), the nobility (the Second Estate), and the professional classes (the Third Estate, by far the largest of the three). Despite its dormancy, the Estates-General loomed large in the French collective consciousness as part of the monarchy's implicit legitimating structure. Especially in the late eighteenth century, the idea of the Estates-General offered a powerful symbol of the nation and held out the possibility for the nation's voice to be heard more directly.

The perceived importance of consulting the nation grew as public confidence in the government declined. The need to reaffirm the monarchy's legitimacy and to bolster its viability became acute in the late 1780s, when the monarchy was nearing bankruptcy. This crisis had both systemic and contingent causes: the resistance of the privileged classes to taxation had stunted the growth of internal revenue; French military support for the recent American Revolution had drained financial resources; and a disastrous harvest in 1788 had sent bread prices soaring, intensifying social and political unrest.[43] The *parlements*, controlled by the aristocracy, created the conditions for their own supersession by obstructing the king's authority, both concretely (by blocking new taxes) and symbolically (by exacerbating and drawing attention to political disputes). The fragility of public confidence made it impossible for the government to raise loans to replenish the country's coffers. Louis XVI admitted in September 1788 that "the State needs the Nation" and that there was "but one recourse for the Nation, the Nation itself."[44] He convoked the Estates-General in a final bid to prevent the kingdom's economic collapse.[45] As Kingsley Martin suggests, "The calling of the States-General was more than a confession that the Government needed popular support; it was also an acknowledgement of the people's right to give or to withhold it."[46]

Paradoxically, although the king's appeal had been supported and even encouraged by the *parlements* as an acknowledgment of the need to consult the nation (their own legitimating platform), his action was largely designed to circumvent parliamentary resistance to new taxes. Having used the nation to justify their own claims to power, the *parlements* could not credibly defend their own political monopoly in the face of the Estates-General, a historically revered representative body. The *parlements* were overtaken by the very forces they had deployed in a process typical of the impending Revolution.

The king's decision to convoke the Estates-General met with widespread enthusiasm, except amongst a few prescient, antidemocratic ministers. His appeal to the nation was prompted by a desire to reaffirm the legitimacy of the monarchy by reattaching it to the founding principle of national consent, and its immediate effect was to bolster his popularity.[47] The meeting of the Estates-General was preceded by the drafting of *cahiers de doléances* (booklets of grievances) by subjects from all parts of France, a process that itself fostered popular involvement in and awareness of politics.[48] Despite widespread devotion to the king (though not to the nobility), his public support was circumscribed by the increasingly widespread idea of the nation's rights: "all cahiers supported monarchy but: *not one* defended royal absolutism. All the cahiers contemplated limitations upon the monarchy, with the States-General as the voice of the sovereign people."[49] The *parlements*' monopoly on the rhetoric of nationhood was coming to an end, and their political and institutional importance along with it.

Contractarian language familiar to readers of the *Encyclopédie*, pamphlet literature, and parliamentary remonstrances resurfaced in the consultative *cahiers*. This language enhanced the political expectations attached to the Estates-General, and it foreshadowed the expansion of this body's mandate from fiscal reform to broader constitutional restructuring.[50] The delegates to the Estates-General, and especially those from the politically voiceless Third Estate, saw themselves as *re*claiming rights that had belonged to them all along.[51] Their sense of entitlement was ill-understood and ill-appreciated by entrenched élites,[52] for whom the political empowerment of the nation and the constitutional adjustments it entailed were indeed "revolutionary."[53] Between 1788 and 1789, the sovereignty of the nation went from being an abstract political conception to a concrete institutional imperative.

The *parlements* had successfully established the habit of invoking the national will and, by implication, the need to consult the nation's representatives in order to make government decisions appear legitimate in the eyes of an evermore exacting public opinion—"*le que dira-t-on*" ("the what will people say"). But *which* representatives to consult?[54] The paradox of constitution—the need to rely on those who claim to speak in the nation's name—threatened to make the new foundations of political legitimacy equally, if not more, susceptible to abuse than the old ones.

The idea of the nation as a collective, rights-bearing entity was developed largely as a means of grounding claims to power in the face of an absolute monarch. However, the recognition and entrenchment of authoritative national spokespeople risked overshadowing, and even undermining, this original contractarian impulse. Once national representatives are recognized and politically entrenched, there is no guarantee that they will resist the temptation of authoritarianism. This tension was not lost on the critics of political reform.

Paradoxically, the authoritarian potential of national representatives enabled champions of absolute monarchy to present themselves as protectors of political liberty. André Chénier (who was guillotined in 1794) remarked in a 1792 article on "la cause des désordres qui troublent la France et arrêtent le développement de la liberté" (the cause of the disturbances that are troubling France and halting the development of liberty):

> Une simple équivoque a suffi à tout: la constitution étant fondée sur cette éternelle vérité, *la souveraineté* du peuple, il n'a fallu que persuader aux tribunes du club qu'elles sont le *peuple*. . . . Et quelques centaines d'oisifs réunis dans un jardin ou dans un spectacle, ou quelques troupes de bandits qui pillent des boutiques, sont effrontément appelés le *peuple*; et les plus insolents despotes n'ont jamais reçu des courtisans les plus avides un encens aussi vil et aussi fastidieux que

> l'adulation impure dont deux ou trois mille usurpateurs de la souveraineté nationale sont enivrés, chaque jour par les écrivains et les orateurs de ces Sociétés qui agitent la France. [A simple equivocation was enough to do the trick: since the constitution was founded on this eternal truth, *the sovereignty* of the people, all that was needed was to persuade the tribunes of the (Jacobin) club that they were the *people*. . . . And a few hundred laggards meeting in a garden or at a show, or a few gangs of good-for-nothing outlaws who pillage the shops, are brazenly called the *people*; and the most insolent despots have never received from their most voracious courtesans such vile and insipid sycophancies as this impure adulation with which two or three thousand usurpers of national sovereignty are intoxicated each day by the writers and the orators of these Societies that are stirring up trouble in France.][55]

André-Quentin Buée agreed in his satirical dictionary: "*Le salut du peuple est la supreme* [*sic*] *loi*: maxime parfaitement vague, et, par cela seul, parfaitement tyrannique" (*The good of the people is the supreme law*: a perfectly vague maxim, and, by that alone, a perfectly tyrannical one).[56] These concerns, present from the beginning, were voiced with increasing urgency as the Revolution progressed. The struggle for political power in the process of constitution exacerbated the theoretical tensions in the paradox of conception. This lent credence to predictions of the authoritarian consequences of (ostensibly) popular rule.

Despite these warnings, which were often retrospectively voiced, the meeting of the Estates-General went ahead as planned. The central goal, as stated in a preparatory decree of July 5, 1788, was to create "une Assemblée vraiment nationale par sa composition comme par ses effets" (an Assembly that is truly national in its composition as in its results).[57] The gathering of delegates was envisaged as a moment of unity for all of France,[58] but it remained unclear how best to implement this vision. As Pierre Louis de Lacretelle, a lawyer from Metz, observed: "Disons la chose comme elle est, nous voulons être assemblés en Corps de Nation, mais nous ne sçavons comment nous y prendre" (Let us state the situation frankly: we would like to be gathered together in a National Body, but we do not know how to set about doing this).[59] Rather than fostering unity, preceding Estates-Generals had actually enshrined the separation of estates in their composition and voting procedures: "[N]ous avons vu que ces convocation [*sic*] représentoient essentiellement des Corps de la Nation, & fort peu la Nation même" (We have seen that these convocations essentially represented Bodies [subdivisions] of the Nation, and hardly the Nation itself).[60] For many observers, it was not monarchy that prevented national cohesion, but rather the division of estates and the preservation of aristocratic privilege. These individuals hoped that a nonhierarchical assembly of the unified nation would reaffirm monarchical legitimacy through a constitution based on national consent.[61]

Other contemporary commentators were much less enthusiastic. One anonymous dictionary author begins his definition of the word "constitution" by noting that this is a strange word in the French language, and redirecting readers to the entry for "royal prerogative."[62] This author insists with respect to the king's decision to convoke the Estates-General:

> Une convocation d'états n'est point, de la part du prince, une abdication de son ministere. Ce n'est point la création d'un minister [*sic*] nouveau ordonné par la nation. . . . que ce soit la nation elle-même, le roi n'est pas étranger à la nation[.] Elle le reconnoît comme l'organe par lequel elle exprime sa voix, et exécute son action. Elle n'étouffe pas son organe, pour agir sans lui. [A convocation of estates is not at all, on the part of the prince, an abdication of his office. It is not at all the creation of a new office ordered by the nation. . . . even if it is the nation itself, the king is no stranger to the nation. It recognizes him as the organ through which it expresses its voice, and executes its action. It does not suffocate its organ, to act without him.][63]

Although this author might seem somewhat hostile to the nation's claims, he reaffirms its legitimate entitlements, wondering only how these should be pursued: "Encore une fois, il ne peut y avoir de question sur les droits de la nation; tout est à elle. Mais *où est la voix de la nation*?" (Let me repeat, there cannot be any question about the rights of the nation; everything belongs to it. But *where is the voice of the nation*?)[64] The paradox of constitution captures this central dilemma.

In registering the king's declaration convoking the Estates-General, the *parlements* specified that the assembly would take the form of its 1614 predecessor: the three estates would send equal numbers of delegates, meaning that the Third Estate, despite representing a vastly greater percentage of the French population, would always be outnumbered two to one. Although the king subsequently consented to double the size of the Third Estate's delegation, votes were taken by estate, preventing the translation of this numerical advantage into political sway. The usages of feudalism threatened to eclipse the ideal of a unified nation, creating disillusionment that fueled agitation for reform.

The perceived subordination and even humiliation of the Third Estate led its members to develop a unified spirit. They directed their collective anger at the nobility and its privileges.[65] The reclamation of the Estates-General had already given the "people," embodied largely in the Third Estate, a concrete platform for identity formation and political mobilization.[66] Unity of identity came from unity of purpose. Paris lawyer and pamphleteer Camille Desmoulins wrote in 1789: "Listen to Paris and Lyon, Rouen and Bordeaux, Calais and Marseille; from one end of France to the other, the same cry (*cri*), a universal cry, is heard. . . . The Nation has everywhere expressed the same will. All wish to be free."[67] Meeting on June 17, 1789, to protest the archaic and unjust protocol of the Estates-General, the members of the Third Estate voted to call themselves the "National Assembly," and they proclaimed this Assembly the source of legality itself.[68]

In a process exemplified by the creation of the National Assembly, Revolutionary demands for political participation became constitutive of the nation in whose name they were made. The creation of the Assembly provides an early example of the circularity of self-constitution through the articulation of nationalist claims. On June 20, 1789, the members of the National Assembly swore the famous "Tennis Court Oath" (so named because they had to gather in an indoor tennis court after having been barred, either deliberately or through miscommunication, from entering the official meeting chamber). They pledged to meet continuously until they established a Constitution.[69] The Tennis Court Oath also enshrined the repudiation of imperative mandates (votes dictated by home constituencies), reinforcing the importance of national solidarity.[70] France was on its way to becoming a constitutional monarchy, and it was edging closer—at least rhetorically—to republicanism.[71]

While the assertion of the nation's importance began as an attempt to reinforce monarchical legitimacy, the conflict between national sovereignty and royal sovereignty turned the competition for political power into a zero-sum game, with the king on the losing side.[72] His reluctance to accept a constitutional mandate that would have circumscribed his absolute power led the nation's representatives to challenge the very legitimacy they had originally intended to reinforce.[73] As Jean-Joseph Mounier, later one of the authors of the Declaration of the Rights of Man and the Citizen, insisted before the Assembly, "[l]e roi n'a pas de consentement à donner à la Constitution; il [*sic*] est antérieur à la monarchie" (the king has no consent to give to the Constitution; it is anterior to the monarchy).[74] The National Assembly, created to represent the nation before the king, ended up institutionalizing the preeminence of the nation itself.[75]

This ideational and institutional transformation had vital repercussions. A role reversal occurred between the king and the nation, culminating in the nation supplanting the king: "Louis par la grâce de Dieu roi de France et de Navarre devint Louis par la grâce de Dieu et de la loi constitutionnelle de l'État roi des français" (Louis by the grace of God king of France and of Navarre became Louis by the grace of God and of the constitutional law of the State king of the French).[76] Conceptual and ceremonial changes went hand in hand. These developments validated the assertion that "d'ores et déjà la souveraineté une et indivisible n'est plus un attribut royal. Elle est réellement nationale" (from this moment, one and indivisible sovereignty is no longer a royal attribute. It is truly national).[77] When the king was presented with the Constitution of 1791 for approval, it was his turn to perform a mere formality, signing: "*J'accepte et ferai exécuter. 14 septembre 1791. Louis*" (I accept and will enact it. September 14, 1791. Louis).[78] The king could no longer pretend to embody the nation; he now not only had to "accept" its laws, but he also had to reconcile himself to a reduced status and to the fate that the nation would assign him. Louis XVI lamented: "Que reste-t-il au roi, autre chose que le vain simulacre de la royauté?" (What is left for the king, besides the vain pretense of royalty?)[79] The delegates of the Third Estate had been summoned by the king as the people's representatives, but they ended up regarding themselves as the embodiment of the nation—the true and legitimate seat of political power.

2.3 The Contribution of the Abbé Sieyès

The creation of a National Assembly was largely inspired by the political thought and rhetoric of Emmanuel-Joseph Sieyès. This priest-*cum*-politician became famous in 1789 with the publication of his provocative pamphlet *Qu'est-ce que le Tiers État?* (What is the Third Estate?). He was subsequently elected as a delegate from the Third Estate of Paris to the Estates-General, and he played a large part in the proceedings of June 17, which culminated in the proclamation of the National Assembly. During the years that followed, Sieyès continued writing, but he was eclipsed by other orators; his apocryphal response to the question of what he had done during the Revolutionary Terror was simply "I survived." Sieyès returned to government under Napoleon but was unsuccessful in implementing his ideas. Exiled in 1815 under the Restoration for having voted for the execution of Louis XVI, Sieyès did not return to France until 1830, where he died six years later.

Alfred Cobban, though mindful of the influence of Sieyès's famous pamphlet, dismisses it as "little more than an assertion of a claim to political power without any theoretical argument."[80] This observation, shared by others, has led to the relative academic neglect of Sieyès's ideas.[81] Sieyès is certainly no Montesquieu or Rousseau: Pasquale Pasquino overstates the case when he credits Sieyès with single-handedly introducing the idea of political representation as the cornerstone of modern European government.[82] Nevertheless, Sieyès's work provides important insights into the mentality and reasoning of those who enshrined the nation as the ultimate source of sovereignty and political legitimacy in late-eighteenth-century France.

In contrast to Rousseau, Sieyès begins with the assumption that the national will cannot manifest itself directly. It must therefore be detected in some other way: "quoique la volonté nationale soit, en ce sens, indépendante de toute forme, encore faut-il qu'elle en prenne une pour se faire entendre" (although the national will is, in this sense, independent of all concrete form, it must still assume one to make itself heard).[83] The "form" Sieyès proposed was a National Assembly, a chamber (or two) of delegates brought together, not as spokespeople for their respective constituencies, but as representatives of the national interest as a whole: "[D]ans un pays qui n'est pas une démocratie (et la France ne saurait l'être), le peuple ne peut parler, ne peut agir que par ses représentants" (In a country which is not a democracy [and France would not know how to be one], the people cannot speak, cannot act except by means of its representatives).[84] Far from distancing governmental decisions from the people, a representative assembly would allow the identification and implementation of a universal national will that transcends local perspectives and prejudices.[85]

For Sieyès, it is not a question of overriding or suppressing local particularities, but simply of institutionalizing what individuals have in common as the basis for legitimate government: "Une malheureuse phrase de Jean-Jacques s'oppose seule à ce concert unanime: 'La volonté, dit-il, ne peut point être représentée.' Pourquoi pas? Il ne s'agit pas ici de la volonté entière de l'homme" (An unfortunate sentence of Jean-Jacques [Rousseau] alone opposes itself to this unanimous chorus: "[The people's] will, he says, can never be represented." Why not? It is not a matter of representing the entire will of humankind).[86] For Sieyès, representation is the key to successful political institutions. His vision relies on a voluntarist conception of the social and political body in which any individual can (in theory) exercise an exit option.[87] This makes the decisions of political representatives even more strongly binding on those members who remain. Citizenship does not consist in making laws, but in exercising the right to choose representatives.[88] Representation does not produce the unity of the people per se, but simply the unitary expression of the content of the national will.[89]

While a Rousseauean polity tends to absorb the private sphere into the public domain, Sieyès insists on a strict public/private divide as an explicit defense against totalitarianism.[90] Sieyès's idea of the national will relates only to public interests, not to all aspects of personal and social life. In a later text suggestively entitled *Contre la ré-totale* ("Against the re-total," in contrast to the re-public), Sieyès clarifies his idea of political society as the uniting of individuals' public interests, not their entire selves: "[O]n ne met en commun que ce qui est nécessaire pour parvenir au but de l'association" ([Members] do not place in common anything but that which is necessary to accomplish the goal of the association).[91] The only act requiring unanimity among representatives is the initial act of association; after that, the decisions of a simple majority are considered binding, within the limits of the rules set out in the associative act: "[C']est à la constitution de nous garantir notre liberté. . . . [I]l faut que le despotisme légal soit impossible" (It is for the constitution to guarantee our liberty. . . . Legal despotism must be made impossible).[92] The people's assembly is the "organ of national sovereignty," but the representatives are not themselves the sovereign: sovereign power belongs to the "ideal universality" of the people, independent of individual members.[93] This distinction is meant to insulate representatives from the temptation of abusing political control.

Sieyès's vision of national unity relies on the idea of delegates to the National Assembly as representatives of the entire nation, not just of their own electoral districts. Strictly speaking, they are not *representatives*, but rather authors of the national will, since the national will can only exist insofar as they articulate it.[94] Sieyès's model of the state is unitary, not federative.[95] Despite his emphasis on the importance of regional delegates, he is adamant that the process of uniting France under a single national administration has nothing in common with the American model of political federation.[96] This is where Sieyès meets Rousseau, by promoting the holistic vision of an internally unified and externally galvanized French nation-state.

Sieyès's arguments crystallized the cause of national sovereignty. As the holder of the "constituent power" (*pouvoir constituant*), the nation is the only source of legitimate political authority.[97] By the nation, Sieyès means the Third Estate and, once it is constituted, the National Assembly. Equality (absence of privilege) and national unity go hand in hand.[98] When Sieyès speaks of the need for "*adunation*," he has in mind the abolition of privilege and the fusion of all parts of the French nation into a unified whole.

Sieyès takes issue with the notion of a two-step contract (the formation of the people, followed by the contractual establishment of government), and even with the idea of a contract existing between the government and the governed at all.[99] He conceptualizes the nation's claims in terms of inherent entitlement rather than the fulfillment of a mutually binding agreement.[100] According to Sieyès, the national interest can only be located in and expressed by the Third Estate.[101] He attempts to support this point with a variety of arguments: (1) that the Third Estate is itself a complete nation,[102] or at least that it "always confuses itself in [his] mind" with the idea of a nation;[103] (2) that only those subject to the common law can be considered part of the common order, thereby excluding the privileged orders from the nation by definition;[104] and, as a last resort, (3) that even if a unitary nation does not actually exist in France because of a lack of civic equality, one should be created.[105] In the end, Sieyès concedes that even if the Third Estate is, in one sense, just one order among three, it can be considered in a second sense (*rapport*) to be the nation itself.[106] Any lack of national unity can be remedied through institutions, with the ultimate aim of joining all the orders in a common social pact.[107]

The stages of state-formation in Sieyès's theory have rarely, if ever, been highlighted or clarified. Broadly speaking, there are three phases, culminating in the creation of a republican government:

1. *le jeu des volontés individuelles* [the interplay of individual wills]: "[O]n conçoit un nombre plus ou moins considérable qui veulent se réunir. Par ce seul fait ils forment déjà une nation: ils en ont tous les droits; il ne s'agit plus que de les exercer." [We imagine a more or less considerable number (of people) who want to join together. By this fact alone they already form a nation: they have all of its rights; all that remains is to exercise them.][108]
2. *l'action de la volonté commune* [the action of the common will]: Individuals come together to discuss the goals and methods of their association. "On voit qu'ici le pouvoir appartient au public. Les volontés individuelles en sont bien toujours l'origine et en forment les éléments essentiels; mais considérés séparément, leur pouvoir seroit nul. Il ne réside que dans l'ensemble. Il faut à la

communauté une volonté commune; sans l'*unité* de volonté elle ne parviendroit point à faire un tout voulant et agissant." [We see that here, power belongs to the public. The individual wills are certainly still the origin of this and make up its essential elements; but considered separately, their power would be null. The community needs a common will; without *unity* of will, (the community) would never be able to constitute a desiring and acting whole.][109]

3. *un gouvernement agissant par procuration* [a government acting by procuration]: The government exercises that part of the common will conferred on it by the constitution. Only the nation possesses the right of conferral as the holder of the constituent power. This creates a need for an authentic national organ to establish the parameters of government by enacting a constitution.[110]

Sieyès is careful to specify that "la nation seule peut vouloir pour elle-même et par conséquent se créer des loix. . . . Si nous manquons de constitution, il faut en faire une; la nation seule en a le droit" (the nation alone can will for itself and consequently create laws for itself. . . . If we are lacking a constitution, it is necessary to create one; the nation alone has this right).[111] He further insists—in an anonymous review of his own pamphlet: "C'est le gouvernement qui est constitué et non la nation" (It is the government that is constituted and not the nation).[112] Nevertheless, as the paradoxes of conception and constitution suggest, it is difficult to point to the existence of a nation without reference to governmental institutions or to administrative boundaries. If the nation is defined by the state, by what leap of faith can we justify assuming that the nation is not in fact dependent on it?

Sieyès defines a nation as "[u]n corps d'associés vivant sous une loi *commune* et représentés par la même *législature*, etc." (a body of associates living under a *common* law and represented by the same *legislature*, etc.).[113] However, his desire to endow the nation with as much independent strength as possible also leads him to portray the nation as an association that exists separate from and prior to positive laws: "La nation existe avant tout, elle est l'origine de tout. Sa volonté est toujours légale, elle est la loi elle-même. Avant elle et au-dessus d'elle il n'y a que le droit *naturel*" (The nation exists before all, it is the origin of all. Its will is always legal, it is the law itself. Before it and above it there is nothing but *natural* law).[114] This second definition is more consistent with Sieyès's account of the origins of political institutions, but it does not answer the question of how to define the nation without reference to the state. Sieyès accepts and enshrines the control of the nation over the state without resolving the question of how to differentiate them. He simply asserts that the nation is self-justifying, while the state is accountable to the nation whose will animates it and from which it receives its authority and legitimacy. His entire political theory rests on this unresolved ambiguity.

In order for the nation to exercise its constitutive power, it must be able to express its will. This creates a practical need for a theory of representation. For Sieyès, the 1789 Estates-General cannot speak in the nation's name because it does not represent the nation. A truly representative body must be formed, one whose composition more accurately reflects that of the nation as a whole.[115] In *Qu'est-ce que le Tiers-État?*, Sieyès contends that only the Third Estate can form a truly *National* Assembly. Only this kind of Assembly is capable of articulating a unified and coherent national will: "Si le Tiers n'y est pas représenté, la nation y sera muette. Rien ne pourra s'y faire validement. . . . [N]ous ne pouvons pas souffrir qu'on dispose de nous sans nous" (If the Third [Estate] is not represented in the Estates-General, the nation will be mute there. Nothing valid could be done there. . . . We cannot tolerate being ruled without our participation).[116] Even if the Third Estate does not comprise all of the nation's members, it is the best placed, being the most numerous, to speak and to make decisions on the nation's behalf. Sieyès's claim may be viewed as conservative, seeking a voice within existing political structures, or as radical, aspiring to transcend or to surpass this institutional framework. If the Third Estate were simply seeking enfranchisement, it would be more accurate to view it as a segment of the population seeking entry into the decision-making sphere. Insofar as its members wanted to create a new or different public sphere, they could be regarded collectively as a nation seeking self-determination, a meta-political project.

Although Sieyès's arguments on behalf of the Third Estate were designed to target the privileged classes, they also had a devastating impact on the status and authority of the king: "Ce sont les élus du tiers état qui peuvent dire maintenant: La nation, c'est nous. . . . Le roi n'a pas d'existence en dehors de la constitution" (It is the elected delegates of the Third Estate who can now say: We are the nation. . . . The king has no existence outside of the constitution).[117] Still smarting from the wounds inflicted by the *parlements*, the king was demoted once again. The power vacuum left by the discrediting of the king was filled by those claiming to speak for the nation. The nation emerged as the principal site of political contestation—the holder of sovereignty and the basis of political legitimacy, a premise implicit in many discussions of domestic and international politics today.

Conclusion

The reaction to this transformation was not uniformly enthusiastic. A 1796 dictionary, published in Germany by a French *émigré*, says of the word "Constitution":

> Vieux mot Français, dont on n'a pas encore su fixer le vrai sens. . . . On a sermenté, on s'est embrassé, on s'est battu, on a égorgé, on a guillotiné, pour l'amour de cette *Constitution*. Mais hélas! elle n'est plus. . . . Peut-être cela arrivera-t'il, avant l'année 2440. [Old French word, whose real meaning we have not yet managed to establish. . . . (The members of the National Assembly and their supporters) took oaths, they embraced one another, they fought one another, they slit throats, they guillotined, for the love of this Constitution. But alas! it no longer exists. . . . Perhaps (the creation of a lasting Constitution) will happen before the year 2440.][118]

France went through four different constitutions between 1791 and 1799.[119] This political turbulence seemed to validate the accusation that "[l']abus de liberté est plus dangereux que l'abus d'autorité" (the abuse of liberty is more dangerous than the abuse of authority)[120]—an admonition that haunted the Revolution, especially in its later years. The Revolutionary experience of liberation followed by repression left an indelible imprint on the French Revolution's popular and political legacy. The trade-off between freedom and authority remains a perennial problem for political theory and practice. This dilemma is complicated by, if not unique to, the constitutional challenge of creating state institutions in the name of a sovereign nation.

The destabilizing effect of the principle of national sovereignty was accompanied by another, seemingly contradictory, dynamic: a tendency to entrench the political status quo. This paradoxical situation arises because political power can only be wielded effectively by those with a political voice. Unless the nation can be identified separately from state institutions, it cannot provide a check on the exercise of state power or a guide for the delineation of state borders, even if the state purports to embody the nation and to act in the nation's name. Viewed in this light, the ideal of national sovereignty contains the very potential for abuse that Sieyès sought to avoid. William Pitt (the Younger) summarized this argument in a prime ministerial speech on May 6, 1793:

> In what is called the government of the multitude, they are not the many who govern the few, but the few who govern the many. It is a

> species of tyranny, which adds insult to the wretchedness of its subjects, by styling its own arbitrary decrees the voice of the people, and sanctioning its acts of oppression and cruelty under the pretence of the national will.[121]

Although political sovereignty in France remained essentially monolithic and unchecked, the principles underlying it were fundamentally transformed, as sovereignty was enshrined in the nation instead of the king. This transformation would prove central, not only to French Revolutionary reforms, but also to the elaboration and entrenchment of the nation-state principle more generally.

Chapter 3

Composition

How to Define Insiders and Outsiders

Introduction

The eighteenth-century reconception of the relationship among nation, state, and king provided a foundation for the development of the nation-state idea. The Revolutionaries' regeneration of the French polity institutionalized the previously implicit contract between governor and governed, and enshrined national, as opposed to royal, sovereignty as the source of political authority.[1] Article III of the 1789 *Declaration of the Rights of Man and the Citizen* proclaimed: "Le principe de toute souveraineté réside essentiellement dans la nation. Nul corps, nul individu ne peut exercer d'autorité qui n'en émane expressément" (The principle of all sovereignty resides essentially in the nation. No body, no individual may exercise any authority that does not emanate expressly from the nation).[2] The French Revolution propounded a vision of world public order in which national sovereignty replaced absolute monarchy as the standard for domestic and international legitimacy.

The idea of national sovereignty provided the theoretical basis for the constitution of the nation-state. But what about the nation's composition? Simply proclaiming the sovereignty of the nation was insufficient to ensure the viability of the state created in the nation's name. Criteria for national membership had to be identified and bonds of solidarity cultivated to foster cohesion, commitment, and compliance within a nation-based regime. This chapter investigates how the Revolutionaries gave content to their idea of nationhood. It explores the implications of a unitary vision of national sovereignty (section 3.1); the criteria for national membership, including the promotion (in theory, if not in practice[3]) of a single national language (section 3.2); and the consolidation of national membership through festivals designed to guarantee exclusive allegiance to the French nation, as defined by Revolutionary leaders (section 3.3).

National cohesion had to be based on more than just a contractual fiction in order to underpin the unity and effectiveness of the Revolutionary state.[4] The conceptual importance of the nation as the only entity capable of establishing a legitimate state could not be operationalized without criteria for identifying its members.[5] National characteristics served both to identify the nation's members, and to solidify—or to create—a sense of common purpose among them.

Where a strong sense of national identity already exists, it seems logical that it could be used as a basis for institutionalizing the more abstract notion of a people's right to govern itself. This intuition depends on the idea of the nation as something concrete, resonant, and compelling—something beyond question. However, it is far from clear that such a French nation existed before the Revolution, especially separate from the body of the monarch. If allegiance to the king could no longer provide a basis for nationhood, something else had to bind individuals together to make the nation a viable platform for political identification and popular mobilization. The paradox of composition encapsulates this imperative and accounts for its potentially illiberal results.

The idea that the French nation existed separate from and even prior to the king, a crucial underpinning of the principle of national sovereignty, was problematic on both the historical and the theoretical levels.[6] Historically, the French nation had been created by French kings. Theoretically, as highlighted by the paradox of conception, it is difficult to imagine a nation without reference to state structures, especially when the nation supposedly rests on voluntarist ideals rather than innate characteristics. For the nation to remain conceptually separate from the state and thus viable as a standard for state legitimacy, the nation must possess an independent identity derived from its own internally generated unity, loyalty, and cohesion. The paradox of composition focuses on the nonpolitical principles of unity that were identified to ensure the viability of the Revolutionary nation as the basis of a regenerated state. It suggests that the view of the Revolutionary nation as purely voluntarist is oversimplified, and it challenges the corresponding tendency to glorify voluntarist nationalism as automatically liberal and benign.

3.1 Implementing National Sovereignty

The monarchical nation had been held together symbolically by the king and delineated territorially by the reach of his administration. The Revolutionary nation was defined more subjectively and even metaphysically, based on the people's will to live together.[7] The will to live together was assumed to exist among members of the French nation (those who spoke the French language or had a French "heart"), but not among counter-revolutionaries, reactionary priests, or those otherwise considered undesirable or subversive.[8] Revolutionary leaders forged national solidarity both positively through symbols, ceremonies, and festivals, and negatively through exclusion, purges, and executions.[9] This section explores the implications of invoking a unitary nation as the basis for the state.

Operationalizing something as indeterminate as a sovereign national will was far from self-evident. Early in Louis XVI's reign, his finance minister Anne-Robert-Jacques Turgot had warned him: "your nation has no constitution. It is a society of orders badly united, and of a people in which there are but very few social ties between the members."[10] The king often referred to his "peoples" in the plural, an acknowledgement of diversity fundamentally at odds with the unitary Revolutionary ideal.[11] Among the king's subjects, great regional and linguistic variation compounded wide and conspicuous differences in social standing, making it difficult to identify commonalities among the French. Hence, the idea of the monarch as the cohesive basis of the nation: Frenchness could at least be defined as submission and allegiance to the French king. As explored in the paradox of conception, the nation could not be used to challenge the king until it was defined as a separate and independent entity. For a nation-based Revolution to succeed, national identity, unity, and cohesion had to be based on something other than the governmental structures it sought to replace.

The French nation, springing as it did from contractualist rhetoric, was born with a pronounced emphasis on voluntarism. However, the Revolutionary leaders had to make the nation as distinct as possible from the state in order to reinforce the nation's viability as a platform for challenging aristocratic and monarchical domination. They did this by fortifying the idea of the nation with its own internal principles of coherence and cohesion. This strategy opened the door to, and even required, a more restrictive view of the bonds of national membership.

Revolutionary leaders found themselves having to fortify their voluntarist conception of a French nation based on will with nonvoluntarist elements in order to strengthen their nation-based claims. This practical imperative forced modification of the nation's theoretical underpinnings. The slippage from voluntarist to nonvoluntarist definitions of the Revolutionary nation resulted from the need to consolidate the Revolutionaries' claim to legitimate control of the French state. This process illustrates the tensions and dangers implicit in the idea of nation-based legitimacy more generally.

The most concrete manifestation of the turn towards nonvoluntarism arose from the need to define and protect the nation's boundaries. Self-consciously adapting their voluntarist rhetoric to the demands of political expediency, the Revolutionaries elaborated a view of national self-determination as a unidirectional process. Once the nation's boundaries had been defined by those in power, ostensibly in accordance with the wishes of the people concerned, the inviolability of national unity precluded the secession of a "part" from the "whole."[12]

The Revolutionaries refused to accept the "slippery slope" of secession as a potential consequence of the consistent application of the principle of national self-determination to self-identified cultural and territorial units within France. By enshrining national sovereignty, and by imagining the population of France as a unitary nation, Revolutionary leaders sought to preclude the possibility of internal threats to their own political supremacy. The indivisibility of political sovereignty reinforced the indivisibility of the nation, the entity said to possess it. In a twist characteristic of the Revolution, this indivisibility, this imperative of unity, and this automatic self-legitimation were claimed by the leaders of the regenerated state once they had defined the state as truly national. The circle of self-validation closed once again.

This paradox arose despite the Revolutionary emphasis on the nation as the starting point for the circle of legitimation. The primacy of the nation was enshrined in Article III of the 1789 *Declaration of the Rights of Man and the Citizen* and in subsequent constitutional provisions.[13] Article III represents the culmination of eighteenth-century contractarianism with a nationalist, as opposed to an individualist, bent: "The principle of all sovereignty resides essentially in the nation. No body, no individual may exercise any authority that does not emanate expressly from the nation." The nation, a unitary actor, could delegate the *exercise* of sovereignty to a government, but it could never transfer sovereignty itself.[14]

Article III boldly affirmed the nation as the holder of sovereignty, but in a very particular fashion: by using the phrase "the *principle* of all sovereignty," this article allowed the National Assembly to claim the right to exercise sovereignty on behalf of the nation, as the nation's authentic representative.[15] As suggested by the paradox of constitution, representative institutions promised to express a truly national will, but they also carried the danger of validating decisions made by those with a monopoly on the ability to speak in the nation's name, regardless of their popular mandate. Although Article III was written in consultation with Thomas Jefferson, the French model of national sovereignty consciously eschewed the institutional checks and balances of the United States Constitution. The leaders of the French Revolution upheld the sovereign nation as unitary and inviolable. They did this both as a means of opposing the absolute monarchy, and in order to consolidate their power in the face of other political and territorial challenges. This strategy engendered nonvoluntarist results at odds with the Revolutionaries' voluntarist ideals.

Article III affirmed that the "essence" of sovereignty, the source of power and legitimacy in the new political order, resided in the nation—the body of French citizens considered as a self-contained and unitary whole—rather than in God, the king, or any other group or institution. The problem with political power exercised in the name of the nation was that it remained difficult to distinguish from other types of unitary power, except in its terms of self-justification. The attribution of indivisible and inalienable sovereignty to the nation dictated a certain monolithic quality in national self-construction and membership.[16] The proclamation of national sovereignty represented an important but insufficient step towards creating a free and politically empowered citizenry.

The French Revolutionary emphasis on individual rights as derivative of national membership (as opposed to the more individualistic, "Anglo-Saxon" conception) stemmed in part from the nature of the entity against which the French nation had to define itself: an absolute and unitary monarchy. The nature of sovereignty as it had been established and enshrined by the French monarchy was such that it could best be wielded by a unified entity free of internal division and dissent.[17] The imperative of national cohesion fostered definitions of national membership based on innate characteristics and loyalties that precluded alternative allegiances. In addition, this internal principle of national sovereignty ultimately provided the basis for the external promotion of national self-determination as an international standard, shaping the configuration of international politics.

The sovereign nation emerged as a unit of delineation and action, identity and power, both within the French state and in the international arena.[18] The sovereignty of the nation as defined in the French model proved ill-suited to accommodating diversity both within and among nation-states. While an emphasis on the strength of the nation played a central role in bolstering the rights of the French people against encroachment by the king, it contained the implicit potential to undermine the very individual freedom it purported to enshrine by making personal liberty a function of national membership, and by making national cohesion a political imperative.[19] This helps explain why declaring the nation the source of the sovereign power traditionally wielded by the king might have involved a tremendous conceptual shift, but it did not replace the monarchy with more liberal or pluralistic institutions. In fact, it ended up justifying repressive policies, contradicting the idea of national empowerment as a guarantee of individual freedom.

3.2 Defining National Membership

The initial voluntarism at the heart of the Revolutionary nation-state was not uniformly sustained. Ostensibly voluntarist definitions of national belonging could be just as exclusive as nonvoluntarist ones, as their terms were equally if not more susceptible to manipulation by political élites. The new civic culture created through symbols and ceremonies fostered social cohesion, but it also entailed justifications for exclusion, particularly on political or ideological grounds. The "unpatriotic" individuals who did not support the current version of Revolutionary ideology were excised from the social fabric, often with the surgical precision of the guillotine. Those whose political views did not keep pace with the visions of those in power became the Revolution's next victims until, as illustrated by one political cartoon, the only person left to execute was the executioner himself.[20]

Abstract conceptions of the nation carry an added potential to become illiberal, as definitions of national membership can be engineered by those in power to preempt opposition by establishing a "légitimité exclusive et excluante" (exclusive and excluding legitimacy).[21] During the Revolution, *lèse-patrie* or *lèse-nation*, treason to the *patrie* or to the nation, became the ultimate political crime.[22] The precariousness of a French national identity based purely on subjective, internal factors (the voluntarist ideal) militated against a national self-definition too accommodating of diversity and dissent. As Maurice Cranston has observed, "au-delà devait s'affirmer l'unité fondamentale de la Nation, voire du peuple, union patriotique et fraternelle qui serait *plus qu'un simple consensus sur quelques principes de base*" (above it all the fundamental unity of the Nation, of the people, had to affirm itself, a patriotic and fraternal union that would be *more than just a simple agreement on a few basic principles*).[23] While a group can have an identity and even an interest defined as the aggregate of the identities and interests of its individual members, in order to have a *will* of its own it must be in some sense a "collective being." It is difficult to reconcile this idea with the notion of voluntary membership and the promotion of individual rights.

The strong, coherent, and independent constitutive principles imputed to the nation can be thought of as the functional equivalent of Rousseau's national character: a set of pre-political social bonds that lend the nation internal coherence and cohesion without recourse to administrative ties.[24] Initially, the strongest evidence for and force behind national unity was the National Assembly. This institutionally based self-definition sat uncomfortably with the idea of the nation as an independent legitimating standard for political structures. Nevertheless, the feeling that the establishment of the National Assembly had itself created a unified French nation was pervasive among contemporaries: "les Français, 'jusqu'alors agrégation inconstituée de peuples désunis, sont véritablement devenus une nation.' . . . 'Il n'y a plus diverses nations dans le royaume, il n'y a plus que des Français'" (the French, heretofore an unconstituted aggregate of disunited peoples, have really become one nation. . . . There are no longer diverse nations in the kingdom, there are no longer anything but Frenchmen).[25] Evolving definitions of national membership reflected its political importance in unifying and mobilizing the population of France. This, in turn, entailed the primacy of national membership over other aspects of individual identity.[26]

Views from France's colonies offer insight into perceptions of the criteria for national membership. Different groups had different ideas about what constituted Frenchness, depending on their particular circumstances. For example, some inhabitants of Sénégal affirmed in 1789: "Nègres ou mulâtres, nous sommes tous Français puisque c'est le sang des Français qui coule dans nos veines" (Negroes or mulattos, we are all French because it is the blood of Frenchmen that flows in our veins).[27] The "blood of Frenchmen," a biological metaphor for national belonging, could not be claimed exclusively by the white colonists. The National Guards of the *île de France* (today Mauritius) insisted in a similar fashion: "L'Amour des François pour la liberté ne tient ni au climats, ni aux lieux qu'il [*sic*] habitent, mais au sang qui coule dans leurs veines. Rien ne peut altérer en nous un sentiment si précieux" (The Love of the

French for liberty is not a product of climates, nor of the places they inhabit, but of the blood that flows in their veins. Nothing can change in us such a precious feeling).[28] Frenchness is physical, psychological, and even spiritual: French blood is a product of nature rather than nurture, but its most salient characteristic is the love of liberty, a subjective feeling rather than a tangible fact.

Biological conceptions of Frenchness were generally inclusive when employed by colonized peoples, but they could prove exclusionary when invoked by French colonists. For example, Brahmanic Indians in Pondicherry were barred from participating in a citizen assembly despite their pleas to assimilate themselves with the French in their territory. Their argument, which was rejected, ran as follows:

> Une longue habitude de vivre sous le doux gouvernement français a transformé notre coeur en celui des Français. Nous envisagions le Roi de France comme la nôtre . . . nous ne faisions d'autre voeux, nous n'avions d'autre désir que celui de revoir notre chère nation. [A long practice of living under the gentle French government has transformed our heart into that of French people. We envisage the King of France as our own. . . . (when the English conquered Pondicherry in 1761) we made no other wish, we had no other desire than that of seeing our dear nation once again.][29]

There were also pragmatic motivations behind this conception of membership, as the Brahmanic Indians sought greater military protection from France. Nevertheless, its underlying vision remains noteworthy: a combination of voluntarism and shared experiences that could, in certain circumstances, forge bonds of common nationality from the viewpoint of the colonized, if not the colonizers.

The importance and effect of civic ceremonies in fostering national unity should not be underestimated. However, more concrete measures were needed to keep the illusion of unity from succumbing to the pressures of internal division. Revolutionary leaders had to demonstrate that the French nation-state, despite its geographical and demographic diversity, was "fait d'une seule et même étoffe" (made from one and the same cloth).[30] Beyond the exclusionary criteria for membership based on political ideology (with national membership restricted to those who embraced the Revolutionary project), a cultural definition of the nation emerged to bolster the nation's claim to political expression in state institutions. The cultural definition had even stronger nonvoluntarist implications than the ideological one.

These two sets of criteria, ideological and cultural, were related. Campaigns to enforce linguistic uniformity became a central means of promoting and disseminating the new regime's policies. Language was envisioned as an essential tool for forging unity and concretizing identity. This was especially true in rural areas that risked becoming counterrevolutionary enclaves under the influence of priests who refused to swear allegiance to the Constitution.[31] As the Revolution progressed, advocacy of linguistic homogenization reinforced the importance of cultural similarity alluded to, but not emphasized, by some prerevolutionary definitions of the nation.

In Revolutionary rhetoric, the French language became both constitutive and emblematic of political and cultural solidarity. The importance of language as a marker of and medium for French national identity blurred the distinction between voluntarist and nonvoluntarist nationalism. The ostensibly voluntarist French nation sought more substantive and permanent foundations that pointed towards a more essentialist and restrictive definition of national membership.

Two individuals, the Abbé Henri Baptiste Grégoire and the Toulouse lawyer Bertrand de Barère, made particular efforts to propagate the French language during the Revolutionary period. Although these proposals were not systematically implemented, they offer insight into the perceived necessity of thicker bonds of identification among members of the French nation, both practically (to facilitate communication) and symbolically (to differentiate members from nonmembers). According to the Abbé Grégoire, for an individual to belong to and participate in the French nation, "il suffit qu'il ait un coeur français" (it was sufficient for him to have a French heart).[32] The question was how to identify and to ensure this: the answer, in part, lay in the French language. Grégoire authored a *Rapport sur la nécessité et les moyens d'anéantir les patois et d'universaliser l'usage de la langue française* (Report on the necessity and the means of obliterating provincial dialects and universalizing the usage of the French language).[33] The report laments the discrepancy between the linguistic reality of "retrograde" diversity and the political reality, or at least the aspiration, of freedom and solidarity.[34] On a practical level, linguistic diversity posed a worrying threat to the integrity of the new nation-state. Grégoire writes: "dans l'étendue de la République, tant de jargons . . . empêchent l'amalgame politique, et d'un seul peuple en font trente" (in the full expanse of the Republic, so many jargons . . . prevent political amalgamation, and out of one single people make thirty).[35] It is evocative that, in the French language, "s'entendre" means both to understand one another and to get along. In this respect, ties of language and communication are both procedurally necessary for national solidarity and substantively constitutive of it.

In Grégoire's conception, language provides both the mechanism for forging and affirming national identity, and the proof of its existence.[36] He emphasizes the centrality of language in his conviction that "l'unité de l'idiome est une partie intégrante de la révolution" (unity of language is an integral part of the revolution);[37] the double connotation of the word "intégrante" as both "integral" and "integrating" highlights the importance and the homogenizing function of language. Grégoire's report culminates in an affirmation of the necessity of linguistic uniformity to the political viability and success of a nation-state:

> Tout ce qu'on vient de dire appelle la conclusion, que pour extirper tous les préjugés, développer toutes les vérités, tous les talents, toutes les vertus, *fondre tous les citoyens dans la masse nationale*, simplifier le méchanisme et faciliter le jeu de la machine politique, il faut identité de langage. [All we have just said calls for the conclusion that, to extirpate all prejudices, develop all truths, all talents, all virtues, *melt all citizens into the national mass*, simplify the mechanism and facilitate the working of the political machine, it is necessary to have unity of language.][38]

In this perspective, language plays an indispensable role as a functional requirement for and symbolic affirmation of unified identity and purpose.

Bertrand de Barère followed Grégoire's study with his own report, the *Rapport du Comité de Salut Publique sur les Idiomes* (Report of the Committee of Public Safety on Languages).[39] According to Barère, the fundamental problem with having multiple languages in France is that "[o]n eût dit qu'il y avait plusieurs nations dans une seule" (one would have said that there were several nations in a single one).[40] This is unacceptable in a unitary nation-state. On a practical level, multiple languages (Bas-Breton, Basque, German, Italian) impede the "propagation of the public spirit" and prevent citizens from learning and obeying the Republic's laws.[41] The provincial idioms in particular are considered an intolerable bastion of counterrevolutionary ideas, because they literally keep individuals from learning about new laws and from forming an attachment to the Revolutionary republic.[42] Language, a key element of identity, is also an important instrument of power.[43] Corroborating Grégoire's apprehensions about linguistic diversity, Barère identifies the lack of communication as the root of an "indestructible federalism" that menaces the unity, and thus the legitimacy and viability, of the French nation-state.[44]

In the Revolution's early years, Revolutionary decrees were translated and distributed in a variety of local languages. The Jacobin centralization characteristic of the later years saw the advocacy and implementation of linguistic uniformity as a key homogenizing measure.[45] Interestingly, even these later policies were largely elaborated as part of a liberal conception of the new political order. Education was seen as essential to the full enjoyment of citizenship.[46] Monolingualism was considered inherently anti-despotic, since citizens could best monitor one another's activities and the activities of their government if they could communicate easily. Barère wrote:

> Le despotisme maintient la variété des idiomes. . . . Dans la démocratie, au contraire, la surveillance du gouvernement est confiée à chaque citoyen; pour le surveiller il faut le connaître, il faut surtout en connaître la langue. [Despotism preserves linguistic variety. . . . In a democracy, by contrast, the monitoring of the government is entrusted to each citizen; to monitor it one must know it, one must above all know its language.][47]

Linguistic homogeneity is equated with political equality, a central Revolutionary ideal.[48] Liberty and unity are upheld as mutually reinforcing, not antagonistic.[49] For Barère, the necessity of linguistic uniformity seems self-evident to promote liberty and to realize the benefits of republican citizenship.

Despite these beneficient intentions, the policies of homogenization required by such a perspective could prove highly inimical to individual rights, since the elimination of provincial languages would mean eradicating smaller cultures and traditions within France.[50] It remained unclear how to reconcile the potentially conflicting Revolutionary goals of liberty and unity. A common language permits the formation and articulation of a shared political will. But language can acquire importance as much more than just an instrument of communication, becoming emblematic and constitutive of national identity itself. The centrality of language to identity-formation trumped the acceptance of cultural pluralism and the individual right to choose one's own linguistic and cultural ties.

On a more general level, the criterion of language poses interesting complications that challenge the possibility of classifying liberal and illiberal nationalisms according to voluntarist or nonvoluntarist definitions of membership. Eric Hobsbawm upholds language as a fairly open and flexible criterion for national membership, noting that "in theory it was not the native use of the French language that made a person French . . . but the willingness to acquire this, among the other liberties, laws and common characteristics of the free people of France."[51] In a similar vein, Will Kymlicka notes that "[f]rom a liberal point of view, language-based nationalism is maximally consistent with freedom and equality, since (unlike religious-based nationalism) it does not presuppose any shared conception of the good; and (unlike racially based nationalism) it is not inherently exclusionary or discriminatory."[52] Despite these observations, language became and has tended to remain part of a cultural, and sometimes even ethnic or racial, conception of nationhood.[53] The paradox of composition helps explain the slippage between open and closed definitions of nationhood, as principles of cohesion become justifications for exclusion in the context of an initially voluntarist national self-definition.

3.3 Consolidating National Identity

National identity, although imagined as separate and preexisting, was fostered by deliberate policies of the Revolutionary state. For example, the formal unity of the French nation, and of the state created in its name, was enshrined by the National Assembly and its proclamations. The Assembly's decrees of August 1789 abolished all forms of privilege and brought all of France under one common law with the goal of creating social and legal uniformity.[54] One deputy, Enjubault de la Roche, commented in 1791 that "depuis que les représentants de la Nation se sont réunis en corps constituant, les parties de l'empire auparavant isolées, se sont fondues en un seul tout" (ever since the representatives of the Nation joined together in a constituent body, the previously isolated parts of the empire have melted together into one single whole).[55] This process operated in two directions: from the bottom-up, since a unitary nation was posited as the basis for a unified state; and from the top-down, since this state, once created, enacted policies of consolidation and unification aimed at bringing national reality into line with Revolutionary ideals.

French national identity was intended to bolster the unity and viability of the French state. Lawyer Guy Jean-Baptiste Target explained in 1789 that "[e]ach man must forget himself, see himself only as a part of the whole [nation] of which he is a member, detach himself from his individual existence, renounce all *esprit de corps*, belong only to the great society, and be a child of the fatherland."[56] This organic conception of the nation was seen as the condition for, not an obstacle to, the political freedom and empowerment that had been lacking, at least for the non-privileged classes, under the old regime.

The anonymous *Crédo du tiers-état* (Credo of the Third Estate), written in 1789, contained the vow: "Je Crois À l'*esprit* de patriotisme qui va remplacer l'*esprit* de corps; À l'union des campagnes, des villes, des provinces & de la France entière, sous Louis XVI, union qui opérera le bien, sacrifiera l'intérêt personnel à l'intérêt général" (I believe in the *spirit* of patriotism that will replace the *spirit* of particular groups; In the uniting of countrysides, towns, provinces, and of all of France, under Louis XVI, a union that will produce good, that will sacrifice personal interest to the general interest).[57] The challenge, as Patrick Riley has phrased it, was to "'denature' particularistic beings *without destroying their (ultimate) autonomy*."[58] The Revolutionaries tried to square this particular circle by presenting national membership as voluntarist, or at least by assuming that the creation of the Revolutionary state as an act of the national will meant that, by proxy, the state had been willed by each member of the nation. At least one contemporary commentator, André-Quentin Buée, was predictably scornful of this vision: "Que prétendre cependant former, avec vingt-cinq millions d'individus, un corps absolument *un*, c'est la plus absurde des chimères" (To claim to form a body that is absolutely *one* out of twenty-five million individuals is the most absurd of chimeras).[59] Nevertheless, the very possibility of making "one body" out of millions of people lies at the heart of the nationalist project. This is precisely what the Revolutionaries set out to do.

The Revolutionary leaders relied largely on festivals and on symbolic enactments of national unification to create and to reinforce a sense of French identity. Although they imagined this identity as preexisting, it was in fact fostered largely by the Revolution itself. For the Revolutionaries, the unity of the nation depended on the solidarity of the Third Estate. Pasquale Pasquino calls the cultural unity of the Third Estate an "espace symbolique d'appartenance" (symbolic space of belonging), which excluded aristocrats and privileged élites (reversing the old regime's bias).[60] The importance of membership in the Third Estate, and thus in the nation, was palpable:

> Lorsque sur leur chemin ils rencontrent quelqu'un: ils lui demandent "es-tu du Tiers-Etat?" ou bien "Etes-vous de la Nation?". . . . Arthur Young raconte comment, après avoir été arrêté par une bande de paysans, il se tire d'affaire en épinglant sur ses vêtements la cocarde nationale. [When they encounter someone on their path: they ask him "are you a member of the Third Estate?" or else "Are you a member of the Nation?". . . . Arthur Young recounts how, after having been stopped by a band of countrymen, he saved himself by pinning the national cockade on his clothing.][61]

Jean-Jacques Clere has described the situation as follows: "Le Tiers n'est plus un ordre mais il constitue à lui seul la Nation, à l'exclusion des privilégiés. Font partie de la Nation ceux qui acceptent la Révolution. L'unité nationale traduit l'adhésion à l'ordre nouveau" (The Third [Estate] is no longer an order but rather constitutes the Nation by itself, to the exclusion of the privileged classes. Those who accept the Revolution are part of the Nation. National unity is the manifestation of adherence to the new order).[62] While an "order" traditionally referred to a socioeconomic class, this usage of the term gave way to a new definition of "order"—a new conception of social and political organization that constituted national identity and defined national membership.

The Revolutionary leaders' first task and central challenge upon assuming control of the French state was to bolster the foundations of the nation that they had championed in their rhetoric. Despite their emphasis on the nation as pre-institutional and largely automatic, the Revolutionaries devoted a great deal of energy to consolidating and reinforcing the national unity they so often invoked. They developed the public festival as the primary vehicle for national consolidation, including processions, the swearing of national oaths, the construction of monuments, and the celebration of Revolutionary principles and heroes. Festivals helped to inculcate a sense of unified identity, purpose, and destiny as part of the Revolutionary regeneration of the French nation-state.[63]

The most remembered ceremony was the 1790 Festival of Federation on the one-year anniversary of the storming of the Bastille.[64] In the month leading up to this celebration, Jean Sylvain Bailly, the mayor of Paris, proclaimed:

> Un nouvel ordre de choses s'éleve & va régénérer toutes les parties du royaume, comme toutes les branches de l'administration. Déjà la division des provinces ne subsiste plus; cette division qui faisoit en France comme autant d'états séparés & de peuples divers. Un grand peuple ne connoît que le nom de Français; c'est le nom d'un peuple libre: il n'y a plus qu'un devoir; celui de la soumission à la loi & au roi; il n'y a plus qu'un sentiment, celui de l'amour et de la fraternité. C'est sur ces bases que vont reposer & la paix & la prospérité de cet empire. [A new order of things is rising up and will regenerate all the parts of the kingdom, like all the branches of the administration. Already the division of the provinces no longer subsists; this division that made France look like so many separated states and diverse peoples. A great people knows no other name than that of the French; it is the name of a free people: there is no longer any remaining duty

> but one; that of submission to the law and to the king; there is no longer but one feeling, that of love and fraternity. It is on these pillars that both the peace and the prosperity of this empire shall rest.][65]

Bailly's speech, like so many others, emphasized the dawn of a new order, both administratively (organization of government, geographical integration) and metaphysically (creation of a great and free people). These changes were important both symbolically and practically, as they were meant to guarantee peace and prosperity—the very goods that the monarchy had proven unable to secure.

The connection between symbolic gestures and practical imperatives was also apparent in the "serment fédératif" (federative oath) administered on this occasion:

> Nous jurons de rester à jamais fideles [*sic*] à la nation, à la loi & au roi; De maintenir, de tout notre pouvoir, la constitution décrétée par l'assemblée nationale, & acceptée par le Roi; De protéger, conformément aux loix, la sûreté des personnes & des propriétés, la libre circulation des grains & subsistances dans l'intérieur du royaume, & la perception des contributions publiques, sous quelques formes qu'elles existent; De demeurer unis à tous les Français par les liens indissolubles de la fraternité. [We vow to remain forever faithful to the nation, to the law and to the king; To uphold, with all our power, the constitution decreed by the national assembly, and accepted by the King; To protect, in conformity with the laws, the safety of persons and of properties, the free circulation of grain and foodstuffs inside the realm, and the levy of public contributions, in whatever form they exist; To stay united to all the French by the indissoluble bonds of fraternity.][66]

Administrative and infrastructural regularity and homogenization went hand in hand with the broader and even metaphysical project of national unity. The ultimate goal, as invoked in a poem written for the 1790 Festival of Federation, was to behold "[t]ous les enfans de la patrie / S'embrassant à la fois sous le même drapeau" (all the children of the *patrie* / Embracing one another at the same time under the same flag).[67] This vision guided the regeneration of the nation-state.

Forging Revolutionary unity involved both creating bonds of identity and loyalty among the Revolution's supporters, and excluding the Revolution's enemies from the definition of the nation itself. The perceived precariousness of successive Revolutionary regimes fostered an increasingly exclusionary and even monolithic definition of national membership. This occurred largely in response to the need to galvanize the nation as a bulwark against competing sources of political authority and allegiance. This experience illustrates how social and political pressures can engender highly restrictive membership criteria, especially in situations of instability and contestation. The process of national consolidation, even if based on ostensibly voluntarist premises, can blur the classic distinction between civic/inclusive nations and ethnic/exclusive ones.

Conclusion

The idea of the nation as a moral and political entity entails the need to delineate members and nonmembers. In theory, principles of delineation can be fluid, including an exit option for those who wish to leave. In practice, such openness tends to work against the emotional resonance and political utility of nationalist platforms. Nationalist leaders may feel that pure voluntarism is simply not enough to hold the nation together and to guarantee support for their control of the state. For a nation to establish a credible claim to its own exclusive territory and political institutions (or, rather, for credible claims to be made in the nation's name), it must be robust and to some extent self-sustaining. This observation cautions against the uncritical championing of nationalist platforms and highlights the challenges of implementing nation-based conceptions of the state.

As the French Revolutionary experience indicates, a nation that is purely voluntary and self-willed cannot easily remain a viable platform for identity formation. History suggests that the need generally arises for reliance on more innate, automatic, and unselfconscious characteristics and ties, even if these have a largely invented or mythical quality. The automaticity of "fellow-feeling" between members of an ideal, preexisting nation precludes a strictly voluntary character, since choice requires an act of will inimical to the ideal of preexisting nationhood.[68] An account of a preexisting nation, the only kind of nation that offers an a priori basis for legitimating the state, must almost necessarily downplay the role of voluntary choice.

In deciding how to define the French nation and construct the nation-state, the Revolutionaries began with a contractualist conception as the basis for challenging the monarchical status quo, using language inherited from political philosophers and from the *parlements*. However, loose contractualism was not the same as pure voluntarism, especially in the absence of an exit option. Even if a nation is ostensibly defined by will rather than by ethnicity (already one step removed from the ideal, "automatic" nation), historical consent often becomes part of a more essentialist understanding of a shared identity based on common origins.[69] Consent, initially the more legitimate for having been given by the people themselves, becomes constitutive of a subsequently unquestionable national identity. The nation-state becomes immune to modification or challenge, even by the principles upon which it was founded, calling into question the practical sustainability of a voluntarist model of nationhood.

Political communities and their institutions serve a number of basic purposes, including coordination, regulation, and redistribution. In "thicker" versions of political association, states are also charged with embodying and fostering cohesion, solidarity, dignity, and a sense of belonging. Nationalist/particularist accounts of communal identity and obligation seem better equipped than cosmopolitan/universalist accounts to provide these foundations. However, there are problems with the nationalist ideal, especially in its exclusionary tendencies. The first known use of the word *nationalisme* in French highlights this difficulty: the word appears in a 1798 history of Jacobinism, in which nationalism is equated with "egotism practiced by a nation," the ultimate form of selfishness.[70]

In an ideal civic nation, voluntarism itself becomes a platform for a sense of identification and loyalty, with common participation, or at least representation, acting as a social and political cement. The will to live together and to participate in government can be both emblematic and generative of cohesive bonds. For example, F. M. Barnard sees Rousseau's notion of a "daily renewal" as foreshadowing Ernest Renan's famous 1882 metaphor of a "daily plebiscite," an ongoing process of national legitimation based on voluntarist principles.[71] In a strong version of this argument, it has been contended that because democracies give citizens the feeling or the illusion that they govern their own destinies, democracies are especially capable of creating the sense of identification and adhesion necessary to demand the ultimate sacrifice of life in war.[72] This stands in contrast to the view that democratic institutions are themselves insufficient to foster loyalty and cohesion without more substantive national foundations grounded in preexisting, or at least strongly imagined, bonds among co-citizens.

The question of whether or not pure voluntarism, with or without an exit option, is a strong enough force to define and to sustain an autonomous political unit remains a contentious one. The Revolutionaries clearly felt that more was needed, as demonstrated by their advocacy of strict language policies and quasi-religious rituals that invoked common historic ties and a shared destiny among the French people. The perceived need for strong bonds among a nation's members, captured in the paradox of composition, continues to plague attempts to develop viable models of inclusive civic nationhood.[73]

The paradox of composition also hinders efforts to implement a solidarist vision of international community. Several decades before the Revolution, Voltaire had lamented: "Il est triste que, souvent, pour être bon patriote, on soit l'ennemi du reste des hommes" (It is sad that, often, to be a good patriot, one has to be the enemy of the rest of men).[74] Rousseau was also aware of this dilemma, noting that "le patriotisme et l'humanité sont . . . deux vertus incompatibles dans leur énergie" (patriotism and humanity are two virtues which are incompatible in their energy),[75] and that "[l']esprit patriotique est un esprit exclusif, qui nous fait regarder comme étranger, et presque comme ennemi tout autre que nos concitoyens" (the patriotic spirit is an exclusive spirit, that makes us view as strangers, and virtually as enemies, all others besides our fellow citizens).[76] This problem tends to characterize nationalist conceptions of political legitimacy and obligation regardless of whether the bonds constitutive of nationhood are envisioned as voluntarist or nonvoluntarist in nature.

This chapter has investigated how, on the domestic level, the ideal of voluntarist nationhood may succumb to more exclusionary visions. This is both because the idea of the nation as the basis for the state requires a certain degree of pre-political solidarity, and because political instability tends to prompt repressive measures. The next chapter explores how similar factors played a role in transforming a well-intentioned vision of cosmopolitan humanism into a universalistic and even imperialistic campaign to spread French ideals and institutions throughout Europe.

Chapter 4

Confrontation

How to Interact with Other Political Units

Introduction

This chapter explores the contradictions and potential abuses of nationalist platforms—even those of the "liberal" or emancipatory variety—in interstate relations. It focuses on the challenges faced by French Revolutionaries in their attempt to implement a universalist nationalism during the Revolutionary Wars of the 1790s: that is, to spread the Revolutionary ideals of national sovereignty and national self-determination in Europe. This ultimately entailed a policy of military occupation and the creation of virtual satellite states.[1] Debates within successive Revolutionary assemblies led to the French declaration of war of April 20, 1792, against the "King of Bohemia and Hungary." This declaration marked the beginning of a series of military conflicts with other European powers that continued until France was finally defeated in 1815 at Waterloo.

The paradox of confrontation involves a nexus of issues central to the conduct of relations among distinct political communities. These include: challenges to the delineation and composition of political units; the possibility and legitimacy of intervention across borders; the tension between transformation and tradition in international relations; and the ways in which international practice shapes the application of political ideas, as the "logic of principles" encounters the "logic of power."

The idea of any country as a "universal nation" (the self-proclaimed identity of Revolutionary France) is itself a paradox, juxtaposing the assertion that all people are subject to a single universal standard with the particularist ethic contained in the idea of nationhood. Viewed in this light, the Revolutionary conception of international relations embodies the classic and enduring tension between cosmopolitan and nationalist visions: between the idea of a single human family and the notion of the nation as a self-enclosed moral and political unit. The Revolutionary wartime experience offers a privileged window into this puzzle and its implications.[2]

The attempt to spread the French model of national self-determination as a universal ideal was particularly antagonistic and destabilizing in eighteenth-century Europe, which was composed of monarchical states. The principle of national self-determination, insofar as it legitimizes and privileges certain forms of political association, has the potential to disrupt existing political orders within and among states. As Jennifer M. Welsh explains in her study of Edmund Burke: "[for Burke,] international legitimacy is premised upon an underlying 'homogeneity' in the international system—an agreement on the acceptable *domestic* social and political composition of states."[3] This philosophy presents a "substantive conception of international legitimacy" whose criteria are *intra*-national: in this case, domestic institutions based on tradition and "conformity with the standards of European civilisation."[4] The idea of a substantive conception of international legitimacy captures the link between principles of constitution (relating to domestic institutions) and those of confrontation (relating to international relations). The Revolutionary principle of national sovereignty lies at the intersection of domestic and international politics, and is in fact *constitutive* of the boundary between them. In the French Revolutionary model, domestic constitutive principles were a matter of international concern. The Revolutionaries sought to enshrine national self-determination as the new criterion for membership in international society.

Revolutionary states operate in and seek to promote a new vision of what international society is (conception), who its legitimate actors are (constitution/composition), and what rules guide their interaction (confrontation). The connection between principles of constitution and those of confrontation in the Revolutionary context was apparent in at least two dynamics: first, emulation, as the French upheld their model of national self-determination as an alternative to absolutism; and second, intervention, as the Revolutionaries spread their political vision through propaganda and military campaigns. Both methods fueled a dynamic of insecurity in Europe, disrupting the equilibrium of stable expectations and contributing to a decade of war.

The Revolutionary reconception and reconstruction of the French nation-state had direct implications for foreign policy and international relations in at least three ways. First, the Revolutionaries saw their principles as relevant not only to the French nation, but also to humanity as a whole. This compounded the implicit challenge the French example posed to the legitimacy of monarchical states in Europe. Second, on a more active level, the French deemed themselves empowered to act on behalf of European peoples whose freedom was compromised (according to the French) by constitutional arrangements that failed to recognize their sovereignty and rights. Third, the Revolutionary conception of international society that flowed from its domestic constitutive principles required the creation of a world of sovereign peoples unencumbered by the despotism of existing states. The Revolutionaries charged themselves with creating this world—when not by invitation, then by military force, with strong echoes in U.S. foreign policy today. The principle of national sovereignty at the heart of the Revolutionary vision was fundamentally at odds with the level of interference required by France's self-appointed liberationist mission, again revealing the connection (and the potential conflict) between principles of constitution and patterns of confrontation. Inspired by a conviction in the moral unity of humankind, the Revolutionaries clung to their emancipatory project, handling its contradictory implications in ingenious and often pernicious ways.

The analysis in this chapter falls under three broad headings, moving chronologically through Revolutionary principles, guiding policies, and wartime practice. This structure permits an investigation of the interaction between Revolutionary principles and international practice. The chapter begins by exploring the underlying principles of Revolutionary foreign policy: most centrally, the idea of the universal nation and its implications at the international level (section 4.1). It then considers three explicit guiding policies: the initial Revolutionary renunciation of wars of conquest and break with the royalist past; the desire to create a democratic peace; and the doctrine of natural frontiers (section 4.2). Finally, it turns to the problem of practice, as the Revolutionaries confronted questions including: How to handle contending claims to sovereignty; How to spread national self-government without the use of force; and How the French army should conduct itself in occupied territories (section 4.3). The final question raises the broader issue of the kind of international order the Revolutionaries believed they were operating in and, when they encountered resistance, attempted to impose.

The primary goal of this chapter is not to offer a detailed historical narrative, but rather to provide an illustration of the quandaries involved in defending and propagating a universalist nationalism. It has often been observed that French Revolutionary intervention in Europe ended up undermining the very ideals it sought to promote, as the Revolutionaries preached emancipation but practiced repression.[5] This contradiction between principles and practice merits further exploration, both in its own right and as a source of insight into current debates, a project pursued in chapter six.

4.1 Revolutionary Principles

As previous chapters have indicated, the cornerstone of Revolutionary political theory was the concept of the nation as the source and first holder of sovereignty, separate from and prior to the king and the state. Within France, the National Assembly drew its legitimacy from its claim to represent the French nation. The problem came when the Assembly and its successors pursued the self-appointed task of speaking on behalf of other nations, acting to uphold the French definition of other nations' interests based on "universal" standards of legitimacy and justice. France's self-perception as the "mother of free nations" generated an active and even interventionist view of French responsibility for the freedom and well-being of peoples throughout Europe. The connection between domestic politics and foreign policy lay at the core of this dynamic: France sought to spread the ideal of national self-determination as an internal *and external* political standard. The Revolutionary idea of what self-determination involved was very restrictive: it demanded both political organization in accordance with a French administrative model, and ideological and material support for the French wartime cause.

The perception of the French Revolution as an international threat was exacerbated by the explicitly universal character of its guiding principles.[6] Although turmoil in France had been welcomed initially by some of France's European neighbors as weakening this traditionally predominant state, continued instability was perceived as a danger in need of containment.[7] The literature on revolutionary states highlights the potential for internal changes in one state to affect surrounding states. This dynamic is compounded in the case of a state whose explicit mission is to make others embrace its own conception of political legitimacy at the national and international levels.[8] Changes to the principles governing life within the state were bound up with challenges to the traditional patterns and premises of international relations.

The implementation of a universalist nationalism is particularly tricky, since the contradictory logics of nationalism and universalism dictate divergent, and potentially irreconcilable, visions of international society.[9] Nationalism tends to consider each nation an island unto itself, with the attendant prerogatives of inviolability and self-determination embodied in the idea of sovereign nation-statehood. Universalism regards national differences as of secondary importance, both to individual identity-formation and to political organization, and it downplays the relevance of national obligations and allegiances. As Montesquieu wrote, "[i]f I knew a thing useful to my nation which was ruinous to another, I would not propose it to my prince, because I am a man before being French, (or what is the same thing), because I am necessarily man, and only French by accident."[10] This is the core of Enlightenment cosmopolitanism, a fundamentally nonnational outlook named for the Greek *kosmopolites* (*kosmos* + *polites*), meaning world citizen.[11] Universalism goes one step further than cosmopolitanism, positing a more ideologically homogenous global society, and not just one in which difference is morally unimportant.

The French Revolutionary conception of international society combined nationalism and universalism, envisaging a family of self-determining nations (states based on the principle of national sovereignty) embedded in a common moral framework. While only the most zealous Revolutionary orators believed that this juxtaposition of national sovereignty and global community was entirely unproblematic, many regarded its desirability as self-evident, even if they were more realistic about its immediate feasibility. It appears obvious in retrospect that realizing universalist ambitions almost inevitably carries imperialist overtones. But this danger was not clear to many who genuinely believed in the justice and benevolence of a regenerated France charged with spreading its constitutive principles to neighboring states. The contradiction involved in universalist nationalism—championing one model as universally applicable despite its particular national origins, especially when that model prescribes national *self*-determination—was not completely hidden from the Revolutionaries, especially when it came to implementation. They reconciled universalism and nationalism in ingenious ways, developing an ideological justification for cross-border intervention in the name of the universal right of peoples to national self-determination as understood and prescribed by the French.

Revolutionary thinkers reconciled national sovereignty with the vision of a common humanity by offering a French definition of what that humanity entailed. The Revolutionaries took their own struggle to be exemplary for the world as a whole. As such, being faithful to their ethical and political principles meant embracing a liberationist mission that reconciled the apparently divergent ideals of cosmopolitanism and French nationalism by defining the first (cosmopolitanism) as the culmination of the second (French nationalism).[12] This formed the ideological basis for the exportation of French principles and institutions during the 1790s, the high point of French "Revolutionary Messianism." The Revolutionaries were nationalist in championing France, and universalist in upholding the French nation as the embodiment of ideals for humanity as a whole.[13] The Revolutionary ethos was so powerful precisely because of this ability to mobilize national sentiment around ideals upheld as universal.

Employing a similar logic, the French envisaged Revolutionary patriotism as the highest celebration of the rights of humankind. The Chevalier de Jaucourt had anticipated this ideal in his definition of patriotism in the *Encyclopédie*: "[L]e *patriotisme* le plus parfait est celui qu'on possede [*sic*] quand on est si bien rempli des droits du genre humain, qu'on les respecte vis-à-vis de tous les peuples du monde" (The most perfect *patriotism* is that which we possess when we are so filled with the rights of humankind, that we respect them with regard to all the peoples of the world).[14] While this vision was compelling, it remained unclear whether or not "respect" for the rights of each people meant that each people would be able to define the "rights of humankind" in its own way. Despite his good intentions, de Jaucourt's language was precisely the kind used to justify bestowing (read: imposing) French constitutional principles on "less fortunate" nations in the guise of universal standards.[15] It is difficult to see how a foreign policy based on this universalist conception could avoid becoming interventionist in its quest to unite, both spiritually and institutionally, the disparate members of the human family.

Paradoxically, the pairing of universalism and French nationalism was expressed most fervently by Anacharsis Cloots, a Prussian orator. Cloots advocated the creation of a "universal republic" with Paris as its capital.[16] In this worldview, "[p]atriotism and cosmopolitanism could conflict only for people who came from countries other than France, since as patriots they owed allegiance to their own country and as men they owed allegiance to France, the incarnation of humanity!"[17] There was some basis for these universalist pretensions besides sheer arrogance: French was the language of diplomacy and "high culture," connecting members of the

European intellectual elite and giving France a position of influence and prestige. It is therefore not surprising to find the opinion expressed by monarchist *émigré* Louis-Gabriel-Ambroise de Bonald that "[u]n ouvrage dangereux écrit en français est une déclaration de guerre à toute l'Europe" (a dangerous work written in French is a declaration of war against all of Europe).[18] Within France, such observations fostered grandiose sentiments such as those of Louis Saint-Just, one of the youngest and most fanatical Revolutionary leaders, who declared in a 1793 draft constitution: "Le peuple français vote la liberté du monde" (The French people votes for the freedom of the world).[19] Initially, it was believed that the French simply had to proclaim emancipatory principles in order for other nations eagerly to follow suit.[20] At times, however, this ideal of voluntary emulation needed an extra impetus, one that ended up looking very much like expansionism.[21] While this danger might seem obvious in retrospect, even those less adamant than Cloots were sometimes blinded by their Utopian and, as they believed, humanitarian visions.

The progression from the idea of a single human family to subsequent episodes of Revolutionary expansion and ideological entrepreneurship was natural, if not inevitable. Just as the Revolutionaries emphasized the need to unify all the "peoples" of France into a single French nation, so did they extend this unifying impulse outward, first to the so-called natural frontiers of France itself and then, at least rhetorically, to the rest of the world.[22] On the first anniversary of the Tennis Court Oath, Georges Jacques Danton, one of the Revolution's great orators, proposed a toast that was applauded by all those present; proclaiming "que le patriotisme ne devant avoir d'autres bornes que l'univers, il proposait de boire à la santé, à la liberté, au bonheur du genre humain" (that since patriotism should have no other boundaries than those of the universe, he proposed to drink to the health, to the liberty, to the happiness of humankind).[23] While this aspiration did not necessarily entail imperialist designs—Maximilien Robespierre, present at the banquet and applauding with the others, was vehemently opposed to an expansionist war—it does represent a peculiar and singularly ambitious mentality. This should be borne in mind when trying to come to terms with and evaluate the foreign policy decisions made by men imbued with these ideas.

The precepts put forward as the basis for Revolutionary policy sought to combine universalist and nationalist ends. Even though Martin Wight has suggested that there was no "Jacobin international theory,"[24] attempts were made during this period to consolidate sets of principles that could guide the foreign policy of France and of other nation-states.

The most notable attempt to consolidate principles was prepared by the Abbé Grégoire, whose report on language policies was explored in chapter three. Grégoire proposed his project for a *Déclaration du droit des gens* (Declaration of the law of nations) twice, first on June 18, 1793, and again on April 23, 1795.[25] As Théodore Ruyssen observes, this declaration is noteworthy as "la première énonciation précise des principes du droit international qui ait été soumise à une assemblée politique" (the first precise enunciation of the principles of international law to be submitted to a political assembly).[26] Grégoire's proposal was never put to a vote, but it is considered by the few who have studied it to express a state of mind common among France's Revolutionaries.[27] Legislative records suggest that Grégoire's declaration embodied principles that were widely agreed upon, but that the Assembly was afraid to enshrine too completely at a time when it was struggling with the contradictions implicit in its new foreign policy and with the pressures of waging a European war.[28]

Grégoire insisted that "si l'homme doit un amour de préférence à la société dont il est membre, toutefois l'égoïsme national est aussi coupable que l'égoïsme individuel" (if man owes a preferential love to the society of which he is a member, nevertheless national egoism is as blameworthy as individual egoism).[29] The goal was to achieve the proper balance between national and cosmopolitan allegiances. Nevertheless, for some, considerations of national security occupied too subordinate a position in Grégoire's declaration, making it dangerous as a practical guide. Bertrand de Barère argued: "Vous n'êtes pas seulement une assemblée philosophique et législative, vous êtes une assemblée politique. . . . [I]l ne faut pas s'extravaser en opinions philanthropiques" (You are not just a philosophical and legislative assembly, you are a political assembly. . . . We must not overflow with philanthropic opinions).[30] Barère's concern highlights the tension between the logic of principles and the logic of power, even in the Revolution's early years.

Despite accusations of idealism, Grégoire's proposal offers a key to unlocking some of the central elements of what could have been a Revolutionary international theory. The proposed declaration contains twenty-one articles that are wide-ranging in both scope and significance. The most notable feature of the document is its insistence on "peoples," rather than states or governments, as international actors. This is fully in keeping with the novel Revolutionary ontology of the nation-state. The proposal is also nonindividualist, making no mention of the rights of *persons*. In this fashion, it combines the features of traditional international law (law between states) with a more innovative view of the law of peoples (which are ontologically separate from and ethically prior to states). Grégoire's view of the basis for an international code of conduct is similarly composite in nature, containing both natural law and positivist components.

Article 1 of the declaration begins with the common observation that peoples can be considered as existing in a state of nature. However, in Grégoire's vision, peoples "ont pour lien la morale universelle" (have universal morality as a bond between them). This qualification introduces a strong element of the international society perspective, positing more substantive "social" ties among states. It raises unanswered questions about the scope and content of these universal moral rules, but it tends to reflect a solidarist, as opposed to a pluralist, view of an international society. Within this common framework of universal morality, article 2 makes clear that each people is "independent" and "sovereign," regardless of the size of its population or territory. By characterizing this sovereignty as "inalienable," article 2 protects peoples from threats by other peoples and by governments, either domestic or foreign—a crucial theoretical weapon against domestic despotism. However, on the international level, Grégoire fails to acknowledge the potential tension between the inalienable sovereignty of peoples and their being embedded in a common moral framework.

By virtue of their common humanity, peoples have an obligation to treat one another well (article 3). In times of peace, peoples have a positive obligation to do the "most good" for one another possible; in times of war, they must endeavor to do the "least harm" (article 4).[31] Grégoire's idea of a positive obligation between nations and the existence of a common human family pushes against the general view that, as summarized by Andrew Linklater, "[w]hile political theory can be 'the theory of the good life,' international theory is limited to 'the theory of survival.'"[32] Grégoire's strict distinction between insiders and foreigners prevents his emphasis on the moral unity of humankind from presenting a direct challenge to the separate existence of states per se. Nevertheless, a potential conflict exists. His dual emphasis on independence and unity makes it more difficult to conduct a consistent foreign policy towards neighbors whom one views as independent and inviolable on the one hand, but bound by basic tenets that they might not have explicitly accepted on the other.

This ambiguity is compounded by article 5, which projects Rousseau's image of the ideal domestic society onto the global sphere: "L'intérêt particulier d'un peuple est subordonné à l'intérêt général de la famille humaine" (The particular interest of a people is subordinate to the general interest of the human family). Like Rousseau, Grégoire seems to assume that this idea of the general interest is unproblematic even though, in the absence of an international Legislator, it is difficult to see how such an interest could be formed, expressed, or acted upon. Grégoire affirms that each people has the right to organize and to change the forms of its own government (thereby keeping open the revolutionary option), but that it has no right to interfere in the government of others (articles 6–7). In case this be interpreted as an injunction against spreading the Revolutionary message, he is careful to specify that only governments founded on equality and liberty are in accordance with peoples' rights and therefore, presumably, legitimate and deserving of the protection of the nonintervention principle (article 8). This provision has echoes in the emphasis on democratic governance as a requirement for membership in international society today, and on the apparently greater willingness to disregard the nonintervention principle when it comes to nondemocratic states.

Article 15 articulates a type of collective security arrangement for peoples against threats to their liberty: "Les entreprises contre la liberté d'un peuple sont un attentat contre tous les autres" (Undertakings against the liberty of one people constitute an attack against all the others). This statement might be considered the mirror image of the Brunswick manifesto, issued by the general-in-chief of the Prussian and Austrian armies on July 25, 1792, that proclaimed the solidarity of monarchical governments against the Revolution. Without reading too much into article 15, one can discern a potential legitimation for collective action against despotic regimes: the omission of a subject for "undertakings" suggests that this provision might extend to action against a government that is deemed to be oppressing its own people. The back-and-forth within Grégoire's declaration between the assertion of national sovereignty and exclusive national jurisdiction on the one hand, and the repeated invocation of a more interconnected and even familial image of the society of nations on the other, illustrate the poles between which Revolutionary foreign policy was operating. These poles pulled Revolutionary foreign policy in opposite directions, both ideologically and in terms of the justifications for actions including intervention and annexation (referred to as "reunion" in the Revolutionary lexicon).

Articles 16–21 regulate diplomacy and warfare, which are still considered important institutions of international society. Article 20 establishes the equality of rank of "public agents" of nations, anticipating the formal equality of states currently enshrined in the United Nations.[33] Article 21, a somewhat pedantic but essential note to end on, affirms the principle of *pacta sunt servanda*—the sacredness and inviolability of treaties. In keeping with the rest of the document, this article invokes treaties "between peoples," not between governments or any other entities.

Grégoire's proposal, although it combines elements of Revolutionary ideology with more traditional precepts, is consistent and adamant in distinguishing between governments and peoples. This distinction proved crucial to legitimating the Revolutionary project within France, and the policies pursued by successive French Revolutionary governments towards "oppressed peoples" in foreign countries. The idea of the king as a mere agent for the execution of the sovereign national will made it easier for the Revolutionaries to dissociate nations from their rulers, and to envisage international relations as direct dealings amongst peoples. This opened the door to policies aimed at delegitimating European monarchs in the name of national sovereignty.[34]

The Revolutionary vision of global society, exemplified by Grégoire's declaration, was fundamentally ambiguous: in one sense, it was underpinned by a cosmopolitan morality in which all individuals were envisioned as members of a common humanity; in another sense, it was more strictly (inter)nationalist, based on the notion of a global society composed of peoples, not of persons. When deputy Constantin Volney exclaimed "O nations, bannissez toute tyrannie et toute division et ne formons plus qu'une seule et même société" (O nations, banish all tyranny and all division and let us no longer form anything but one and the same society),[35] he seemed to have in mind a society of *nations* and, what is more, a society of nations in which "those" still plagued by tyranny would join "us," the group embracing Revolutionary self-government and national liberation. This "in-group" comprised the only legitimate members of the new international society—a society of distinct nations, rather than a universal republic. The Revolutionaries tended to assume that national self-government alone would be sufficient to create a degree of doctrinal homogeneity in the international system. However, nationalist arguments more often view nations as embodying distinct, and potentially incompatible, conceptions of the good. Embedding the particular within the universal was (and is) more easily said than done.

Volney issued his own proposal for an international society of self-determining nations to the National Assembly (also referred to as the National Constituent Assembly) on May 18, 1790.[36] He urged the Assembly to declare that the "universality of humankind" forms only one and the same society whose goals are peace and the happiness of all and each of its members; that peoples and states are the members of this society, possessing natural rights and subject to rules of justice as if they were individuals;

that no people has the right to invade the territory of another people or to deprive another people of its liberty and its natural advantages; and that the only just wars are defensive wars, meaning that any act of aggression against one state will be regarded as a threat against them all. Volney's proposal to renounce wars of conquest was essentially reproduced in the *Déclaration de paix au monde* (Declaration of peace to the world) of May 22, 1790, which became an article of the 1791 Constitution. Alphonse Aulard celebrates this provision as enshrining "le principe du libre consentement des peuples, reconnus maîtres de disposer de leur destinée" (the principle of the free consent of peoples, recognized as masters of deciding their own destiny), adding (apparently unselfconsciously): "Ce principe fut bientôt invoqué et appliqué pour l'annexion d'Avignon et du Comtat" (This principle was soon invoked and applied for the annexation of Avignon and the Comtat).[37] Many of the Revolution's proponents and its subsequent apologists seem blind to the ways in which principles could be corrupted by practice, a process explored in sections 4.2 and 4.3 below.

One final example completes this sketch of the ideological backdrop for Revolutionary foreign policy. On April 23, 1793, Robespierre proposed his own articles for completing the *Declaration of the Rights of Man* with a *Declaration of the Rights of Peoples*. He insisted that the ideals of fraternity and mutual assistance should bind peoples worldwide, not just those "parqué sur un coin du globe" (corralled in one corner of the globe).[38] This proposal (like Volney's) was not put to a vote, but it remains an interesting and informative exposition. The Declaration begins by asserting that men of all countries are brothers, and that different peoples should help one another according to their ability, as would the citizens of a common state. Unlike Anacharsis Cloots, Robespierre does not envision an actual universal republic, but merely an international society in which the bonds of fraternity link different nations, much as they link individuals within nations. For Robespierre, as for Grégoire and Volney, this leads to principles of collective security between peoples against tyrants. Although Robespierre himself thought that the international dimension of the Revolution should be played down until Revolutionary gains were consolidated within France, his long-term vision led in the same direction as more overtly belligerent and expansionist policies. The absolute and sweeping delegitimation of monarchy could not help but have international repercussions, since it posed a challenge to the foundations of other European governments—both in theory by the spread of ideas, and in practice through military campaigns.

While the Revolutionaries tended to speak in abstract, grandiose terms, they did not lose sight of the national interest of France, defined by them as the triumph of a particular kind of national self-determination in France and, ultimately, throughout the world. It was easy for them to speak in general terms precisely because they believed that France was the purest incarnation of, and the guiding light for, humanity as a whole. Only as the war progressed did practical pressures force choices and modifications. As the above analysis has indicated, the seeds of imperialism were contained in even the most ostensibly liberationist rhetoric. The ideal of unity based on reason entailed a certain assumption of doctrinal and institutional uniformity, as Martin Wight's description of "Revolutionism" as a strand of international theory suggests.[39] For the French Revolutionaries, the need for collective mobilization in the face of internal and external threats made this assumption an imperative. Their ideology had an (inter)nationalist ontology (international society composed of distinct nations), a cosmopolitan morality (with those nations joined by bonds of "fraternity," based on ideals of liberty and equality), and universalist ambitions (concerned with spreading and implementing the Revolutionary interpretation of liberty, equality, and fraternity on both the domestic and the international levels). It is precisely this combination that makes the French Revolutionary case so instructive as a universalist nationalism based on cosmopolitan ideals, with echoes in liberal universalist rhetoric and U.S. foreign policy today.

4.2 Revolutionary Policies

This section highlights three explicit principles that guided foreign policy making during the Revolution: the renunciation of wars of conquest and the break with the royalist past; the idea of a democratic peace; and the doctrine of natural frontiers. Despite the apparent innocuousness of at least the first two of these ideas, all were considered threats to the existing order in Europe. The first posed a direct challenge to the legitimacy of monarchical governments not based explicitly on the people's consent. The willingness of political factions within other countries to seize this legitimating platform for their own purposes further destabilized the relationship between France and the governments of neighboring countries. The second idea, the eighteenth-century version of a "democratic peace," fueled the Revolutionaries' perception of the importance of being surrounded by governments based on the principle of national self-determination, leading to policies of intervention to implement this vision. Finally, the doctrine of the "natural frontiers" of France, which was revitalized during the Revolutionary years despite its association with the monarchy, exacerbated the push for a more outward-looking foreign policy and intensified the Revolutionaries' missionary zeal. The idea of France as a universal nation blurred the boundaries between benign cosmopolitanism and the aggressive spreading of the French national ideal. The doctrine of natural frontiers compounded this tendency by expanding the geographical definition of the nation itself.

The decision often cited as marking the rupture with the royalist past came in response to a Spanish request for French assistance in April 1790. A conflict had arisen between Spain and England over the attempted capture of British installations by Spanish warships in the Nootka Sound Bay (California): the court of St. James demanded reparation, and the issue risked provoking war. The King of Spain requested help from the King of France based on the *Pacte de famille* (Family Compact) concluded on August 15, 1761, between the Bourbon cousins Charles III and Louis XV. The deputies of the National Assembly met to consider (1) if this treaty was valid; and (2) on what grounds they could justifiably risk war.[40] The arguments presented in the Nootka Sound debates reinforce the link between principles of constitution and confrontation, as the deputies explicitly upheld the new foundations of political legitimacy in France as the basis for international relations. In the end, the Assembly decided that, notwithstanding treaty engagements, the King could not be authorized to engage in an unjust war, and it refused to allow the dispatch of French ships.

This position sent a strong message both internally and externally, marking a symbolic break with royalist politics and alerting foreign rulers to the Assembly's "unpredictability." T. C. W. Blanning notes of this episode: "most importantly, the debates showed that many members of the National Assembly believed that a new era in international relations had begun. The regenerated revolutionary state, it was argued, should shun the brutal expansionism and squalid horse-trading of the old regime powers."[41] Even though the Revolutionaries did not live up to their anti-expansionist ideals, the grounds and justifications for French actions did undergo a profound and important shift during this period as part of a more general reconceptualization of international politics.

The Nootka Sound debates led to a broader discussion of the criteria for just war. This resulted in the *Declaration of Peace to the World*, incorporated as Title VI of the 1791 Constitution. The Declaration states: "la Nation française renonce à entreprendre aucune guerre dans la vue de faire des conquêtes, et n'emploiera jamais ses forces contre la liberté d'aucun peuple" (the French nation renounces the possibility of undertaking any war with the aim of conquest, and will never use its military strength against the liberty of any people).[42] The wording of this Declaration makes it much less restrictive of war than its title promises, suggesting the propriety of a more nuanced judgment about its implications. The Assembly resolved not to undertake war *for the purpose* of territorial conquest, or against the *liberty* of any people. In fact, the exportation of Revolutionary doctrines and administrative structures ended up looking like conquest, and the fundamental distinction between the government and its population permitted war against the government in the name of the often uninvited liberation of the people.

Registering these caveats does not require overstating the cynical case. In reading the speeches and debates of the Assembly, one does not come away with the impression that its members were intentionally sophistical or duplicitous. While many of them manipulated arguments for their own political purposes in maneuvering against domestic factions, this does not amount to a deliberate campaign of malicious expansionism. The Assembly drew its own legitimacy from its claim to represent the French nation, based on the arguments explored in chapter two. The problem came when it and its successors pursued the self-appointed task of speaking on behalf of *other* nations. France's universalist ambitions made its brand of nationalism singularly provocative to neighboring states.

The belligerent implications of this posture were not immediately recognized by its proponents. As Alfred Cobban has observed, "War, the revolutionaries believed, was a wicked habit of despots: a nation could not be aggressive."[43] This belief formed the centerpiece of a version of democratic peace theory, the second principle animating Revolutionary foreign policy. As part of the discussion of the Assembly's war-making powers, Monsieur le curé Jallet, a deputy of the clergy from Poitou, made the following argument:

> Toute agression injuste est contraire au droit naturel; une nation n'a pas plus le droit d'attaquer une autre nation qu'un individu d'attaquer un autre individu. Une nation ne peut donc donner à un roi le droit d'agression qu'elle n'a pas; le principe doit surtout être sacré pour les nations libres. *Que toutes les nations soient libres comme nous voulons l'être, il n'y aura plus de guerre*. [All unjust aggression is contrary to natural law; a nation has no more right to attack another nation than an individual has to attack another individual. A nation cannot therefore give a king the right of aggression that it does not have itself; the principle should above all be sacred for free nations. *Were all nations free as we wish to be, there would be no more war*.][44]

This logic captures several important elements of the prevailing mentality: first, that the principles guiding foreign policy can be deduced from a natural law that governs relations between nations, as it does those between individuals; second, that the relationship between the nation and the king is one of delegation of powers, and that freedom consists in recognizing this relationship; and third, that if all nations organized themselves according to the French model of self-determination, the result would be perpetual peace.

This widely held conviction seemed impervious to challenge.[45] For the French Revolutionaries, universalist nationalism and pacifism automatically went hand in hand, even in the context of war.[46] This tendency to associate universal democracy with peace remains prevalent, even though the French Revolutionary *levée en masse* is viewed as the epitome of bellicose mobilization, prefiguring the total wars of the twentieth century. Pierre Vergniaud proposed a national festival to honor the success of the French army after its victory over Belgium at Jemappes on November 9, 1792, urging:

> Chantez donc, chantez une victoire qui sera celle de l'humanité. Il a péri des hommes; mais c'est pour qu'il n'en périsse plus. Je le jure, au nom de la fraternité universelle que vous allez établir: chacun de vos combats sera un pas de fait vers la paix, l'humanité et le bonheur des peuples. [Sing then, sing of a victory that will be that of humanity. Men have died; but it is so that no more ever will. I swear it, in the name of the universal fraternity that you will establish: each of your battles will be a concrete step towards peace, humanity and the happiness of peoples.][47]

The Revolutionaries mistakenly assumed that emulation of their model would be automatic.[48] When their optimism was discredited, they resorted to war to promote their vision of peace.

Belief in a democratic peace reinforced the desire for a buffer zone of "ideologically friendly" states, which the Revolutionaries undertook to create, even at the cost of further fighting. Jean-Louis Carra, a Girondin journalist and cofounder of the *Annales patriotiques*, concluded:

> *Que la France soit entourée au plus tôt dans toute sa circonférence d'une bordure de peuples libres et indépendants*; qu'elle n'ait aucun contact avec les rois qui pourraient conserver encore leurs trônes pendant quelques années. Point de paix avec les puissances voisines, jusqu'à ce que la Belgique, le pays de Liège, les rives inférieures du Rhin

> jusqu'à la Hollande exclusivement, les Alpes extérieures, la Catalogne et la Biscaye n'aient planté avec des racines l'arbre de la liberté! [*Let France be surrounded as soon as possible along all its circumference by a border of free and independent peoples;* let France not have any contact with the kings who might still hold onto their thrones for another several years. No peace with neighboring powers, until Belgium, the country of Liège, the lower banks of the Rhine exclusively as far as Holland, the outer Alps, Catalonia and Biscay have planted with roots the tree of liberty!][49]

This idea combined the more traditional notion of a defensive perimeter with the ideological imperative of converting neighboring regions to the Revolutionary cause, both for their own benefit and to prevent cross-border "contamination." Peace in the short term was subordinated to the longer-term goal of creating a Europe in the image of Revolutionary France, with or without Europe's consent.

The Revolutionary model could be spread either by exporting French ideals and institutions to foreign states, or by defining foreign territories as part of France. The latter tactic was facilitated by the third noteworthy policy: the doctrine of natural frontiers. In a speech on January 31, 1793, Danton issued the classic proclamation of this Revolutionary doctrine:

> Je dis que c'est en vain qu'on veut faire craindre de donner trop d'étendue à la République. Ses limites sont marquées par la nature. Nous les atteindrons toutes des quatre points de l'horizon; du côté du Rhin; du côté de l'Océan; du côté des Alpes. [I say that those who want to make us fear extending the reach of the Republic do so in vain. Its bounds are demarcated by nature. We shall reach them all from the four points of the horizon; from the Rhine; from the Ocean; from the Alps.][50]

Especially after the French took the offensive at Valmy in September 1792, the desire grew for France to consolidate and to extend its territorial gains, despite the potential association of this program with the monarchy.[51] In addition to the pressures of an international environment characterized by military competition and conquest, the perceived precariousness of the Revolutionary regime and the Revolutionaries' siege mentality made expansion seem attractive, and even necessary. Domestic fear bred international ambition.

Talk of frontiers excited the "national enthusiasm" of the French, especially if they had in mind Pierre Gaspard Chaumette's 1792 prediction that "[l]e terrain qui sépare Paris de Pétersbourg et Moscou sera bientôt francisé, municipalisé, jacobinisé" (the terrain that separates Paris from Petersburg and Moscow will soon be frenchified, municipalized, jacobinized).[52] The idea of France as a universal nation blurred the distinction between ideological and territorial ambition, much as it conflated the interests of France with the good of humanity as a whole. This compounded the tendency for French nationalist fervor to overflow its initial bounds, and for universalist aspirations to trump principles of noninterference and restraint.[53]

The desire for a perpetual peace based on French principles imagined as universal proved to be self-undermining in theory and in practice. It provoked suspicion and fear in the other states of Europe, and it imposed a standard for the internal affairs of other countries that could not be guaranteed without French interference and control.[54] This tension was particularly acute during the Revolution, when legitimacy and membership in the international system were based on opposing domestic arrangements: for the Revolutionaries, national self-determination; for their opponents, monarchical tradition. During the 1790s, the principles upheld as the cornerstone of peace became a rationale for war.

4.3 Revolutionary Practice

While the tensions explored above may be difficult to avoid, the Revolution did not become aggressive in a vacuum. Expansionism and interventionism were largely implicit in the vision of a universal nation, but internal factors (fear of political rebellion and organized attacks by *émigrés*) and external pressures (ideological and military competition with monarchical states) fueled a dynamic of belligerence. More and more, ideology became a tool of war. While the perceived foreign threat certainly provided an occasion for hostilities, this was not the only consideration: the Girondin/Brissotin faction wanted war to solve their internal problems and to consolidate power, while the royalists and the King thought that fighting a war would allow them to regain the confidence and support of the French people.[55]

Neither Girondins nor royalists had specific war aims beyond fortifying their own positions. Nevertheless, the Legislative Assembly declared war on April 20, 1792, against the "King of Bohemia and Hungary," "on behalf of the King of the French and in the name of the Nation."[56] The stated reason for war was to defend the liberty and independence of the French nation, but Revolutionary principles fostered an expansive definition of this task: for the Revolutionaries, defending France required transforming Europe. As Jacques Pierre Brissot, a vocal deputy to the Legislative Assembly and a leader of the Girondin party (also referred to as the Brissotin party), announced:

> [T]ous n'attendent que votre explosion pour commencer la leur. . . . Le moment est venu pour une autre croisade et elle a un objet bien plus noble, bien plus saint. C'est une croisade de liberté universelle. [All are waiting only for your explosion to initiate their own. . . . The moment has come for another crusade and this one has a much nobler, much more saintly, object. It is a crusade of universal liberty.][57]

Brissot's picture of restless nations "waiting in the wings" for their cue from France proved overly optimistic. Wartime efforts to spread the French ideal soon shifted from a policy of *exemplarité* (leading by example) to outright interference and ultimately occupation. This shift occurred as a response both to apathy and intransigence among targeted populations, and to the monarchical coalition's attempts to block Revolutionary gains.

Three central issues faced the Revolutionaries in conducting their "crusading" foreign policy: first, how to handle contending claims to sovereignty; second, how to reconcile the ideal of national self-government with the use of force to promote it; and third, how to instruct French armies regarding their conduct in occupied territories. The responses to these problems developed over time, shaped both by principles (the imperative of "liberation" and the importance of national self-determination) and by pragmatic considerations (the failure of occupied populations immediately to follow suit, and the need to feed and provision the French armies). At the beginning, prudentialism tended to prevail, for example, in the National Assembly's 1789 refusal to intervene on behalf of Belgian insurgents, and in its 1790 refusal to recognize a new "Belgian republic."[58] While Corsica was integrated into France on November 30, 1789, at the request of a Corsican deputy, Christophe Saliceti, who emphasized the "will of the people" and the principle of self-determination,[59] this early action was the exception rather than the rule. Only gradually did the National Constituent Assembly (and its successor bodies, the Legislative Assembly and the National Convention) overcome its reluctance to implicate itself in potentially antagonistic and provocative enterprises.

Two examples relating to claims over territorial sovereignty help illustrate this evolution: the debate over the status of Avignon and the Comtat Venaissin (two papal enclaves within France), and the question of the treaty rights of German princes in Alsace. The status of Avignon and Venaissin plagued the members of the National Assembly through the first year of their tenure and beyond.[60] Not only were the wishes of the inhabitants unclear, but the deputies were also divided on whether or not to recognize papal authority and control.[61] The issue was significant because it called into question the law of treaties, and it involved a right to national self-determination separate from the demonstration of governmental abuses.[62] Most deputies were initially hesitant to question the age-old arrangements governing the papal enclaves. However, the Pope's refusal to grant Avignon and the Comtat constitutions similar to that of France following a request by local representatives aggravated the situation, strengthening the case for some form of intervention by France.[63]

In November 1790, the National Assembly once again took up this question. The deputies placed increasing emphasis on the idea of the people's right to self-determination. Robespierre exclaimed:

> On vous a dit qu'Avignon était la propriété du Pape. Juste ciel! les peuples, la propriété d'un homme! . . . On vous a dit que par un décret vous avez renoncé à toute conquête. La réunion libre d'un peuple à un autre a-t-elle quelque chose de commun avec les conquêtes? . . . Ce n'est pas sur l'étendue du territoire avignonnais que se mesure l'importance de cette affaire, mais sur les hauteurs des principes qui garantissent les droits de l'homme et des nations. La cause d'Avignon est celle de l'Univers. [You have been told that Avignon was the property of the Pope. Good heavens! peoples, the property of a man! . . . You have been told that by a decree you have renounced all wars of conquest. Has the free joining of one people to another anything in common with conquests? . . . It is not on the stretch of Avignon territory that the importance of this affair shall be measured, but on the heights of the principles that guarantee the rights of man and of nations. The cause of Avignon is that of the Universe.][64]

In October, in response to violent insurrections in Avignon, the Assembly decided to ask the King to send troops to help the municipal authorities reestablish order. The intervention was short-lived, but it was interpreted by the faction of Avignon patriots as signifying their incorporation into France.[65] The National Assembly finally formalized annexation of the two enclaves in September 1791, primarily to ensure civil order. Despite its concrete motivation, the theoretical justifications for this action had lasting and important implications.[66]

As the French deputies had foreseen, annexation was condemned by other European states as a threatening precedent. Count Mercy, the Austrian ambassador to France, regarded it as a virtual declaration of war against all other governments.[67] T. C. W. Blanning observes that, precisely to avoid this reaction, the annexation decree had combined both traditional and Revolutionary arguments:

> L'Assemblée Nationale déclare qu'en vertu des droits de la France sur les Etats réunis d'Avignon et du Comtat Venaissin, et que, conformément au voeu librement et solennellement émis par la majorité des communes et des citoyens de ces deux pays pour être incorporés à la France, lesdits deux Etats réunis d'Avignon et du Comtat Venaissin font, dès ce moment, partie intégrante de l'Empire français. [The National Assembly declares that by virtue of the rights of France over the united states of Avignon and the Comtat Venaissin, and in accordance with the freely and solemnly expressed wish of the majority of the communes and citizens of these two territories to be incorporated into France, the said two united states of Avignon and the Comtat Venaissin are, from this moment on, an integral part of the French Empire.][68]

By unearthing an old parliamentary decree to support France's rights over Avignon, the deputies tried to avoid plunging directly into a policy of disregarding treaties: they attempted to ground their actions to some extent in principles that others could accept as authoritative.[69] However, they also took advantage of the opportunity to invoke and to reinforce the emerging standard of the popular will as the basis for legitimate political arrangements, a step towards a more revolutionary foreign policy.[70]

In October 1790, the Assembly considered the question of the rights of German princes over the territories of Alsace. While feudal rights had been guaranteed to these princes in the acts by which sovereignty over the region had been ceded to the King of France, these stipulations were in conflict with the Assembly's abolition of all remnants of feudal privilege.[71] In his report on the subject, Merlin de Douai struck a note consonant with the Nootka Sound principles: he rejected arguments based on "conventions from the time of despotism," and he reaffirmed the union of the Alsatian people with the French people based on the Alsatian popular will.[72]

Frictions in the French borderlands exacerbated the regional instability created by the Revolution. The ever-present threat of aristocratic *émigrés* plotting to regain control of France with the assistance of neighboring monarchies, coupled with Louis XVI's unsuccessful attempt to flee France in June 1791, heightened the siege mentality. On November 29, 1791, the Legislative Assembly decreed:

> Dites-leur [aux puissances étrangères] que si des princes d'Allemagne continuent de favoriser des préparatifs dirigés contre les Français, nous porterons chez eux non le fer et la flamme, mais la liberté. C'est à eux de calculer quelles peuvent être les suites du réveil des nations. [Tell the foreign powers that if the princes of Germany continue to support the preparations directed against the French, we will bring to them, not the sword and the torch, but liberty. It is up to them to calculate what the consequences of the awakening of nations might be.][73]

Peaceful coexistence no longer seemed possible between states operating in such different registers—adherence to treaty rights versus popular will—especially where questions of political and territorial sovereignty were concerned.

The Revolutionaries found themselves having to justify war in a manner consistent with their pacifist proclamations. They recognized that, paradoxically, spreading their ideals might ultimately undermine them, but they were loath to abandon the principles for which they had fought their domestic political battles. As a result, they attempted to reconcile aggression with the renunciation of war by creating a loophole derived from their own Constitution, emphasizing the sovereignty of the people and the strict separation between the authentic nation and the extraneous privileged classes. The latter distinction was enshrined in some of the Revolution's most remembered slogans: "Il faut déclarer la guerre aux rois et la paix aux nations!" (We must declare war on kings and peace to nations!),[74] and "Guerre aux châteaux, paix aux chaumières!" (War on the castles, peace to the cottages!).[75] The declaration of war in 1792 was addressed to the "King of Bohemia and Hungary," not to the Empire's peoples. It is often noted that the semantic separation between kings and peoples made little difference in practice. However, it is less often appreciated just how innovative this distinction actually was as a justification for foreign policy. Even if Revolutionary practice was inconsistent with its ideals, this did not impair the potency and resonance of its new legitimating standard. As explored below, the language of national self-determination was in fact appropriated by opponents of the Revolution, contributing to the centrality of this principle as a basis for political and territorial claims.

In keeping with their view of international society as composed of free and sovereign peoples, the Revolutionaries sought to establish direct relations with peoples over the heads of governments. Pierre Samuel Dupont de Nemours exclaimed: "plus de diplomatie; plus d'ambassadeurs; rien que des 'pactes nationaux' avec 'des peuples libres'!" (no more diplomacy; no more ambassadors; nothing but "national compacts" with "free peoples"!).[76] This view was reflected in the declaration issued by French generals on invading foreign lands:

> *Le peuple français au peuple* . . . Frères et amis, nous avons conquis la liberté, et nous la maintiendrons: notre union et notre force en sont les garans. . . . Vous êtes, dès ce moment, frères et amis, tous citoyens, tous égaux en droits, et tous appelés également à défendre, à gouverner et à servir votre patrie. [*The French people to the ______ people*: Brothers and friends, we have conquered liberty, and we shall maintain it: our union and our strength are its guarantors. . . . You are, from this moment on, brothers and friends, all citizens, all equal in rights, and all equally called to defend, to govern, and to serve your country.][77]

It is difficult to imagine bolder language.

Not surprisingly, however, the French generals did not mean exactly what they said—or, rather, they meant it in their own way. The *patrie* that occupied peoples were called on to serve was not the one to which many of them thought they belonged. The first act of the invading Revolutionary armies was to abolish existing "feudal and despotic" civil, military, and social structures. This did not leave occupied peoples with much to call their own.[78] Revolutionary committees were set up in the invaded territories to emulate the French model of citizenship and government, without consideration for indigenous structures and preferences. Resistance was perceived as backward, misguided, subversive, and in need of suppression in the name of the "universal *patrie*."[79] This was a more abstract but nevertheless imposing version of Anacharsis Cloots's universal republic, centered around the guiding light of France.

This vision of "natural frontiers *plus*" ran into difficulty, especially as few foreigners were as enthusiastic as Cloots had been to embrace the French model. Reluctance and resistance in occupied territories led to the imposition of more forceful "emancipatory" measures.[80] While the French had justified intervention by distinguishing existing governments from their peoples and by assuming that peoples invariably wanted to be liberated, popular indifference and opposition were impossible to ignore. The conceptual separation of governments and peoples was meaningless for French armies faced with hostile populations. Added to the fact that the French armies engaged in pillage despite contrary orders, the stage was set for violent conflict—not only with monarchical governments, but also with peoples themselves.

This leads to the question of occupation policy, central to the confrontation dynamic. Once again, intentions were more praiseworthy than actions. Johann Wolfgang von Goethe, reflecting on the Revolution, noted of General Adam Philippe Custine's advances into Mainz: "Les Français arrivaient, mais ils ne semblaient apporter que l'amitié. . . . Ils promettaient à chacun son droit et son gouvernement propre" (The French arrived, but they did not seem to bring anything but friendship. . . . They promised that each [people] would have its own law and government).[81] The French General Charles François Dumouriez (who later defected) expressed a similar position upon his entry into Belgium:

> Brave nation belge! Nous entrons sur votre territoire pour vous aider à planter l'arbre de la liberté, sans nous mêler en rien à la constitution que vous voudrez adopter. Pourvu que vous établissiez la souveraineté du Peuple et que vous renonciez à vivre sous des despotes quelconques, nous serons vos frères, vos amis, vos soutiens. Nous respecterons vos propriétés et vos lois. [Brave Belgian nation! We enter your territory to help you plant the tree of liberty, without meddling at all in the constitution that you wish to adopt. As long as you establish the sovereignty of the People and renounce living under any despots whatsoever, we will be your brothers, your friends, your supporters. We will respect your proprieties and your laws.][82]

Without reading too finely between the lines, one immediately notices the conditionality built in to the second part of this definition: "*as long as you establish*. . . ." As Sophie Wahnich observes, "[l]e geste de souveraineté, se donner des lois qui consacrent la liberté, est la *condition* de la fraternité républicaine" (the act of sovereignty, to give oneself laws that consecrate liberty, is the *condition* for republican fraternity).[83] Fraternity between peoples is not just a function of their common humanity, but a bond that exists between one sovereign people and another, as implied by Volney's declaration cited earlier. This emphasis on conditionality came to overshadow the primacy of consent as a basis for domestic legitimacy and the criterion for membership in the new international society.

The decrees of November and December 1792 instructing French generals in the occupied territories to proclaim the sovereignty of the people "made it clear that the 'freedom' of the conquered peoples only extended as far as their willingness to select a form of government that was compatible with French principles."[84] C. J. H. Hayes summarizes this problem: "Apparently other nationalities were to be free to exercise the right of self-determination, if they exercised it in accordance with French models, but not otherwise."[85] The Revolutionaries were aware of the contradiction involved in this idea but, for them, imposing a French model was simply part of their emancipatory mission. Jacques Nicolas Billaud-Varenne wrote in a report to the National Convention:

> L'établissement de la démocratie chez une nation qui a longtemps langui dans les fers peut être comparé à l'effort de la nature dans la transition si étonnante du néant à l'existence. . . . Il faut, pour ainsi dire, recréer le peuple qu'on veut rendre à la liberté. [The establishment of democracy in a nation that has long languished in irons may be compared to nature's effort in the astonishing transition from nothingness into being. . . . It is necessary, so to speak, to recreate the people one wants to emancipate.][86]

Georg Forster, a German supporter of the French cause, was more prosaic on this issue: "il faudra leur ordonner d'être libres" (it is necessary to order them to be free).[87] This assertion crystallizes the paradoxical and dangerous coupling of liberty and force.

The French Revolutionaries believed that the only path to "real" freedom for other peoples was by way of French tutelage. This view stands in sharp contrast to John Stuart Mill's position in his classic essay "On Non-Intervention": "if they have not sufficient love of liberty to be able to wrest it from merely domestic oppressors, the liberty which is bestowed on them by other hands than their own, will have nothing real, nothing permanent."[88] Jean Jaurès in his *Histoire socialiste de la Révolution* characterized the Revolutionaries' situation as follows: "Terrible dilemme: ou laisser subsister autour de soi la servitude toujours menaçante, ou faire de la liberté imposée une nouvelle forme de la tyrannie" (Terrible dilemma: either let ever-menacing servitude subsist around oneself, or turn imposed liberty into a new form of tyranny).[89] Letting "servitude" subsist would be both morally irresponsible and threatening, but intervening to overcome it would involve aggression and, worse, might undermine the very principles of autonomy and sovereignty at the heart of the Revolutionary mission.

Perceptions of threat pushed Revolutionary principles towards the interventionist end of the spectrum.[90] For example, even before the outbreak of war, aristocratic *émigrés* who fled or were forced to leave France in the early stages of the Revolution sought external support to help restore the French monarchy. These efforts created a vicious circle whereby French Revolutionary belligerence could be justified with reference to this concrete threat. Foreign reactions were then intensified by a perception of increasing French ambitiousness in exporting its ideals and institutions, compounding a cycle of suspicion that fueled hostile wars.[91]

Faced with this situation, the French opted for interventionism, concretized in the Revolutionary decree of November 19, 1792: "La Nation française accordera *fraternité et secours à tous les peuples qui voudront recouvrer leur liberté*" (The French Nation will grant *fraternity and support to all peoples who wish to regain their liberty*).[92] While historian Albert Mathiez praises this decree as "the apogee of the cosmopolitan and humanitarian policy" of the Revolution, he admits:

> Désormais, la propagande émancipatrice prenait la forme d'une tutelle, presque d'une dictature. La France révolutionnaire reconnaissait que les peuples libérés laissés à eux-mêmes étaient incapables par leurs seules forces d'imiter son exemple. Elle était obligée "de se substituer à eux et de faire pour eux, sans eux, au besoin contre eux leur Révolution." [From (November 19) on, emancipatory propaganda took the form of a tutelage, almost of a dictatorship. Revolutionary France recognized that free peoples left to themselves were incapable of imitating its example on their own. It was obliged "to substitute itself for them and carry out their Revolution for them, without them, if need be against them."][93]

From the Millian perspective referenced above, this approach was ill-fated from the start. Not only did it undermine the very freedom it purported to bestow, but it also sparked a backlash against the Revolution. This intensified a vicious circle of repression, breeding draconian policies both at home and abroad.[94] For example, a strong disincentive for military defeat among French generals was the possibility that they would be executed for treason upon their return from the battlefront.

The intensity of the backlash against the Revolution was in large part a function of the ambitiousness of the Revolution's self-proclaimed mission: hypocrisy added insult to injury, making occupation in the guise of liberation a worse crime than occupation alone.[95] Forster wrote to General Custine on January 4, 1793, about the pillage experienced by German towns at the hands of French armies:

> Le brigandage des employés subalternes n'a déjà que trop bien réussi à aliéner les esprits et à les détourner du projet de se donner à la France. La loyauté de la Nation, l'équité, la justice et la générosité de la République sont mille fois compromises. . . . Ah! les habitants auraient été moins cruellement trompés si on leur eut dit en arrivant: "Nous venons tout vous prendre." [The banditry of subordinates has already succeeded all too well in alienating souls and diverting them from the project of giving themselves to France. The loyalty of the Nation, the equity, the justice and the generosity of the Republic are compromised a thousand times. . . . Alas! the inhabitants would have been less cruelly deceived if the troops had told them upon arrival: "We have come to take everything from you."][96]

As Robespierre had cautioned, nobody likes armed missionaries: "C'est à la puissance de la raison, non à la force des armes de propager les principes de notre glorieuse Révolution. . . . La liberté ne s'apporte pas à la pointe des baïonnettes" (It is up to the power of reason, not to the force of arms to propagate the principles of our glorious Revolution. . . . Liberty cannot be brought in on the blades of bayonets).[97] Sparking both passive and active resistance, the war for liberty became as vicious and divisive as a war for more "traditional" objectives.[98]

While French "universal principles" were applauded by certain political minorities in other countries, attempts to spread this model bred resentment and hostility among populations at large. Universalism went from being a Revolutionary fantasy to a concrete international threat. The alleged beneficiaries of emancipation would feel very much like victims of French domination.[99] This led Edmund Burke to dub intervention "the homicidal philanthropy of France."[100] The banner of universalist nationalism could only be carried so far until the antiuniversalist nationalism of other countries rose up in reaction against it.[101]

The strength of this resistance was reflected in new instructions to French generals, who had initially been charged with exercising military restraint. On September 15, 1793, deputy Jeanbon Saint-André pushed through a decree that the Republican generals "'renonçant désormais à toute idée philanthropique,' pratiqueraient la loi des représailles et exerceraient à l'égard des pays et des individus subjugués par leurs armes, les droits ordinaires de la guerre" ("renouncing from now on every philanthropic idea," would practice the law of reprisals and would exercise with respect to the countries and individuals subjugated by their arms, the normal rights of war).[102] General Dumouriez, whose initial emphasis on relative nonintervention in the local affairs of occupied territories was noted above, foresaw the following situation:

> où malheureusement quelque province, ville ou bourg serait assez avili par l'esclavage pour ne pas saisir avec enthousiasme l'arbre de la liberté que les Français veulent établir . . . [alors] cette province, cette ville, ce bourg, ce village seront traités comme les vils esclaves de la maison d'Autriche. [where unfortunately some province, city or town would be depraved enough by slavery to fail to seize enthusiastically the tree of liberty that the French want to establish . . . then this province, this city, this town, this village will be treated like the vile slaves of the house of Austria.][103]

This was not the language of the Revolution's early years. It reflected the theoretical contradictions involved in exporting a particular brand of universalism based on the idea of national liberation, combined with the practical imperatives of fighting a large-scale war.

Wartime actions might have betrayed Revolutionary ideals, but these actions were still framed in terms of Revolutionary principles defined in opposition to the old order. A new and distinctive set of justifications, understandings, and perceptions was articulated and entrenched. This process created legitimating standards for international relations founded on national self-determination that, despite their apparent discrediting in the Revolutionary experience, remain potent and resonant in the present-day. The greatest tribute to the Revolutionary movement on the international level was not the adherence of other peoples to the French national mission: it was their appropriation of French rhetoric as a weapon *against* the imposition of French rule.[104] This is the phenomenon underlying the perspective of those who associate nationalism as a political doctrine with the reaction against the French Revolution, rather than with the Revolution itself.

Disillusionment among occupied populations did not result in the rejection of national self-determination, but only of the French version of it. (In this sense, liberty *was* brought in by bayonets, though not in the way the pro-war Girondins had imagined.) In fact, the French occupation and creation of virtual satellite states prompted local populations to draw on, consolidate, and even romanticize their own indigenous identities and traditions as a bulwark against French influence. This is the paradox or contradiction that arises in the attempt to implement a universalist doctrine of national self-determination: as long as the French Revolutionaries insisted that neighboring nations "determine themselves" exclusively in France's own image, their posture as self-styled liberators was bound to undermine itself and appear naïvely hypocritical, if not intentionally duplicitous. Danton's January 31, 1793, call to other peoples to "organize yourselves like us"[105] was only partially accepted. The French Revolutionary rhetoric of liberation and national self-determination did imprint itself on political discourse and on the popular imagination. However, these ideas were more likely to be used against France than for it, in an act of ideological appropriation that foreshadowed the dynamic of twentieth-century anticolonial movements.[106]

Revolutionary France was notable not just because it was a revolutionary state, but because it promoted national self-determination as an international political standard. As Volney declared to his fellow deputies in the opening stages of the Revolution: "Vous ne souffrirez plus que des millions d'hommes soient le jouet de quelques-uns qui ne sont que leurs semblables et vous rendrez leur dignité et leurs droits aux nations" (You will not tolerate any longer that millions of men are the playthings of a few who are really their equals, and you will restore to nations their dignity and their rights).[107] This commitment was the basis for a new "legitimate right of revolutionary intervention," the most dangerous of the Revolutionary innovations from the perspective of other European powers.[108] This "right" was based on the solidarity of free peoples, an idea that was central to Grégoire's declaration and to other Revolutionary texts.

The most concrete expression of this right of intervention was the tendency for the French nation to embrace and even engulf neighboring peoples in the name of solidarity and self-determination. Jacques Dehaussy calls this impulse towards *la Grande Nation* "la première expression pratique du '*principe des nationalités*'" (the first practical expression of the "nationality principle").[109] However, the French creation of a circle of virtual satellite states looked much like imperialism; the more genuine expression of the "nationality principle" was instead the resulting consolidation of other European national identities as a reaction against France.[110]

Despite expansionist projects, there were limits to French universalism, defined primarily in pragmatic and prudential terms. Danton worried about the precedent of intervention on behalf of oppressed peoples, noting that it might lead to a "politique d'intervention continuelle" (policy of continuous intervention).[111] The fear of overextension was real for the Revolutionaries despite their globalist rhetoric, highlighting the practical impediments to implementing even the most fervently held ideals.

In some interpretations, this concern for the French national interest became not just a restraint, but the core of the French project itself. Historian C. J. H. Hayes suggests: "Embarking upon the Great War of 1792 in order to make the world safe for liberty, equality, and the right of national self-determination, it was not long before they were waging it primarily for the greater glory of France."[112] Alexander Hamilton leveled the accusation against the Revolutionaries in 1797 that "[t]he specious pretense of enlightening mankind and reforming their civil institutions is the varnish to the real design of subjugating them."[113] While the cynical argument says that this was the case all along, the evidence presented in this chapter tends to mitigate this harsh evaluation. The Revolutionaries were generally sincere in their intention to create a more just and free international society based on the principle of national sovereignty. However, they were largely (if not entirely innocently) trapped by the logical consequences and practical dilemmas involved in their ambitious rhetoric, and caught up in the momentum of their bold ideals.

The forces underlying what became a wide-scale conflict with neighboring countries stemmed not only from power-political imperatives, but also from the dictates of a universal nationalist ideal. The idea of universalist nationalism is problematic, as it is largely unable to reconcile a thicker vision of international solidarity with the preservation of heterogeneity and freedom. This latent contradiction is exacerbated, but not created, by concrete internal and external challenges. The French Revolutionary example illustrates the ways in which nationalist arguments can be used to legitimize particular domestic and foreign arrangements and actions. It suggests how the pressures of international practice can combine with nationalist principles to shape the constitution and composition of political and territorial units in international society, and the patterns of confrontation among them.

Conclusion

While the French Revolution is remembered primarily as a domestic political uprising, it had lasting repercussions in the international sphere. It was perceived as embodying a clash between two radically different conceptions of international order or, in the words of Austrian statesman and diplomat Baron von Thugut, between order and anarchy.[114] As Martin Wight suggests, "[i]nternational revolutions generate revolutionary wars, in the sense that their wars are tinged with doctrinal ferocity, and have unlimited aims."[115] In this perspective, Revolutionary states tend to be interventionist by nature, not only because of their ideological convictions and "crusading spirit," but also because consolidating their own legitimacy requires securing recognition from other international actors. If necessary, Revolutionary states attempt to secure this recognition by transforming the principles underlying the international system itself.[116] Albert Sorel observes: "la guerre est inévitable. Elle éclate précisément parce qu'il n'existe plus de droit commun entre la France et l'Europe" (war is inevitable. It breaks out precisely because there no longer exists any common law between France and Europe).[117] France became a menace to the homogeneity of international society as it had developed in the eighteenth century, and a threat to the very existence of that "society," which was based on common rules.

This process highlights certain continuities between ideological and more "traditional" forms of international confrontation, whether belligerent or otherwise. For example, the French Constitution of Year I of the Republic (1793) announced a return to the principle of nonintervention, except in already occupied territories.[118] This measure has been construed by jurist Jacques Dehaussy as demonstrating a desire for recognition and legitimation of the Revolutionary regime by more traditional powers, "le désir de *montrer que la République se comporte en État avec les autres Puissances*, en sorte que celles-ci soient amenées à la traiter elle-même comme un État" (the desire to *show that the Republic is acting in a State-like fashion with the other Powers*, such that these are brought around to treating it like a State).[119] This dynamic is reminiscent of the Revolutionaries' appeal to treaty rights as a basis for annexing Avignon, and it was evident in more "conventional" wartime measures including the suspension of treaties, the taking of prisoners, and the extraction of payments from occupied territories. These features of Revolutionary policy blurred the line between the "new" and "old" diplomacies.

The legacy of the Revolution for French diplomats could therefore be seen as ambiguous: "When Talleyrand was asked in 1832 to explain the real meaning of the word nonintervention, he replied: 'C'est un mot métaphysique, et politique, qui signifie à peu près le [*sic*] même chose qu'intervention'" (It is a metaphysical and political word that means about the same thing as intervention).[120] There is a danger, however, in assimilating Revolutionary policy too closely to Old Regime politics, and thereby neglecting its innovative features. A similar conflation characterizes the tendency to uphold Napoleon as the epitome of unmasked Revolutionary cynicism, an unfair assessment given Napoleon's habit of disregarding his instructions and carrying out expansionist projects on his own initiative.[121]

International relations in the aftermath of the Revolution were not devoid of power politics, as the most Utopian Revolutionary thinkers might have desired. But it was balance-of-power politics with a twist, namely, a new international legitimating discourse based on national sovereignty. Arguments about age-old treaties and hereditary ties gave way to struggles between different versions of liberationist rhetoric and competing conceptions of nationhood. The French Revolutionaries could not ensure the triumph of their own version of what national sovereignty meant or the political configuration they thought it should entail. Even so, they succeeded in popularizing the ideal of national self-determination in international political discourse, both through their own rhetoric and practice, and through reactions against it.

While the French Revolution might be accorded excessive doctrinal importance by those who hail it as "the birth of the modern nation-state," it remains an important source of insights for those seeking to understand the nation-statist model. Martin Wight has suggested that "[t]he Versailles Settlement was the final victory in Europe of the French Revolution over the Holy Alliance," in that a nation-based principle of international order (in theory) was finally established as the basis for settling conflicting territorial claims.[122] However, as violence in the Balkans and elsewhere has confirmed, either the Versailles Settlement did not follow the national self-determination principle very well, or this principle does not offer a viable solution. Despite these caveats, self-identified "oppressed peoples" continue to look to national self-determination as a basis for their grievances and a potential motor for change.[123] T. C. W. Blanning has suggested that "[i]t was not the French Revolution which created the modern world, it was the French Revolutionary wars."[124] This chapter has suggested that this is a false dichotomy, since domestic constitutive principles gave rise to international policies and standards designed to transform the foundations of world public order.

The conjunction of principles of constitution and those of confrontation, mediated by ideas of national self-determination and legitimate intervention, lies at the intersection of politics and international relations. The story is told of Napoleon who, upon his return from Italy in 1797, announced to Sieyès: "J'ai fait la grande nation."—"C'est, lui répondit Sieyès, que nous avions d'abord fait la nation" (I have created the great nation.—It is, responded Sieyès, because we had first of all created the nation).[125] These words, apocryphally exchanged by the general charged with executing Revolutionary foreign policy and the philosopher-priest who elaborated the basis for Revolutionary domestic politics, capture the crucial link between how a nation conceives of and organizes itself, and how it engages with—and potentially transforms—the international system.

The above exploration of Revolutionary foreign policy and wartime practice suggests some implications of promoting a "substantive conception of international legitimacy,"[126] as opposed to a merely procedural or formalistic one. The final chapters investigate more recent incarnations of this "thicker" conception of international society, which underpins principled justifications of intervention across borders and the idea of a right to democratic governance.

Chapter 5

Synthesis

Introduction

The preceding chapters offered an overview of the core tensions and trade-offs involved in the conception, constitution, composition, and confrontation of nation states during the French Revolution. This historical analysis provides a framework for exploring the nation-state principle as a basis for world public order. Even if the contemporary international political map does not reflect a pure application of the nation-state model, understandings based on the nation-state idea continue to shape international perceptions, attitudes, expectations, and demands. The historical development of the idea of national self-determination offers insight into both the internal structure of nationalist ideas and arguments, and the ways in which the imperatives of political practice can shape the application of these ideas, particularly in a heterogeneous international system.

The first section of this chapter provides an overview of the uses and abuses of nationhood as a political platform, as illustrated by the preceding study of the French Revolution (section 5.1). The rest of the chapter considers the ways in which models of "benign national" or "post-national" political communities appear viable or problematic in light of the insights gleaned from the French Revolutionary experience. Section 5.2 situates the nation-state principle in the broader context of debates about the relevance of group identity to political boundaries and institutions. Section 5.3 examines the common distinction between civic and ethnic nations, and explores three attempts to reduce the exclusionary potential of nation-statism: civic nationalism, constitutional patriotism, and multiculturalism. Having identified pitfalls in these three attempts, it suggests possible (though certainly not infallible) modifications.

5.1 Drawing Insights from the Four Paradoxes

The paradoxes of conception, constitution, composition, and confrontation can provide a framework for analyzing and evaluating claims based on national entitlements and aspirations. Each "paradox" highlights a valuable use of the idea of the nation as a platform for identity-formation and political mobilization. However, each benefit entails a corresponding warning that should form part of any inquiry into the legitimacy of claims on the part of actual or would-be nation-states.

The first set of tensions revolves around the issue of conception. The question "Which came first, the nation or the state?" might seem pedantic, but its answer (in the popular consciousness, if not the historical record) is crucial in substantiating nation-based political claims. Only if nations can be conceived of as separate from states can appeals to the nation be used to legitimate or to challenge state institutions and boundaries; for example, without the ability to conceive of a Kurdish nation, it would be very difficult for Kurdish separatists to advocate an independent Kurdish state.

Voluntarist definitions of nationhood based on the will to live together in a given territory and to share a common government implicitly assume the existence of a nonpolitical "we" capable of possessing such a will. If state institutions provide the only means of defining national borders and regulating national membership, then the concept of nationhood loses its independent legitimating value. For example, it would be difficult to conceive of a *nation*-based argument for the secession of Ontario from the rest of Canada; this is why Québec nationalism focuses on other markers of belonging, such as language. Conceiving of nations separate from existing governments creates the possibility of appealing to the governed as the source of political authority and legitimacy, especially in the face of authoritarian or imperial rule. However, both voluntarist and nonvoluntarist models encounter the paradox of conception, in which the idea of the nation risks becoming detached from the actual welfare and concerns of constituents. The need to be able to define a strong, cohesive "we" risks pushing voluntarist self-definitions towards less voluntarist models.

The theoretical potential for the idea of a preexisting nation to become exclusionary is exacerbated by the practical tendency to use claims on behalf of the nation as weapons in political power struggles. This leads to the paradox of constitution: the need to rely on those who claim to speak in the nation's name. For example, the political aspirations of the people of Northern Ireland or of the Palestinians may be articulated by the leaders of Sinn Fein or the Palestinian Authority, respectively. On the positive side, the paradox of constitution underscores the value of having people see themselves reflected in and represented by their political leaders and institutions. However, in international relations, the ability of national spokespeople to monopolize nationalist rhetoric suggests a need for caution in taking their claims at face value. The nonintervention principle fosters a tendency to view the "people's representatives" as legitimate de facto, regardless of the extent or nature of their popular mandate. The paradox of constitution captures both the need for the nation to have a political voice, and the dangers involved in giving it one.

The claim to represent the people can be used both to promote and to undermine democratic governance. It is important for individuals to see themselves reflected in their political institutions, so that they accept the results of the political process as fair, legitimate, and binding. This can be a complex proposition in heterogeneous societies, where simple majority rule might not ensure adequate representation of minority groups. The nation-state idea presumes a certain uniformity in basic political and social values such that no particular subset of the population is categorically relegated to minority status, and all members of the polity are able to participate in and influence the outcome of political decisions. The fact that many, if not most, states today have heterogeneous populations suggests the inadequacy of a purely nation-statist model in ensuring legitimate governance.

During the French Revolution, a demographic majority, the Third Estate, protested its exclusion from political decision making and asserted its right to govern itself. In France today, the most salient demographic cleavages tend to be ethnic and religious, as well as socioeconomic. Confronted with the persistent myth of a unitary nation-state, individuals may turn to substate identities and associations to create order and find meaning in their daily lives. This phenomenon could challenge the ability of the French polity to foster sufficient cohesion, commitment, and compliance among its members to ensure the smooth and stable functioning of the state.

Where identifiable substate minorities exist, an excessive emphasis on the idea of a unitary nation can prevent the development of more flexible and plural forms of governance. The nation-state principle in its pure form precludes the need to address the problems of "deeply divided" societies precisely because national and state boundaries are assumed to be congruent. The simultaneous liberal discrediting of assimilationism and the reluctance to endorse secession create an urgent need to find acceptable and effective ways of fostering cohesion, compliance, and commitment within the framework of existing states with heterogeneous populations.

These challenges lead directly to the paradox of composition, another site of political contestation in the French Revolution and today. In the United States, which prides itself on an open and inclusive model of citizenship based on common allegiance to a set of political principles (albeit an increasingly contested one), low voter turnout rates, intergroup violence, and the literal walling-off of private communities testify to a high degree of socioeconomic stratification and a lack of social and political cohesion among individuals and groups. It took a national tragedy in the attack of September 11, 2001, to regenerate a strong feeling of American identity. At the time, most American political figures did their best to affirm the inclusiveness of this identity. Nevertheless, the overt hostility of certain members of the public towards Muslim and Arab Americans, and other so-called visible minorities, revealed the exclusionary potential of a strong collective identity, even one ostensibly grounded in shared principles rather than common physical or genealogical traits. Voluntarist nations also carry the potential to exclude nonvisible minorities based on selective definitions of membership that exclude perceived nonconformists or dissidents, as illustrated by the French Revolutionary "Reign of Terror." In the twentieth century, McCarthyism epitomized the abusive manipulation of voluntarist definitions of membership based on loyalty to those in power.

Broadly speaking, the dilemma of composition turns on the perceived trade-off between cohesion and openness in national self-definitions, especially in an allegedly voluntarist model. Once the nation has been constituted, its leaders often find it necessary to consolidate national identity as a means of bolstering their political support by facilitating popular mobilization against internal and external threats. This phenomenon was evident during the course of the French Revolution, and it characterizes U.S. political rhetoric during World War I and World War II, the Cold War, and the so-called war on terror. It is difficult to dispute the desirability of some degree of shared values and/or identity among members of a polity so that they can enjoy a sense of collective belonging and cooperate to pursue their substantive conceptions of the good. However, nationalist rhetoric is often shaped by perceived limitations on the nation's capacity for inclusiveness. Fears of social fragmentation can lead to more restrictive and exclusionary definitions of national identity.

The nation-state model exacerbates exclusionary tendencies by linking state sovereignty to national distinctiveness. National membership tends to be valued in proportion to its status as something special, something crucial to an individual's sense of self that makes that individual part of a united "we," distinguishable from an alien "they." The potency and resonance of nationhood stems in large part from the convergence of human psychology (receptivity to identity-based platforms that create or reinforce a sense of belonging) and political expedience (cementing obligations to co-members and to leaders). This fuels recourse to nationalist platforms and policies, particularly in times of actual or perceived insecurity.

The final paradox, confrontation, involves the tension between particularism and universalism in international relations. The universalist impulse is grounded in the assumption that human beings have certain desires, aspirations, and capacities in common; nationalism, by contrast, privileges traits that distinguish members of the nation from everybody else. As the French Revolutionaries discovered, nation-statism relies for its theoretical consistency and practical viability on the primary nature of identification with the nation, as opposed to humanity as a whole. This makes nationalism difficult to reconcile with a universalist perspective. While identities might be overlapping and complementary much of the time, crisis situations often force action based on hierarchical allegiances that reveal the incompatibility of competing obligations, most strikingly in times of war.

On a normative level, the nation-state principle only makes sense if nations are assumed to be internally cohesive and in some sense unitary, because there is no other apparent reason to look to nations as the basis for territorially separate and politically independent states. Even with the development of customary international law and the emergence of concepts such as universal jurisdiction for crimes against humanity, nonintervention among states remains a fundamental tenet of international relations. The nation-state principle requires recognizing and providing space for completely different and encompassing ways of life that, so far, continue to find their highest political expression in the aspiration for or reality of a sovereign state. The fact that nation-states are inevitably embedded in a heterogeneous international system creates the possibility for open, participatory societies to provide positive examples of individual liberty and democratic governance, and it forces recognition of the inevitable interdependence among states in contemporary international relations. However, the paradox of confrontation captures the danger of particular states viewing their own political models and values as intrinsically superior, and the risk of universalism leading to ideological and/or military imperialism, as explored in chapters four and six.

The preceding observations can be summarized as follows (table 5.1):

TABLE 5.1
Implications of the Four Paradoxes

Paradox	*Importance*	*Danger*
Conception	possibility of appealing to the governed as the source of political authority and legitimacy, especially in the face of authoritarian rule	potential for the idea of the nation to become detached from the actual welfare and concerns of constituents
Constitution	emphasis on the need for people to see themselves reflected in and represented by their political leaders and institutions so that they accept the results of the political process as fair, legitimate, and binding	tendency to view the "people's representatives" as legitimate de facto, regardless of the extent or nature of their popular mandate
Composition	desirability of some degree of shared values and/or identity among members of a polity so that they can cooperate to pursue their substantive conception(s) of the good; positive aspects of a sense of collective belonging	perceived limitations on the capacity for inclusiveness in any given polity; tendency for fears of social fragmentation to lead to more restrictive and exclusionary definitions of national identity; ability of those in power to manipulate membership criteria
Confrontation	possibility for open, participatory societies to provide positive examples of individual liberty and democratic governance; recognition of interdependence and the need to view one's own polity as part of a larger global society	tendency to view one's own political model and values as superior; risk of universalism leading to ideological and/or military imperialism

While the four paradoxes describe theoretical tensions implicit in the idea of nationhood, they are not sufficient in themselves to explain exclusionary and belligerent outcomes. Rather, perceptions of internal and external threat activate illiberal tendencies over time. Internal pressures include governmental instability, lack of social unity, and economic precariousness. External forces include insecurity in the face of globalization and market pressures; military and terrorist threats; upheavals in neighboring states; and, on the offensive rather than defensive side, the desire for territorial or other forms of expansion, which can fuel irredentist or liberationist claims. These pressures can foster outcomes at odds with the liberal motivations often underlying support for nation-based claims.

The circumstances and tenor of a particular nationalist argument will shape to what extent its positive potential (fostering cohesion, commitment, and compliance) is maximized, and its dangers (exclusion, extremism, and belligerence) avoided. The French Revolutionary experience corroborates the intuition that the more insecure or contested a nation-based regime perceives itself to be, the more likely it is to adopt a closed self-definition. Even so, the nation-state model itself, even apart from threatening circumstances, tends to entail certain assumptions and claims that work against more porous and flexible political and territorial arrangements: first, that nations can at least be imagined as nonpolitical and defined independently of their institutions; second, that nation-states will be more internally cohesive and externally legitimate than other political models; and third, that a nation that does not control its own exclusive state has a presumptive right to secure one, both for its own benefit and in the name of a stable and just international order. The next sections examine these assumptions in the broader context of debates about the relevance of group identity to political boundaries and institutions.

5.2 Re-examining the Nation-State Principle

Both political theory and international relations (IR) tend to take states for granted, each in its own way. Political theorists generally focus on authority within politically organized communities (states) without problematizing its external dimension or boundaries. IR has been defined as the study of interaction between states, generally insulating state boundaries themselves from normative scrutiny. Although liberal and neoliberal IR theorists challenge the neo-realist "billiard ball" view of the international system, few critically examine the nation-state principle itself: that is, the criteria for delineating and legitimating the entities that comprise international society.

Despite the tendency to compartmentalize the study of IR and politics, national self-determination can best be examined by combining insights from both disciplines, especially insofar as this principle partly constitutes the boundary between them. Internally, national self-definitions are crucial in legitimating and maintaining political and territorial control. For example, the Turkish government's view of Kurds as "Mountain Turks" or "Eastern Turks" defines them as part of the Turkish nation, thus undermining Kurdish claims to political and territorial autonomy, while the Kurds' definition of themselves as a nation fundamentally alters their presumed political and territorial entitlements. Although the French Revolutionary nation was not based on ethnicity, allegiance to Revolutionary principles tended to become a functional substitute for such supposedly automatic bonds. Internally, the French vision of the nation (and thus the nation-state) was, and remains, fundamentally unitary.[1] Externally, the rhetoric of national self-determination remains prominent, even if this principle is only selectively observed.[2] As the four paradoxes (especially those of conception and constitution) suggest, nationalist leaders often rely for their domestic and international success on the fiction of a preexisting nation, and on their own ability to establish a credible claim to speak on the nation's behalf.

The implications for international relations of constructing nation-states run much deeper than simple matters of administrative and territorial delineation. Nation-based theories of state legitimacy emphasize the importance of pre-political identity and belonging to the viability and moral value of political arrangements. Isaiah Berlin articulates his view of the psychological underpinnings of the nationalist impulse as follows:

> Like Herder, I regard cosmopolitanism as empty. People can't develop unless they belong to a culture. . . . [J]ust as people need to eat and drink, to have security and freedom of movement, so too they need to belong to a group. Deprived of this, they feel cut off, lonely, diminished, unhappy. To be human means to be able to feel at home somewhere, with your own kind. . . . [L]oneliness is not just the absence of others but far more a matter of living among people who understand what you are saying; they can truly understand only if they belong to a community where communication is effortless, almost instinctive.[3]

From a nationalist perspective, it is not enough simply to belong to a culture: a fully "self-actualized" individual must be part of a politically empowered nation.[4] Nationalism grounds normative political prescriptions in a particular account of human psychology.

The nation-state principle assumes that political institutions ought to embody and express substantive forms of belonging, in order to promote the well-being of individuals and the viability of states. This assumption appears to be borne out, at least in part, by the crumbling of multinational empires (such as the Soviet Union) once the threat of forceful repression has disappeared, and the apparent difficulty of imposing constitutional arrangements on heterogeneous populations (such as the Dayton accords in Bosnia). These examples represent strong if imprecise counterfactuals that suggest the value of internalized and even sentimental attachment to the state to ensure its sustained viability.

Of course, not all identities and loyalties are preexisting, nor are they eternal or immutable. Most self-identified nations are in fact the products of historical evolution, often guided by state centralization, as in Western Europe.[5] However, the attribution of moral value to existing national identities tends to militate against embracing assimilationism, especially when coupled with a view of identity-formation as a zero-sum game in which current identities would necessarily be subordinate to or replaced by future ones. While identity per se may not be exclusive, allegiance often is, especially in situations that force action based on a hierarchical sense of obligation to potentially competing "selves" (for example, the decision faced by Socialist internationalists called upon to fight for their respective countries in World War I).

An emphasis on the importance of cultural belonging, and especially national belonging, focuses on the constitutive role of political and social communities in giving their members a sense of common identity, and in endowing members' actions with meaning in a context of shared values, mutual comprehension, and instinctive empathy. This focus distinguishes "thick" conceptions of membership from theories that acknowledge the importance of cultural belonging, but that seek to relegate this to the private sphere, preserving a formal, neutral public space for interaction and decision making based on procedural agreements.[6] For nationalists, individuals cannot flourish, and states cannot survive, unless public political institutions reflect and express a substantive conception of national membership.

The debate about how much internal homogeneity is needed to make political structures viable is an ongoing one, often characterized as that between "communitarians" and "cosmopolitans." With regional integration projects such as the European Union on the one hand, and secessionist movements within states such as Spain and Canada on the other, the possibility for overlapping, multiple, or postnational identities has assumed a high degree of contemporary political relevance. Eric Hobsbawm observes:

> Men and women do not choose collective identification as they choose shoes, knowing that one could only put on one pair at a time. They had, and still have, several attachments and loyalties simultaneously, including nationality, and are simultaneously concerned with various aspects of life, any of which may at one time be foremost in their minds, as occasion suggests. . . . It is only when one of these loyalties conflicted directly with another or others that a problem of choosing between them arose.[7]

If Hobsbawm is correct, then the question is not "Can men and women have multiple and overlapping identities?" but rather (1) Which identities are *politically* relevant, and which must be reflected in government institutions for these institutions to be ethically defensible and practically sustainable?, and (2) Will government institutions that encompass multiple identities prove strong enough to override the tendency for conflicts over political and territorial control to polarize and galvanize diverse identities in destructive ways? The psychological and political resonance of nationhood cannot simply be ignored or wished away, no matter how reductionist an emphasis on national identity, as opposed to other identities, might appear. Any model that seeks to modify or to transcend the nation-state must not simply criticize its abuses, but must endeavor to understand and to incorporate its *uses*, as well.

5.3 Exploring Alternatives to Nation-Statism

The tension between the appeal and the danger of the nation-state principle is reflected in the ambiguity of international legal provisions on self-determination. The attraction of state leaders to the nation-state idea as a legitimating principle (with nations reinforcing the prerogatives of states) has been balanced by their fear of national self-determination as a potential threat to their territorial and political control. The tendency has therefore been for national self-determination to be upheld in principle, but for nations and states to be defined as coextensive in practice, thereby limiting the potential for national self-determination to challenge the integrity of existing states.

Examples of this strategy abound. The French Revolutionaries propagated a contractualist view of political authority, but they did not accept the implication that a part of France could use contractualist arguments to break the "indissoluble" bonds uniting the French nation. Similarly, in 1920, an International Commission of Jurists was convened to consider whether the inhabitants of the Aaland Islands could secede from Finland and join Sweden. Its first report cautioned: "The recognition of this principle [of self-determination of peoples] in a certain number of international treaties cannot be considered as sufficient to put it upon the same footing as a positive rule of the Law of Nations."[8] Its second report was even more adamant:

> To concede to minorities, either of language or religion, or to any fractions of a population the right of withdrawing from the community to which they belong, because it is their wish or their good pleasure, would be to destroy order and stability within States and to inaugurate anarchy in international life; it would be to uphold a theory incompatible with the very idea of the State as a territorial and political unity.[9]

U.S. President Woodrow Wilson's draft of the League of Nations Covenant reflects a similar concern for stability: "The Contracting Powers accept without reservation the principle that the peace of the world is superior in importance to every question of political jurisdiction or boundary."[10] However, without a crystal ball to predict the outcomes of various political arrangements, the insulation of state boundaries from revisionist claims is no more certain a guarantee of peace and stability than their "preemptive" adjustment along national lines.

During the era of decolonization, the language of self-determination became a primary vehicle for claims by leaders of colonized territories to political emancipation and empowerment. In most United Nations documents, the principle (and, in its strongest form, the "right") of self-determination applies to "peoples," not to "nations."[11] If "peoples" are synonymous with "countries" (as in the context of decolonization), then this right cannot pose a challenge to the territorial status quo: secession is precluded, and the exercise of self-determination is confined to the accession to sovereign statehood of former colonies and, in a more recent reading, to the guarantee of representative institutions and elections within existing states.[12] This state-based definition of the "people" underlies minimalist or conservative interpretations of national self-determination.

One strategy for handling national self-determination, then, is simply to assume that nations are coextensive with independent states or "salt-water" colonies (colonies separated from the imperial power by an ocean). This definitional solution addresses the question of national self-determination by begging it. A second strategy acknowledges the disintegrative potential of national self-determination, but attempts to separate this from its ability to reinforce state legitimacy. For example, Martti Koskenniemi opposes the "classical/Hobbesean" conception of national self-determination to the "romantic/*rousseauesque*" idea.[13] These categories approximate the common distinction between "civic" and "ethnic" models of nationhood, discussed further below.

Koskenniemi's description represents an attempt to separate the state-legitimating power of national self-determination from its potential to challenge existing political institutions and borders. This allows its legitimating potential to be preserved, while its revisionist potential is rejected. Koskenniemi explains:

> The classical view has a strong preference for the statehood of existing States. It tries to reconcile self-determination claims with statehood by dealing with them as claims for the entitlement of national minorities to participate in public life within the State on an equal footing with others. By contrast, the romantic view sees nationhood as primary. Thus it contains an inbuilt preference for secession and independence within a community that one can identify as properly one's own.[14]

Koskenniemi's explanation tends to underestimate the extent to which the premises underlying the state-legitimating and the revisionist aspects of national self-determination are related. For example, the French Revolution (upheld by Koskenniemi as an example of "classical" nationalism) contributed to forging the French nation, but its rhetoric explicitly construed this nation as a preexisting entity with natural and inviolable rights—a fundamentally "romantic" approach. On a prescriptive level, it is unclear to what extent the "classical view" could promote the political participation of "national minorities . . . on equal footing" without making concessions to a communitarian or collectivist vision of group identity more often associated with a "romantic" model. If such communitarian conceptions are resisted, a classical model of participation must entail an assumption or a requirement of assimilation.

Despite these complications, a pervasive distinction between Western or "civic-territorial" and Eastern or "ethnic-genealogical" nations has emerged as a strategy for redeeming national self-determination as a legitimating basis for states.[15] Like the proposed dichotomy between classical and romantic versions of national self-determination, the civic-ethnic distinction classifies nations according to their membership criteria. In the civic-territorial model, nationhood rests on voluntarist foundations, and the nation remains in principle open to all those who seek to belong to it. The civic-territorial model of allegiance (as opposed to the ethnic-genealogical version) is considered appealing for three main reasons: first, it avoids the awkward theoretical possibility of secession by using the institutional structure of the state to define the nation (recalling the definitional strategy of equating nation and state); second, it assumes that the civic nation will prove more inclusive and flexible than nations based explicitly on race or ethnicity; and third, it asserts that the kind of national identity produced in a civic nation will preserve the benefits of cohesion, compliance, and commitment, while remaining internally tolerant and externally benign.

The ethnic-genealogical model, by contrast, takes the nation as a preexisting and fundamentally closed unit. Diversity is seen as a source of weakness and impurity; belonging is not a matter of choice, but of destiny. This view does not necessarily entail claims to national supremacy: Johann Gottfried von Herder, for example, viewed separate nations as flowers in the garden of humanity.[16] However, the contemporary discrediting of ethnically based nationalist platforms stems largely from their potential to entail assumptions of racial supremacy and corresponding policies of exclusion and even genocide.[17]

Despite the apparently clear-cut distinction between civic and ethnic nationalism, civic and ethnic nations represent ideal types, not concrete entities. Drawing such a stark distinction between politically based and culturally based nations is not always helpful, either descriptively or normatively. National self-definitions generally combine elements of both models, and they can also evolve over time. As the French Revolutionary example indicates, once a civic nation has been defined, it can easily acquire exclusionary characteristics through attempts at mass socialization designed to create a distinct and internally unified political culture. This potential challenges the civic/ethnic distinction as a straightforward basis for endorsing or rejecting nationalist platforms, and for adjudicating amongst conflicting political and territorial claims.

Like Koskenniemi's effort to distinguish between statist and antistatist versions of the self-determination argument, the attempt to separate civic from ethnic nations and to uphold the former while condemning the latter fails because the distinction it draws is largely between two sides of the same coin, not between two entirely distinct and competing principles. In addition, an excessive reliance on the idea of civic or state-based nationalism poses a problem for the theory of national self-determination more generally, since it erodes the distinction between "nation" and "state." It either conflates them entirely, positing the two terms as synonymous, or it uses "nation" as the equivalent of the state's population—the people distinct from, but still defined as a unit by, their political institutions. Although perhaps historically accurate (since many nations have been created by policies of centralization and homogenization engineered by states), the viability of the nation as a legitimating platform for political authority presupposes on a conceptual level that the nation precedes the state, rather than being created by it, as captured by the paradox of conception.

In national self-determination arguments, the "fit" between nation and state is itself the central issue: as a result, the use of the term "nation" to denote "state population," like the civic nationalist assumption that nations and states are congruent, can lead to a false confidence in the compatibility of national self-determination with the political and territorial status quo. In an "ideal" nation-state, political institutions embody and perpetuate the very beliefs and ways of living that form the substance of nationhood. But if nations and states are not congruent, then these different bases of loyalty may compete and conflict if they are differentially mobilized by those who seek to claim or to maintain political power.

Mindful of this potential for nations to challenge existing states, leaders of states have construed national self-determination as an antidote to "salt-water" colonialism—a one-time right for territorially distinct colonies to independent statehood, to be exercised if possible within existing colonial boundaries. For example, in characterizing the international status of East Timor before the International Court of Justice in a case relating to control over offshore natural resources, Portugal (the former colonial power, acting on behalf of East Timor) described East Timor as a former colony that had *not yet* exercised its right to self-determination, rather than a nation with a more fundamental, lasting claim.[18]

The notion of a "one-shot" right to national self-determination might be practically appealing, but it is not theoretically sound. For the right of self-determination to exist in a strong sense, it must be ongoing. As John Stuart Mill emphasized in *On Representative Government*, "[o]ne hardly knows what any division of the human race should be free to do if not to determine with which of the various collective bodies of human beings they choose to associate themselves."[19] The "one-shot" model of national self-determination rejects this basic intuition without any conceptually coherent justification for doing so, other than the pragmatic desire to avoid redrawing the political map.

Within existing states, three noteworthy models attempt to explain how cohesion, commitment, and compliance can develop in the absence of explicitly ethnic national self-definitions, and without endorsing secession by national minorities (which, in any event, is only viable where such minorities are relatively territorially distinct). The first, civic nationalism, is anchored in a particular view of citizenship that emphasizes the importance of psychological and emotional attachment to the state. Proponents of civic nationalism assume an identity between nation and state, and therefore tend to view national allegiance as all-encompassing and urge identification with republican, state-based values. The second, constitutional patriotism, tends to see the civic nationalist notion of the state as romantic and outdated. Instead, it envisages a less encompassing version of political allegiance to the constitutional framework of a given state. The third, multiculturalism, lies somewhere in-between, straddling the desire and the demand for public recognition of different group memberships within the state, and the fear that an overemphasis on diverse memberships will erode the legitimacy and integrity of overarching state structures. All of these models offer valuable insights, but all also involve potentially problematic assumptions. Attempts to shape existing and future states must grapple with both the insights and the limitations of these models.

Civic nationalism erases the nation/state distinction in an attempt to preserve nationhood as a legitimating principle for states, while preventing national cohesion from degenerating into xenophobic excess. It defines civic nationalism as synonymous with state patriotism, that is, allegiance to state institutions and to fellow citizens. However, it does not explain what characteristics state institutions must have in order to foster cohesion, compliance, and commitment; instead, it tends to assume that a sense of common feeling among co-citizens will arise automatically, while at the same time precluding by definition the dangers of a closed and inflexible national identity. This is trying to have it both ways. Either one should adopt a political theory that begins and ends with the state and attempt to show why and how states can foster tolerance, allegiance, compliance, and participation to promote a good life for their inhabitants (as attempted by proponents of constitutional patriotism), or one can choose to retain the idea of a more automatically cohesive nation as the basis for state loyalty, but then be prepared to face the challenges this entails.

Neither of these options is an easy one. The exaggerated vision of a Rawlsian liberal state composed of atomized individuals behind a "veil of ignorance" whose interests can be rationally accommodated in mutually advantageous institutions has given way even within liberal political theory to a view of individuals as situated, contextualized, and embedded in cultural and other associative groups that are too important to their identity, and hence to their well-being, to relegate to the strictly private sphere. In addition, it is not clear that a purely administrative state, even one based on popular consensus, could generate the kind of loyalty and identification generally upheld as a prerequisite for successful political institutions. The idea of nation-building assumes a virtuous circle of effective state institutions generating loyalty and compliance, but problems arise when preexisting historical or other forms of substate or trans-state identity are mobilized against state structures. The kind of nation a state would have to create to counter such threats would need to engender a fairly deep level of commitment and empathy. Consequently, the so-called civic nation, if it is to retain conceptual independence as something other than a mere synonym for the state, will likely end up creating many of the same problems more frequently associated with ethnic nationhood.[20]

Assuming that civic nations are congruent with or even equal to states also tends to beg the substantive question of why the intervening concept of "nationhood" might be needed to legitimate states to begin with. This subtle circularity underlies Michael Ignatieff's description of the challenge facing contemporary Germany:

> Its task now is not, as some liberals suppose, to pass beyond nationalism altogether and move into bland Europeanism, but instead to move from the ethnic nationalism of its past to the civic nationalism of a possible future. . . . In practical terms, this would mean moving away from identification with the nation towards identification with the state, i.e., away from a citizenship based on the fiction of ethnic identity towards one based on allegiance to the values of democracy.[21]

Ignatieff articulates a perceived need to preserve nationalism as an animating force of political life, contrasting "nationalism" with "bland Europeanism." This mirrors Rousseau's concern two centuries earlier that "il n'y a que des Européens" (there are nothing but Europeans):[22] both point to a worry about the sustainability of political institutions in the absence of some concerted focus for identity and loyalty on more than just an administrative level. However, it is difficult to see what would make "allegiance to the values of democracy" any less "bland" on the state level than it would be on the European level. It appears from this passage that Ignatieff would encourage allegiance to the values of *German* democracy, not merely to democracy in some abstract sense. The problem of how to achieve this strong identification without tipping the scales towards more exclusionary and particularist definitions of belonging remains a critical one, both conceptually and practically. This problem cannot be resolved by simply equating the nation with the state and assuming that the state will foster loyalty that is both appropriately potent and benign.

In general, advocates of civic nationalism attempt to harness the pre-political bonds of solidarity characteristic of nations, while associating these with the institutions of the state. Maurizio Viroli's *For Love of Country* represents a particularly clear example of this strategy.[23] His first step of assimilating the idea of a civic nation ("understood as sovereign people united in an independent political community"[24]) to that of the republic would be acceptable if he did not then invoke the very pre-political bases of solidarity in a nation to argue why the republic would be unproblematically self-sustainable. His argument relies on the premise that patriotism, that is, allegiance to the republic, "works on bonds of solidarity and fellowship that like feels towards like to transmute them into forces that sustain liberty instead of fomenting exclusion or aggression."[25] This emphasis on the centrality of "bonds of solidarity that like feels towards like" suggests the need for a shared, particularistic culture to generate strong identification among co-members. Indeed, Viroli explicitly rejects the notion of a "purely political republic," postulating that such a republic "would be able to command the philosopher's consent, but would generate no attachment, no love, no commitment."[26]

Viroli's civic nation seems to rely on assumptions similar to those underpinning the cohesion and viability of more overtly ethnic models. His particularistic conception even appears to endorse chauvinism, relying on the feeling that "liberty among our own people has a sweeter taste."[27] Viroli's admission—indeed, his insistence—on the need to appeal to something outside the state to sustain the community it embodies jeopardizes the conceptual coherence of his model of civic nationalism and its alleged benefits. Viroli's model ends up sharing many features with the type of ethnic nationalism that Viroli, like many contemporary political theorists, views as dangerous.

Constitutional patriotism, by contrast, contains more explicit guarantees against this kind of slippage towards features of ethnic nationalism, making it a more serious option for handling the identity conundrum in contemporary states. Jürgen Habermas, its most noted exponent, tends to downplay the need for emotional attachment to the state.[28] Habermas, unlike Viroli, observes that "the republican strand of 'citizenship' completely parts company with the idea of belonging to a prepolitical community integrated on the basis of descent, a shared tradition and a common language."[29] For Habermas, political community is based on the *demos*, defined by political institutions, not the *ethnos*, based on the reality or the fiction of pre-political bonds.[30] The question is: even under this model, will the *demos* become a functional equivalent of an *ethnos* as a source of solidarity, cohesion, and allegiance, making it susceptible to similar tensions and abuses when used as a platform for political mobilization?

Habermas comes closer to getting around this problem than Viroli because Habermas downplays the need for a strong sense of personal identification with the state. He is therefore less vulnerable to charges of trying to have it both ways. Nevertheless, both in practical and conceptual terms, one wonders whether Habermas's model of civic relations based on formal/procedural agreement and mutual respect is robust enough to nourish and sustain states as distinct political and territorial entities. It would be congenial to accept Habermas's assertion that citizens can respect each other both as individuals and as members of various groups. Unfortunately, continuing debates about individual vs. group rights, and the degree to which group identity ought to be enshrined in political institutions, suggest that these issues are more problematic than the Habermasean model of constitutional patriotism seems to allow.

Any incarnation of universal liberal democratic values in a particular constitution must be sufficiently concrete and accessible to citizens to make them feel part of a common political project. Allegiance to a particular constitution, like allegiance to a civic nation, must be sufficiently robust to generate the cohesion, commitment, and compliance necessary to sustain the state. The existence of a framework for dialogue, without a perception of common interests (if not common identity) among members and participants, is likely to remain insufficient. Dominique Schnapper suggests the need for certain elements of commonality among members, even in a minimalist state (leaving aside the question of whether Schnapper appropriately labels this minimalist model "Habermasian"). These elements include a shared language, culture, and "at least a few common values" to permit the formation of an "intersubjective" space for democratic discussion and decision making:

> Si la société démocratique implique, pour reprendre des termes habermassiens, qu'il existe un espace communicationnel et intersub-

> jectif où citoyens, hommes politiqes et experts puissent se parler, se comprendre et tenter de se convaincre pour traiter des problèmes de la vie commune, elle ne peut exister si tous les membres ne partagent pas un langage, une certaine culture et, au moins, quelques valeurs communes. Sinon, comment établir cet espace communicationnel? [If democratic society implies, to use Habermasian terms, that a communicational and intersubjective space exists where citizens, politicians and experts may converse, understand one another, and attempt to convince one another to address the problems of common life, this cannot exist if all members do not share a language, a certain culture and, at least, a few common values. Otherwise, how does one establish this communicational space?][31]

This argument highlights the crucial dilemma underlying attempts to theorize more open yet allegiance-generating political institutions. Even participation itself may require a "thicker" basis for common membership than cosmopolitan theorists allow. Habermas's characterization of citizenship as functioning "merely as administrative criteria,"[32] taken at face value, underestimates the feeling of attachment and understanding that citizens may have—and are generally expected to have—towards their particular states and their co-citizens.

Habermas cites the examples of the United States and Switzerland as proof that citizens do not need a common language or common origins to share a single state. It is debatable whether these examples are sufficient to make the case for constitutional patriotism. For example, in the Swiss federation, disputes still arise over the allocation of powers, and cultural differences among cantons can still overshadow feelings of a common, overarching Swiss identity. The United States is, except for indigenous peoples, a country of immigration where an overarching, largely noninterventionist political structure and capitalist economic ethos provide a common framework within which cultural identities can, in theory, coexist without being politically mobilized (even the civil rights movement on behalf of African Americans focused largely on obtaining equal political status within existing American institutions). However, Michael Billig has argued that, in fact, the minimal American state framework is buttressed by all of the symbols and rituals of nationhood (the flag, the national anthem, public holidays, and other manifestations of "banal nationalism"), more akin to Viroli's model than to Habermas's.[33] Although many of these trappings go unnoticed on a daily basis, they arguably reinforce a sense of shared identity, belonging, and purpose among co-citizens. These omnipresent symbols are meant to represent and to create a broader consensus that evokes not only procedural compliance, but also emotional commitment. Without such commitment, the minimalist state risks fostering a largely passive citizenry and creating a persistent possibility of social dislocation for marginalized groups and classes.[34]

On an international level, Habermas's model would preclude nationalist challenges to state borders and institutions by draining the concept of statehood of its nation-based foundations, as evidenced in his vision of European—and potentially world—citizenship. This diffuse allegiance is made possible by capitalist development, which has rendered obsolete the republican participatory models more appropriate for ethnically homogenous states:

> Nowadays, the sovereignty of the people has constrained itself to become a procedure of more or less discursive opinion and will formation. . . . This provides a model of a deliberative democracy that no longer hinges on the assumption of macro-subjects like the "people" of "the" community but on anonymously interlinked discourses or flows of communication.[35]

By decoupling the personal and political spheres, much as in the prototypical Rawlsian argument, Habermas opens up the possibility for a cosmopolitan ethic, in which diversity and difference pertain more to the realms of art, literature, and philosophy than to political life.[36] The preservation of cultural diversity alongside political integration would, in his view, insulate him from charges of succumbing to Ignatieff's "bland Europeanism."

Habermas's proposal is intriguing, but still unsatisfying to those who believe in an intimate connection between culture and politics (a connection gestured towards, but not fully realized, by the concept of "political culture"). In part, this is what makes French Revolutionary political discourse so compelling, as it sought to combine Enlightenment cosmopolitanism with a republican nationalism, just as contemporary liberal theorists try to reconcile identity-blind political structures with an emphasis on the ethical and political importance of groups. As long as elements of both of these approaches remain politically persuasive, attempts will continue to find some sort of conceptual and practical middle ground, fueling continued ambiguity in the normative status of national self-determination as an international political standard.

A third set of proposals for handling the challenge of cohesion in modern states comes under the heading of "multiculturalism." The concept of multiculturalism as a political program is a tricky one, since the idea of nationhood carries with it not only the notion of a distinctive culture or set of values and social practices, but also the demand for (and expectation of) self-government. In this sense, multi*cultural* countries such as the United States (with the possible exception of Puerto Rico) are fundamentally different from multi*national* countries such as (arguably) Canada. Definitions and self-perceptions are all-important when used to create expectations and to legitimate claims: if one is committed to implementing a nation-statist model, then whether one defines Spain and Belgium as multicultural or as multinational will have serious political consequences, since only the latter definition would create an entitlement to some degree of self-government by the state's component nations. Theories of multiculturalism tend to underplay this issue, focusing instead on how to recognize diverse practices, customs, languages, and beliefs within the framework of a single state.

Multiculturalist theorists promote the idea of "unity in diversity." Unlike Viroli, they assume—and, indeed, advocate—a pluralistic nation, and unlike Habermas they explicitly emphasize the importance of a sense of belonging to and identification with the state, beyond a commitment to constitutional principles. In a multiculturalist perspective, for state institutions to be effective and legitimate, they must reflect and reinforce the very diversity they are charged with governing. Bhikhu Parekh explains,

> All societies today are multicultural, and need to find ways of reconciling the demands of unity and diversity. Without unity, they cannot hold themselves together, take and enforce collectively binding decisions, and generate a spirit of community. As for diversity it is not only inescapable but also enriches and contributes to the collective well-being of society. Besides human beings are culturally embedded, and respect for them requires that we also respect their cultures. . . . [The best way to do this is] by encouraging its cultural communities to evolve a plural national culture that both reflects and transcends them. Such a multiculturally constituted and constantly evolving common culture both unites them and gives them secure spaces for growth.[37]

Parekh emphasizes that "[t]he society should be so defined that it belongs to all its citizens and not to its dominant ethnic or religious group."[38] Multicultural institutions are meant to be identity-encompassing, not identity-blind. Parekh advocates fostering a strong sense of unity "in the sense of a strong sense of mutual commitment and belonging," without requiring a "shared comprehensive national culture."[39] The challenge of resisting a "comprehensive" culture while fostering a "strong" sense of mutual belonging confronts all multicultural states.

There are at least three obstacles to the conceptual coherence and practical viability of the multiculturalist vision as a political solution to the challenge of diversity in contemporary states and the problem of borders in international relations. First, multiculturalism assumes a basic compatibility between different symbols, practices, beliefs, and values. This undercuts its concurrent view of distinct cultures as worth embodying and preserving in political institutions precisely because of their uniqueness, and their potential incommensurability. Second, there remains a basic tension between a social and political system based on individual rights and one based on collective rights, a contradiction that advocates of multiculturalism often downplay or ignore. The argument that individuals can best flourish when their cultures are protected can lead to policies that restrict individual freedom of choice in the name of cultural preservation, such as restrictions on the use of the English language on outdoor signs and on the ability of immigrants to send their children to English-language schools in Québec. However, as suggested above, purely individualist political models fail to provide an account of the intragroup ties of obligation and allegiance that are generally considered necessary to ensure cohesion, commitment, and compliance. Third, multiculturalist solutions must choose between simply advocating the public recognition of cultural diversity without enshrining it in political institutions, and adopting measures such as allocating political positions and responsibilities to members of the state's constituent communities.[40] The former may be criticized as token gestures; the latter enshrines group differences, undercutting the idea of a unified state.

The above dilemmas are not easily resolved; it is always easier to identify obstacles than to overcome them. That said, canvassing existing approaches to the problems of defining and accommodating nations and states can help isolate core tensions that merit continued attention and analysis. The central tensions set forth in the above discussion can be summarized as follows:

1. The failure to acknowledge the connection between national self-determination and the nation-state principle, leading to potentially inconsistent attempts to separate the nation's "integrative"/legitimating power from its "disintegrative"/revisionist potential.
2. The failure to recognize the importance of the conceptual distinction between nation and state. The dilemmas that flow from this include the following unanswered questions:
   a. Why is state-based allegiance necessarily better than nation-based loyalty: that is, more open and less belligerent?

   b. What will prevent civic nations from becoming the functional equivalents of ethnic nations in their quest to ensure internal cohesion and external distinctiveness?
   c. If we reject the nation-state model, what mechanisms will produce alternative social and political bonds to ensure state viability, and what principles will serve to delineate states and legitimate their separate existence?
3. The tendency to overestimate the potential for "symbolic inclusiveness" to act as a substitute for more substantive forms of power-sharing, and to underestimate the possibility that recognizing differences will in fact entrench and consolidate existing cleavages as sites for political power struggles.

The search for a conceptually coherent and practically viable balance between cohesion and openness in delineating and maintaining distinct political and territorial entities remains a core constitutive dilemma for international relations, and a continued source of tension on the global stage.

Finding creative solutions to these persistent problems presents a central and enduring challenge for theorists and practitioners alike. The following preliminary observations seem warranted:

1. ONGOING RIGHT. National self-determination does not make sense as a "one-shot" proposition. On a theoretical level, it is inconsistent to affirm that a given nation has an inherent right to independent self-government while maintaining that this right can be lost by a decision at one point in time to become part of a larger political and territorial entity. On a practical level, nations can be expected to have different needs, aspirations, and capabilities at different points in time that will affect their desire and ability to form independent states. For these reasons, if a right to national self-determination exists, it must be ongoing.

Multiple options short of sovereign statehood exist for self-identified nations seeking greater recognition and autonomy. If the members of a given nation seek to change their international status, the argument that the nation has "already" exercised its right to national self-determination must be rejected as a basis for preventing political and territorial change. The right to national self-determination is not, however, unconstrained. Conditions associated with its exercise might include:

1. a sufficient degree of territorial distinctness to make political independence viable. For example, in the cases of the former Czechoslovakia, the former Yugoslavia, and the former USSR,

disintegration largely occurred along existing political boundaries, with intrastate borders between republics or provinces being upgraded to the status of international frontiers;[41]
2. nonviolent procedures for determining the will of the population involved, supervised by the international community; and
3. guarantees that minority populations in the newly formed state will enjoy basic legal protections.

Even where these criteria are met, sovereign statehood is not the only model. Various international options exist under which self-governing nations delegate the exercise of certain competencies to more powerful states, for example in the various compacts of free association that exist between the United States and its former trust territories in the Pacific islands.[42] Such arrangements can be particularly attractive for small, territorially distinct entities.

2. Subsidiarity and participation. A self-identified nation might not be territorially distinct, or might not seek to or be able to form a viable independent or associated state. In such circumstances, options for enhanced self-governance should be based on the principles of subsidiarity and participation. *Subsidiarity* encourages decision making at the most localized level possible, with local decision-making bodies having the "final word" on decisions within their delegated areas of competence, subject only to judicial scrutiny for compliance with constitutional and other human rights guarantees. *Participation* means involving all individuals and groups in political decision making. This can require more than just "one person, one vote." State institutions should endeavor to reflect and accommodate substantive identities through mechanisms including proportional representation, consultative bodies, cultural autonomies over particular policy areas, and, if politically necessary, minority veto rights.

A majority culture does not have the right unilaterally to exclude a minority culture from political participation, but the shape of that participation might vary depending on historical, demographic, and other circumstances. Existing states must be able to generate sufficient cohesion, commitment, and compliance to ensure their continued viability. They should therefore aim to develop complementary forms of identification and allegiance that accommodate subgroup identities while ensuring that members of different subgroups recognize themselves—and each other—as belonging to a common whole. Experiments in allocating decision-making authority by issue-area, rather than dividing it strictly along geographical lines, exemplifies the creative accommodation of group aspirations for control over important aspects of communal life within the overarching framework of a multinational or multicultural state. The Framework Convention for the Protection of National Minorities adopted by the Council of Europe enumerates principles that could govern such arrangements, while recognizing the desire of existing states to maintain their territorial and political integrity.[43]

3. International involvement. States' respect for the principles of national self-determination, subsidiarity, and participation are a matter of inclusive international concern, because these principles fundamentally implicate basic human dignity and the ability of individuals to define and pursue their own ends. However, unconstrained disregard of the nonintervention principle in the name of supporting national self-determination cannot be supported. To avoid abuses, military intervention by one or several states to support national self-determination or self-governance claims affecting another state must be authorized by an appropriate international body. In addition, steps should be taken to further develop international and supranational bodies charged with monitoring the implementation of, and ensuring compliance with, the principles of self-determination, subsidiarity, and participation. Possible models include consultative and adjudicative bodies in the Inter-American and European systems, such as the Inter-American Court of Human Rights, the European Court of Human Rights, and the Council of Europe's Secretariat of the Framework Convention for the Protection of National Minorities.

Conclusion

Politics is not just about the exercise of power, but about its justification. Power can best be exercised and compliance ensured when those subjected to it perceive it as legitimate. The use of the nation as a political platform was and is more than just a rhetorical device: it is a way of mobilizing individuals by shaping their conceptions of their political entitlements and their corresponding expectations about what constitutes a cognizable grievance, and what avenues are available for seeking redress. This observation, borne out by a study of the French Revolutionary experience, suggests at least two possibilities for reducing the instability caused by incompatible political and territorial claims: first, reducing the sense of entitlement to sovereign nation-statehood built into current understandings of the international system, and second, creating viable alternatives that maximize political autonomy while minimizing competition over limited resources, and especially territory.

Isolating the historical origins of certain understandings about the moral value and political entitlements of nationhood can help pave the way for these endeavors. It suggests: (1) what political uses nation-based arguments fill, and thus what incentive structures need to be changed to diminish their attractiveness; and (2) what abuses these arguments can entail, thereby encouraging the search for less exclusionary ways of accommodating group desires for political recognition and enfranchisement.

The stakes and the costs involved in nation-based arguments can be devastating: civil wars and confrontations over disputed territory have proved some of the world's most intractable conflicts, with questions of state sovereignty and the international legitimacy of political actors complicating attempts at negotiation with the goal of peaceful settlement. These issues gained particular importance during decolonization and following the end of the Cold War, and they continue to dominate discussions about the best way to handle "rogue" and "failed" states. Although these questions might become especially salient in the context of specific crises, they are endemic to any international system founded on the assumption that individuals can best define and pursue their own well-being within territorially delineated political units that are separate, sovereign, and, to a certain extent, monolithic and self-legitimating.

As long as nations (or their functional equivalents) are regarded, by definition, as ethically meriting states of their own, it will be very difficult to implement and to uphold compromise solutions (including confederalism and autonomy short of sovereign statehood). This is true even in a world where state sovereignty is no longer what it used to be, and thus perhaps less appealing as a political absolute. The task is to demythologize nationhood while remaining mindful of both the benefits national membership can offer, and the needs and pressures that fuel exclusionary and aggressive nationalism.

It has often been observed that we live in a world characterized by simultaneous unification and disintegration, resulting in more complex webs of obligations and institutions than the nation-state model allows. There are certainly other possible frameworks for the organization of global life besides the nation-state, from local self-government, to the deterritorialized regulation of cultural communities, to the idea of an integrated "global village" with some form of world government. Continued experimentation with alternative models of governance can help reshape expectations and assumptions about the desirability and viability of unitary nation-statehood. Emerging norms of humanitarian intervention and nascent supranational structures also challenge conceptions of indivisible sovereignty and the inviolability of frontiers at the heart of the nation-state principle.

Transformation should be welcomed, but the lessons of the nation-state experiment should not be lost: if a political community is to be more than an arbitrary association (in order to promote cohesion, compliance, and commitment), some perception of common aims and common identity needs to be captured or created. This serves the goals of internal viability and external legitimacy, something lacking in many struggling states today. Unless and until we have a world government, the question of political boundaries and their significance will remain a central puzzle for theorists and practitioners alike. Meanwhile, the nation-state idea will continue to inform our understandings and imaginings of what international political life is, and what it can aspire to become.

Chapter 6

Epilogue—Confrontation Revisited

Introduction

The dilemmas canvassed in the preceding chapters—including the questions of whether democracy can be exported, and whether non-exclusionary forms of solidarity can be forged in multinational and pluri-ethnic states—have taken on even greater urgency in the wake of the U.S.-led effort to replace Iraqi dictator Saddam Hussein's regime with a functioning representative government. This chapter offers some preliminary observations on the striking parallels between U.S. rhetoric leading up to and during the invasion of Iraq, and the French Revolutionary rhetoric explored in chapter four. The French Revolutionary experience of attempting to export the ideal of national self-determination foreshadows the likelihood of backlash against liberty brought uninvited on "the blades of bayonets"—or the barrels of M16s.

The parallels between French Revolutionary rhetoric and the White House's proffered rationale for war—particularly following the discrediting of the allegation that Saddam Hussein was stockpiling weapons of mass destruction—indicate the persistence of the paradoxes of conception, constitution, composition, and confrontation. Alexander Hamilton leveled the accusation against the French Revolutionaries in 1797 that the "specious pretense of enlightening mankind and reforming their civil institutions is the varnish to the real design of subjugating them."[1] The U.S.-led invasion of Iraq in March 2003 prompted similar criticism.

It is frequently observed that the post-Cold War United States enjoys virtually unprecedented global influence through military, economic, and political channels. When, whether, and how it should use this influence is a subject of ongoing debate. Setting aside the important questions of whether and to what extent existing U.N. Security Council resolutions provided a legal basis for military intervention in Iraq, and whether and under what circumstances there is an international right to preemptive self-defense, the United States's declared interest in promoting the global spread of democracy is, in many ways, revolutionary. It challenges the norm of nonintervention and reinforces the emerging notion that only democratically governed states can enjoy equal membership in contemporary international society. As President Bush declared in his Second Inaugural Address, "it is the policy of the United States to seek and support the growth of democratic movements and institutions in every nation and culture, with the ultimate goal of ending tyranny in our world."[2] Secretary of State Condoleeza Rice echoed this commitment in a speech at the American University in Cairo: "The ideal of democracy is universal. . . . We are supporting the democratic aspirations of all people."[3] Although the United States has certainly used the promotion of democracy as a justification for military intervention in the past, the explicit declaration of universal democracy as a goal of foreign policy represents a new commitment and a notable component of the "Bush doctrine."

The limited goal of this chapter is to examine the stated reasons for invading and occupying Iraq within the context of the normative and conceptual framework elaborated in the preceding chapters. The Bush administration has characterized the "war against global terrorism" as a battle "for our democratic values and way of life."[4] In addition to protecting these values at home, the United States has committed itself to promoting them abroad. Like the French Revolutionaries, however, the U.S. government appears to have overestimated the enthusiasm and ease with which an occupied people can be expected to embrace and institutionalize the occupier's political model.

The long-term prognosis for Iraq remains unclear, but the short and medium-term consequences in terms of civilian casualties and lack of basic infrastructure have been disastrous. Given the unique demographic and historical circumstances surrounding each country's democratic transition, there is likely no single formula for the successful and lasting establishment of democratic institutions. In some circumstances, the less drastic techniques outlined as part of the Bush administration's *National Security Strategy*, such as support for nonviolent democratic movements and working through international institutions to put pressure on repressive governments, might be better suited to achieving lasting results.[5]

Experience and common sense teach that external intervention can breed resentment and backlash. In this respect, U.S. policy makers would have done well to remember the late eighteenth century before sending tanks into Baghdad.

6.1 Exporting American Ideals

Speeches made by U.S. President George W. Bush in the aftermath of the terrorist attacks of September 11, 2001, and in the months leading up to and during military operations in Afghanistan and Iraq offer a guide to the administration's public rationale for its foreign policy decisions. This rationale shares the following core elements and assumptions with the French Revolutionary discourse explored in chapter four:

1. *Popular sovereignty:* Peoples can be treated separately from their governing regimes.
2. *Transnationalism:* Freedom-loving peoples share transnational bonds.
3. *Universalism:* The ideals of democracy and self-government are universally applicable.
4. *Democratic peace:* A world composed of self-governing peoples will be more peaceful than a world composed of authoritarian states.
5. *Collective security "plus":* Collective security arrangements can best promote the goal of security through democracy, but they do not preclude unilateral action.

This section examines each of these core principles in turn.

1. POPULAR SOVEREIGNTY: PEOPLES CAN BE TREATED SEPARATELY FROM THEIR GOVERNING REGIMES. Like the Abbé Grégoire's *Déclaration du droit des gens* discussed in chapter four, the Bush doctrine distinguishes peoples from their governments, particularly when those governments are perceived as hostile to the United States. For example, in a September 20, 2001, address to a joint session of Congress, Bush emphasized: "The United States respects the people of Afghanistan . . . but we condemn the Taliban regime."[6] Similarly, in discussing Iraq in October 2002, Bush stated: "We have no quarrel with the Iraqi people. They are the daily victims of Saddam Hussein's oppression, and they will be the first to benefit when the world's demands are met."[7] This approach recognizes that political leaders do not always represent the interests of their constituents, as

captured by the paradox of constitution. The trouble from a foreign policy perspective is determining when to ignore leaders and appeal directly to peoples.

The Bush administration began paving the way for direct appeals soon after September 11. In a September 25, 2001, speech, Bush proclaimed that "[t]he coalition of legitimate governments and freedom-loving people is strong."[8] This statement foreshadows the Bush administration's notion of a natural collective security arrangement among a select group of "legitimate governments" dedicated to protecting the interests of people in their own countries and in other countries. People are presumed to be "freedom-loving" and deserving of protection. However, only governments determined (by the United States) to be "legitimate" are presumptively entitled to the benefits of sovereignty and freedom from external intervention.

In March 2003, Bush acted on this distinction between the Iraqi government and its population. Like the French Revolutionary generals who propagated decrees from the French people to the people of neighboring monarchies, Bush claimed to speak directly to the people of Iraq, negating Saddam Hussein's prerogative of speaking on their behalf or acting as their interlocutory:

> Many Iraqis can hear me tonight in a translated radio broadcast, and I have a message for them. If we must begin a military campaign, it will be directed against the lawless men who rule your country and not against you. As our coalition takes away their power, we will deliver the food and medicine you need. We will tear down the apparatus of terror and we will help you to build a new Iraq that is prosperous and free. In a free Iraq, there will be no more wars of aggression against your neighbors, no more poison factories, no more executions of dissidents, no more torture chambers and rape rooms. The tyrant will soon be gone. The day of your liberation is near.[9]

This strategy of appealing directly to the Iraqi people continued during the military campaign. However, as it became clear that not all Iraqis supported the overthrow of Saddam Hussein, the presumption that all people are inherently "freedom-loving" gave way to a distinction between those who support democratic ideals and those who reject them. Speaking on the occasion of Saddam Hussein's capture by U.S. armed forces, Bush announced:

> And this afternoon, I have a message for the Iraqi people: You will not have to fear the rule of Saddam Hussein ever again. All Iraqis

> who take the side of freedom have taken the winning side. The goals of our coalition are the same as your goals—sovereignty for your country, dignity for your great culture, and for every Iraqi citizen, the opportunity for a better life.[10]

This statement draws a clear dividing line between two camps: on one side, the United States, "legitimate governments," and "freedom-loving people"; on the other, authoritarian rulers and those who support them. The Bush administration's rhetoric makes clear that there is no in-between.

2. TRANSNATIONALISM: FREEDOM-LOVING PEOPLES SHARE TRANSNATIONAL BONDS. Like the French Revolutionaries, the Bush administration has articulated a transnational conception of freedom-loving people that transcends political and geographic borders. As Bush stated in an interview on September 19, 2001: "Again I repeat, terrorism knows no borders, it has no capital, but it does have a common ideology, and that is they hate freedom, and they hate freedom-loving people. And they particularly hate America at this moment."[11] This statement reflects two important themes: first, the administration's recognition that the security challenges of the twenty-first century cannot be addressed solely by ensuring a balance of power among rival states or by operating through traditional diplomatic channels; and second, its identification of the United States as the embodiment of a transnational ideology of freedom, rather than simply the product of a particular set of political choices made by a geographically bounded constituency.

The Bush administration's rhetoric proclaims a set of principles and a platform for political action. It reflects and reinforces a binary worldview that, on its face, leaves no room for compromise—recalling successive French Revolutionary regimes that defined their enemies in categorical terms, both within and outside of France. As Bush announced in a September 20, 2001, speech to a joint session of Congress: "Every nation, in every region, now has a decision to make. Either you are with us, or you are with the terrorists."[12] This theme has featured consistently in Bush's remarks, for example at a graduation speech at the U.S. Military Academy at West Point on June 1, 2002:

> Moral truth is the same in every culture, in every time, and in every place. Targeting innocent civilians for murder is always and everywhere wrong. Brutality against women is always and everywhere wrong. There can be no neutrality between justice and cruelty, between the innocent and the guilty. We are in a conflict between good and evil, and America will call evil by its name.[13]

The idea of a conflict between good and evil is a familiar trope in foreign policy rhetoric: in U.S. rhetoric, one need only recall the "Evil Empire" of the Cold War era. Similarly, the United States's claim to be pursuing military action in the name of a higher ideal is not unique to the war in Iraq. What is striking, if not unique, is the United States's expressed conviction in its singular claim to represent and to promote these ideals, and its explicit declaration that those who are not "with us" are "with the terrorists."

3. UNIVERSALISM: THE IDEALS OF DEMOCRACY AND SELF-GOVERNMENT ARE UNIVERSALLY APPLICABLE. The idea of transnational bonds among freedom-loving people (whether conceived of as bonds among "people" as individuals, or "peoples" as groups of individuals) is closely tied to a conviction in the universal validity of certain principles that ought to govern interactions among individuals and groups. The 1776 *Declaration of Independence*, the 1789 *Declaration of the Rights of Man and the Citizen*, and the 1948 *Universal Declaration of Human Rights* all reflect this idea. The question that the French Revolutionaries confronted, and that the United States now faces, is whether and under what conditions the advocacy of "self-government" by one people on behalf of another can be ethically and conceptually coherent, particularly when advocacy involves the use of military force.

The basic idea that all individuals are entitled to certain fundamental rights by virtue of their humanity is no longer controversial, even absent universal agreement on the scope and content of these rights, and despite pervasive failures to respect them. Bush emphasized in 2002: "America believes that all people are entitled to hope and human rights, to the non-negotiable demands of human dignity. People everywhere prefer freedom to slavery; prosperity to squalor; self-government to the rule of terror and torture."[14] In 2005, he gave content to this ideal of self-government: "Like free people everywhere, Iraqis want to be defended and led by their own countrymen. We will help them achieve this objective so Iraqis can secure their own nation."[15] The conceptual and practical problem, of course, is how to find means of intervention that do not fundamentally contradict or undermine the end of independence. It is difficult to conceptualize any theory of liberation for a people's "own good" that does not, on some level, deny that people's right or ability to determine its own destiny. That is one reason why, fundamentally, intervention with the goal of political liberation, like most foreign policy decisions, is never entirely (or even mostly) altruistic. This leads, in part, to the important role of democratic peace theory in justifying efforts to spread democratic institutions.

4. Democratic peace: A world composed of self-governing peoples will be more peaceful than a world composed of authoritarian states. As explored in chapter four, the French Revolutionaries justified their military undertakings in neighboring states in part by insisting that a Europe composed of "free and independent peoples" would be more hospitable to France and more peaceful overall. The specter of monarchists amassing on France's borders with neighboring states was ever-present in the minds of the Revolutionaries, much as the specter of Al Qaeda operatives plotting without fear of apprehension in nondemocratic states animates the Bush administration's foreign policy. This concrete security concern dovetails with the ideological promotion of self-government to produce a foreign policy of promoting liberation from authoritarian rule.

The idea of a link between democratic institutions and global peace, whose incarnations are often referred to under the rubric of "democratic peace theory," received attention in the United States as part of President Bill Clinton's foreign policy rhetoric. For Clinton, democratic peace theory provided an additional rationale for encouraging the development of democratic institutions and free markets in the states of the former Soviet bloc. Clinton stated in his January 1994 State of the Union address:

> Ultimately, the best strategy to ensure our security and to build a durable peace is to support the advance of democracy elsewhere. Democracies don't attack each other. They make better trading partners and partners in diplomacy. That is why we have supported, you and I, the democratic reformers in Russia and in the other states of the former Soviet bloc. I applaud the bipartisan support this Congress provided last year for our initiatives to help Russia, Ukraine and the other states through their epic transformations.[16]

Clinton's rationale for supporting the "advance of democracy elsewhere" still focuses on states as the central actors—and source of insecurity—in international relations. The terrorist attacks of September 11, 2001, demonstrated that nonstate actors could pose an equally great, if not greater, security threat. Accordingly, the Bush administration has deployed democratic peace theory as a foreign policy rationale in a less state-centric form, invoking the benefit of spreading freedom in "all the world" and in "societies" everywhere.

Like the French Revolutionaries, the Bush administration has invoked both emulation and intervention as methods for advancing the spread of self-government. In particular, Bush has advanced the hypothesis that intervention to establish democracy in Iraq will lead to emulation by other Middle Eastern states. In an address on the eve of the U.S.-led invasion, Bush announced: "Unlike Saddam Hussein, we believe the Iraqi people are deserving and capable of human liberty. And when the dictator has departed, they can set an example to all the Middle East of a vital and peaceful and self-governing nation."[17] He later elaborated on the assumptions underlying this calculation:

> The establishment of a free Iraq at the heart of the Middle East will be a watershed event in the global democratic revolution.
>
> Sixty years of Western nations excusing and accommodating the lack of freedom in the Middle East did nothing to make us safe—because in the long run, stability cannot be purchased at the expense of liberty. As long as the Middle East remains a place where freedom does not flourish, it will remain a place of stagnation, resentment, and violence ready for export. And with the spread of weapons that can bring catastrophic harm to our country and to our friends, it would be reckless to accept the status quo.
>
> Therefore, the United States has adopted a new policy, a forward strategy of freedom in the Middle East. This strategy requires the same persistence and energy and idealism we have shown before. And it will yield the same results. As in Europe, as in Asia, as in every region of the world, the advance of freedom leads to peace.[18]

Despite the difficulties encountered in attempting to establish stable democratic institutions in Afghanistan and in Iraq, the theme of a democratic peace has become a mantra for the Bush administration during its second term.

To its credit, the administration has, at least in speeches, accepted the principle that other peoples need not "determine themselves" in the United States's image—a common criticism of the French Revolutionary campaigns. For example, in the speech cited above, Bush acknowledged:

> As we watch and encourage reforms in the region, we are mindful that modernization is not the same as Westernization. Representative governments in the Middle East will reflect their own cultures. They will not, and should not, look like us. Democratic nations may be constitutional monarchies, federal republics, or parliamentary systems. And working democracies always need time to develop—as did our own.[19]

That said, this tolerance for difference in theory has not yet been tested in practice. For example, the Bush administration failed to offer a satisfactory answer to concerns that the Iraqi constitution would privilege certain dictates of Islam at the expense of secular freedoms. The process of democratic deliberation does not itself guarantee any particular outcome, let alone one that enhances human freedoms and dignity. At the time of writing, no final product had yet been agreed upon by the Iraqi National Assembly. The success or failure of the Iraqi constitutional process was widely perceived as a test of the Bush administration's policy of exporting democracy to the Middle East.

Bush's rhetoric makes clear that the emphasis on global democracy is, primarily, a product of the desire for global peace. Such statements include: "The survival of liberty in our land increasingly depends on the success of liberty in other lands. The best hope for peace in our world is the expansion of freedom in all the world;"[20] and "The heart of our strategy is this: Free societies are peaceful societies. So in the long run, the only way to defeat the ideologies of hatred and fear, the only way to make sure our country is secure in the long run, is to advance the cause of freedom."[21] The perceived link between security and democracy makes promoting democracy a foreign policy priority. However, the lesson that "working democracies always need time to develop" pushes against the urgent concern for displacing authoritarian rule. In times of perceived crisis, gradualist approaches are likely to be rejected in favor of more direct, and even aggressive, methods—even at the expense of the long-term success of a given democratization project.

The initial rationale for the war in Iraq had much more to do with the allegation that Saddam Hussein was concealing weapons of mass destruction than it did with the global promotion of democracy. That said, it is not surprising to find that military intervention in the name of promoting democracy—which, by definition, involves risking the lives of the intervening state's soldiers—must generally be justified in terms of a more concrete perceived security threat. As Bush indicated in his speech on the eve of the U.S.-led invasion of Iraq in response to Iraq's alleged "stockpil[ing of] biological and chemical weapons" and "longstanding ties to terrorist groups," "[i]f . . . the Iraqi regime persists in its defiance, the use of force may become unavoidable. Delay, indecision, and inaction are not options for America, because they could lead to massive and sudden horror."[22] Like the French Revolutionaries, the Bush administration's link between peace and democracy, combined with a perceived threat to domestic security, became a rationale for war.

5. Collective security "plus": Collective security arrangements can best promote the goal of security through democracy, but they do not preclude unilateral action. The universalist rhetoric of the French Revolutionaries and the Bush administration in championing freedom raises the concrete policy questions of when, how, and whether to take steps to implement this ideal. The proactive agenda that flows from an emphasis on the importance of building democratic institutions worldwide is tempered by the need to be selective in committing a state's resources to pursuing this goal in various parts of the world: both because these resources are finite, and because more traditional security arrangements based on mutual respect for the principles of sovereignty and nonintervention continue, in large part, to support the edifice of international relations.

The Bush administration, mindful of criticisms of U.S. unilateralism and of the finite (though unparalleled) capacities of the U.S. military, has elaborated two components of its proactive strategy for promoting democracy: collective security and intervention. The collective security element of this strategy recalls article 15 of the Abbé Grégoire's *Declaration of the Law of Nations*: "Undertakings against the liberty of one people constitute an attack against all the others." Bush declared in September 2001:

> This is not, however, just America's fight. And what is at stake is not just America's freedom. This is the world's fight. This is civilization's fight. This is the fight of all who believe in progress and pluralism, tolerance and freedom. . . . Perhaps the NATO Charter reflects best the attitude of the world: An attack on one is an attack on all.[23]

Defining French or U.S. interests as coextensive with the interests of the world as a whole enables political leaders to portray their actions as furthering the interests of humanity, and to portray opponents as impeding the global march towards freedom. As Saint-Just declared in his draft constitution of 1793, "The French people votes for the freedom of the world." Similarly, in October 2001, Bush declared of the war in Afghanistan and the "war against terrorism" more broadly: "We are supported by the conscience of the world."[24] When bombs exploded in London in July 2005, Bush announced: "The attack in London was an attack on the civilized world."[25]

Although the emphasis on common interests did not succeed in generating unanimous support for the U.S.-led invasion of Iraq, it remains a core component of the United States's view of international relations post-September 11, supporting the notion of an ongoing global role for the U.S. military. Alongside this emphasis, the United States has also made clear its willingness to act alone to promote its security interests:

> While the United States will constantly strive to enlist the support of the international community, we will not hesitate to act alone, if necessary, to exercise our right of self-defense by acting preemptively against such terrorists, to prevent them from doing harm against our people and our country.[26]

The United States has taken the position that alliances are preferred, but not required. The Bush administration's justification for its actions in Iraq has consistently focused on security concerns, but the nature of these concerns has shifted from the allegedly urgent threat of weapons of mass destruction, to the longer-term benefits of a democratically self-governing Middle East. At no time has U.S military action been justified purely in liberationist terms, even though the rhetoric of freedom and democracy-promotion has figured prominently (and increasingly) in the Bush administration's justification for its actions in Iraq.

Despite fundamental transformations in global communications and military technology, striking continuities persist in the theoretical and practical challenges associated with universalist nationalism and exporting the ideal of self-government. The French Revolutionary campaigns generated resentment and backlash in Europe in part because of the discrepancy between the means of force (including pillage) and the purported end of freedom. The United States can be accused of a similar disjunction between means and ends, particularly in view of its wide-scale detention and mistreatment of civilian detainees in occupied Iraq. It is difficult to envisage how the United States can succeed in championing the rule of law and respect for human rights while flouting them. Many a dictatorship has thrived on the excuse that disregard for democratic principles and basic human rights is justified because of a state of emergency. Unless the United States practices what it preaches, the strategies of emulation and intervention are unlikely to produce their desired results.

6.2 Building an Iraqi Democracy

Many of the challenges associated with building democratic institutions in Iraq flow from the political vacuum and infrastructural deficiencies brought about by the U.S.-led removal of Saddam Hussein from power and the ensuing (and, as of the date of writing, continued) military occupation.

Other challenges reflect the particular historical, geographic, and demographic characteristics of the Iraqi territory and population. Two sets of tensions appear particularly salient in discussions about creating a viable and legitimate constitutional framework for the Iraqi state: whether the state will be secular or theocratic, and whether it will be unitary or federal. Both sets of tensions relate conceptually to how members of the Iraqi population define their political identities and their relationships with co-citizens, and practically to debates about power sharing and resource allocation among Iraq's self-identified component groups.

The shape and content of these core dilemmas are particular to Iraq at this historical juncture, but their broader contours reflect common issues in building sustainable participatory governments in postcolonial and pluralistic states. These challenges involve the conception, constitution, and composition of the Iraqi people and state:

1. Conception. Although it has become common to speak of "nation-building," the activities that come under this heading most commonly involve *state*-building: that is, building effective and legitimate governing structures within the borders of existing or newly formed states. The promotion of self-government in Iraq has focused on ensuring adequate representation and political participation for Iraq's component religious and ethnic groups within the borders inherited from the United Kingdom's League of Nations mandate. While proposals for regional autonomy have been advanced by both Kurdish and Shiite leaders, the continued territorial integrity of the Iraqi state as an international entity has by and large been assumed, at least in the immediate future. As in most postcolonial self-determination arguments, the borders of the existing state delineate the Iraqi people, rather than vice versa.

The nation-state model assumes a unitary state, in which the right of self-determination belongs to the "nation," envisioned as a cohesive whole coextensive with the state population. In Iraq, the existing precedent of limited Kurdish autonomy, combined with the tendency for self-identified groups to be concentrated in different geographic regions (the Kurds in the north, and the Shi'a in the south), pushes against this model. Resistance to federal proposals has come mainly from the Sunni population, which fears being deprived of the revenues from these oil-rich regions.

Conceptual differences between a unitary vision of the Iraqi state and a federal vision in which regional allegiances predominate carry significant practical consequences, both for Iraqis and for neighboring states. A federal model might be best equipped to generate cohesion, commitment, and compliance among members of each distinct region, but it can also impede efforts to foster these same attributes at the state level. The central government must provide citizens with symbolic and practical benefits not provided at the substate level (such as an internationally recognized identity, favorable redistribution of resources, enhanced security, and so forth); otherwise, particularly if the state is not supported by the idea or the reality of a cohesive nation, the state will likely face secessionist challenges from groups that do not perceive advantages to a federal arrangement.

2. CONSTITUTION. The question of who speaks for the people of Iraq is a difficult one, particularly given the recent history of oppression by the Sunni-dominated Ba'ath Party under Saddam Hussein. Although the creation of a Presidency Council on April 6, 2005, put a face on the Iraqi executive, the transitional nature of this arrangement and persistent divisions over a permanent Iraqi constitution detract from the perceived legitimacy and authoritativeness of this body. Similarly, the earlier decision by parties representing Sunni Muslims to boycott the legislative elections of January 30, 2005, in which members of a Transitional National Assembly were chosen, threatened to undermine the legitimacy and authoritativeness of that body. The original fifty-five member constitutional committee selected by the Assembly from among its members included only two Sunni delegates. To address concerns about the impact of this under-inclusiveness on the perceived legitimacy and viability of any draft constitution, the committee was later expanded to include fifteen additional Sunni representatives and one representative of the Sabean sect. The committee was charged with drafting a permanent constitution for submission to a popular referendum. This constitution would replace the Transitional Administrative Law issued by the short-lived Iraqi Governing Council in conjunction with the U.S.-run Coalition Provisional Authority.

This proliferation of representative bodies recalls the creation and dissolution of successive assemblies during the French Revolutionary period. Unlike rival French Revolutionary leaders, however, rival leaders in Iraq have focused less on claiming to speak for the entire Iraqi people, and more on claiming political influence in the name of their respective groups. The paradox of constitution operates within each of these groups, manifested in part in the struggle between those who would institutionalize secular values, and those who would enshrine a central role for Islamic law.

The division between secular and religious authorities risks becoming blurred where religion is explicitly entrenched as a source of collective values and standards of conduct. At the time of writing, the drafters of the Iraqi constitution appeared likely to reject the model of separation of church and state, leading to unresolved concerns about the potential for the Iraqi legal order to foster exclusion and curtail individual rights in the name of religious principles.

3. Composition. Debates about the inclusiveness of the new Iraqi legal order suggest the implications of the process of constitution for that of composition. Inclusiveness relates both to the representation of Iraq's component ethnic and religious groups in the new Iraqi government, and to the degree of protection afforded by Iraqi laws and legal institutions to all citizens and residents, including non-Muslim or nonobservant Iraqis and women.

The risk that instituting self-government will produce illiberal or exclusionary outcomes requires tempering an emphasis on self-determination with the imperative of protecting basic human rights. The Bush administration's rhetoric reflects this tension between affirming the right of the Iraqi people to choose their own destiny, and ensuring that this choice complies with standards rooted in the Western liberal political tradition. In 2002, Bush declared:

> The 20th century ended with a single surviving model of human progress, based on non-negotiable demands of human dignity, the rule of law, limits on the power of the state, respect for women and private property and free speech and equal justice and religious tolerance. America cannot impose this vision—yet we can support and reward governments that make the right choices for their own people.[27]

Condoleeza Rice echoed in 2005:

> There are those who say that democracy is being imposed. In fact, the opposite is true: Democracy is never imposed. It is tyranny that must be imposed.
>
> People choose democracy freely. And successful reform is always homegrown.[28]

While Rice makes a valid point about the "homegrown" nature of successful reform, her comments underestimate the extent to which, even in the absence of tyranny, political processes can produce results at odds with the United States's vision of a liberal democratic state, and with the goals of rights-promoting groups within a democratizing country. The question is: What constraints, if any, can be placed on the conduct and outcomes of such processes to ensure results consistent with a particular conception of fundamental rights and human dignity?

If one looks at political self-determination as an end in itself, then any external constraints on the outcome of popular deliberation within a particular state would appear unjustified. However, if one views self-determination as a means to the end of protecting human dignity and promoting human flourishing within politically autonomous communities, then the case for a certain degree of international scrutiny becomes easier to make—particularly where local groups themselves express concerns, as have Iraqi women's groups about the detrimental effect on women's rights of a constitution that enshrines Islamic principles. Despite the valid observation that Western ideas of democracy depend on economic foundations and societal understandings that are not necessarily present in many parts of the world, the universalist impulse should not be condemned whole-scale. Rather, as suggested in chapter five, the promotion of self-determination within a framework guaranteeing respect for basic human and minority rights can aim to reconcile the demands of particularism with the recognition of a moral obligation to protect individuals and groups from marginalization and persecution.

The risk, of course, is that any constraints will be perceived as hallmarks of foreign interference that undermine the legitimacy of a new Iraqi government and, consequently, compromise its ability to generate sufficient cohesion, compliance, and commitment among the population to sustain a functioning state. This trade-off may be the inevitable cost of ensuring that self-determination enhances, rather than curtails, the dignity and well-being of the individuals concerned.

Conclusion

The above discussion suggests certain continuities in the tension between universalism and particularism in international relations, particularly in the context of attempts to export a particular political ideal. These tensions are magnified when that ideal itself emphasizes the value of self-government. The contradiction involved in a policy of "forcing a people to be free" will not be lost on its intended beneficiaries, and can be expected to generate resistance, particularly where the methods used in the name of promoting freedom in fact disregard the desires and well-being of the population involved, and where the intervening state's motives appear more self-interested than benevolent. That said, this conceptual contradiction should not breed complacency in the face of oppressive dictatorships. As suggested in chapter five, abuses can best be minimized by ensuring broad international support for any intervention, and continued international supervision of its results.

In practice, intervention in the name of another people's best interests is most likely to come about when the intervener perceives that its *own* interests are threatened or at stake. In this sense, intervention purely in the name of promoting self-government is bound to be somewhat disingenuous. The task of state-building cannot be a mere afterthought. As the United States could and should have foreseen in Iraq, the existence of a functioning and vibrant civil society ready to take the reins of responsible and responsive government cannot be assumed, particularly in societies emerging from a long period of suppression of dissent and citizen participation. As the French Revolutionary experience confirms, the idea that "sovereignty resides in the people" is easier to proclaim than it is to implement. Any attempt to create stable and lasting institutions for self-governance in the Middle East or elsewhere must acknowledge and take account of this reality. The United States's apparent underestimation of the difficulties involved in this process, including the likelihood of prolonged armed resistance, has meant that Iraq's democratic transition has been both more precipitous and more precarious than it otherwise might have been.

Whether the United States's policy will vindicate itself in the long run remains to be seen. In the meantime, skeptics might recall the satirical definition of the word "constitution" in a 1796 dictionary by Charles-Frédéric Reinhard, an aristocratic *émigré*:

> Vieux mot Français, dont on n'a pas encore su fixer le vrai sens. . . . On a sermenté, on s'est embrassé, on s'est battu, on a égorgé, on a guillotiné, pour l'amour de cette *Constitution*. Mais hélas! elle n'est plus. . . . Peut-être cela arrivera-t'il, avant l'année 2440. [Old French word, whose real meaning we have not yet managed to establish. . . . (The members of the National Assembly and their supporters) took oaths, they embraced one another, they fought one another, they slit throats, they guillotined, for the love of this *Constitution*. But alas! it no longer exists. . . . Perhaps (the creation of a lasting Constitution) will happen before the year 2440.][29]

Three years later, in 1799, Reinhard enjoyed a short-lived tenure as foreign minister of France immediately following Napoleon's coup of 18

Brumaire (after four months in office, he was replaced by Charles-Maurice de Talleyrand). Reinhard's experience—from ousted aristocrat to foreign minister—evokes another aspect of the French Revolutionary experience with potential lessons for the situation in Iraq: the failure of a democratic experiment, followed by an opportunistic dictatorship.

France's Fifth Republic, created in 1958, has now lasted almost half a century. The good news is that the seeds planted by the 1789 Revolution eventually bore fruit; the bad news is that it took close to two centuries. Zhou Enlai, the first Premier and Foreign Minister of the People's Republic of China, reportedly opined in response to a question from Henry Kissinger about the impact of the French Revolution that it was "too soon to tell." The same is no doubt true of the U.S.-led intervention in Iraq. That said, the vicissitudes of history do not provide an excuse for failing to foresee the likelihood of backlash and the danger that instability will pave the way for a new authoritarianism. Continued support and vigilance will be required to prevent Iraq's constitutional process and its aftermath from vindicating the skepticism of contemporary Reinhards—and facilitating the rise of new Napoleons.

Conclusions

The paradoxes of conception, constitution, composition, and confrontation offer a framework for exploring the tensions involved in building nation-states and imagining alternative models. The political utility of nation-based platforms, and the pressures that push national self-definitions and policies toward exclusionary extremes, stem largely from the coupling of nationhood with control over territory and resources. *De*-coupling these concepts is no easy task. The idea of the nation has become bound up with political and territorial claims through historical processes such as those explored in chapters one through four. The assumptions and expectations associated with the nation-state idea continue to limit our international political vocabulary and to shape political and territorial goals.

Nations are politically salient in a world of sovereign states because they are thought to mark the boundaries of affective and effective communities. Nationhood (whether preexisting or constructed) is thought to generate and promote cohesion, commitment, and compliance, and to enhance the legitimacy and effectiveness of nation-based political institutions. The link between nationhood and political power, though historically contingent, remains widely entrenched. Historical and psychological forces have resulted in the sedimentation of obligation and identity at the national level in many parts of the world, challenging the likelihood of radical transformation in the international system.[1]

As an increasing awareness of global interdependence challenges the myth of absolute state sovereignty, state governments must adapt to maintain the confidence and support of their constituent populations. The European experiment, a significant example of adaptation, suggests both the potential for political transformation and its outer limits. The populations of France and the Netherlands rejected a proposed European constitution in 2005, notwithstanding progressively deeper and wider integration among European countries in a range of issue areas, including the widespread adoption of a single currency. The rejection of the proposed constitution testifies, at least in part, to the continued symbolic and practical appeal of the nation-state.

Even apart from proposed political integration, debates about the evolving content of state sovereignty abound. In the United States, these debates have taken the form of competing views about participation in a permanent International Criminal Court; concerns about the trade deficit with China; discussions about the democratic legitimacy of U.S. judges citing foreign and international law in constitutional adjudication; and debates over adherence to international treaties such as the Convention on the Elimination of All Forms of Discrimination Against Women, and the Kyoto Protocol to the United Nations Framework Convention on Climate Change, among other issues. These wide-ranging questions implicate core functions of government, namely, regulating conduct and allocating resources. A government's ability successfully to perform these functions creates a virtuous circle of enhanced legitimacy and effectiveness which, in turn, tends to reinforce cohesion, commitment, and compliance among the population; perceived governmental incompetence or inequity undermines these positive attributes and fuels agitation for political change.

What are the longer-term implications of shifting understandings of sovereignty and the role of the state? Will they lead to more malleable definitions of nationhood and its entitlements, or to alternative political models? One hypothesis is that, if nations are to coexist peacefully in a world composed of less-than-sovereign states, the international political system will tend towards empire in response to the need for a metropolitan power to hold together such diverse communities.[2] However, a global empire that still enshrined national divisions would be susceptible to the same risks of fragmentation as the multicultural models explored in chapter five. It is difficult to imagine why the ethical and power-political arguments for linking nationality and self-government would not reemerge in the future for the same reasons they developed in the past: that is, why a "new medievalism" would not lead eventually to a "new nation-statism."

Some leverage might be gained by emphasizing, both symbolically and practically, the conceptual distinction between allegiance to a prepolitical nation (nationalism) and allegiance to the state (patriotism). In 1813, after Napoleonic imperialism had succeeded French Revolutionary nation-statism, an accused traitor to the French Empire defended the compatibility of German nationality and French imperial citizenship:

> Les membres de ma société idéale en doivent remplir les lois partout où ils se trouvent: chacun doit exercer l'ancienne loyauté et fidélité germaniques envers le gouvernement dont il est sujet. C'est ce que les Allemands ont pratiqué effectivement depuis des siècles et ce qu'ils font aujourd'hui en Hongrie, Transylvanie, Livonie, le Holstein, et particulièrement en Alsace; et c'est ce que les habitants des provinces allemandes incorporées nouvellement à l'Empire français ne manqueront pas de faire à leur tour; tout comme les réfugiés français à Berlin, Leipzig, Hanovre, Cassel, sont comptés parmi les meilleurs citoyens d'états allemands, sans avoir cessé d'être Français et de s'en faire honneur; cet attachement à la nation, qu'on pourrait appeler NATIONALISME, s'accordant parfaitement avec le patriotisme voué à l'état dont on est citoyen. [The members of my ideal society must carry out the laws of that society, wherever they find themselves: each must exercise the ancient Germanic loyalty and fidelity towards the government of which he is a subject. This is what the Germans have effectively practiced for centuries and it is what they do today in Hungary, Transylvania, Livonia, Holstein, and particularly in Alsace; and it is what the inhabitants of the German provinces newly incorporated into the French Empire will not fail to do in turn; just as the French refugees in Berlin, Leipzig, Hanover, Cassel, are counted among the best citizens of German states, without having ceased to be French and to take pride in this; this attachment to the nation, which we could call NATIONALISM, being in perfect harmony with the patriotism pledged to the state where one is a citizen.][3]

This quotation comes from a letter written to the Duke of Rovigo (Napoleon's Minister of Police) on January 24, 1813, from the journalist and bookseller Rodolphe Zachqrie Becker, who had been apprehended under instructions from Napoleon at Gotha in 1812 for trying to form a secret German league (*deutscher Bund*). Becker's enthusiasm for and conviction in the possibility of noncompeting identities was likely driven in no small part by the need to defend himself against charges of subversion. Nevertheless, Becker clearly articulates the possibility of maintaining distinct but compatible allegiances based on nationhood and statehood, respectively.

The notion of complementary identities and allegiances is appealing and, in many instances, unproblematic. However, in situations of international conflict, states must be able to count on the ultimate and undivided allegiance of their citizens. Becker's description does not contemplate such crisis situations. Moreover, his allegedly seditious conduct suggests that the asserted "perfect harmony" between German nationality and

French political control might not have been as straightforward as his letter claims. The French Revolutionaries' emphasis on festivals of unity and oaths of allegiance highlights the perception that complementary identities cannot be coequal, particularly if they are envisioned as all-encompassing. The more the state asks of and provides for its citizens, the more encompassing the national identity supporting the state must be. Conversely, the more states can delegate functions of governance upward to supra-state structures and downward to substate units, the greater the possibility for meaningfully complementary identities among members of diverse populations.

These observations reinforce the close, but often neglected, connection between political theory and international relations. Any theory of international relations must ultimately include a theory of the state, and vice versa. Such ideas do not evolve in a historical vacuum. As scholars of the English School of IR have long recognized, international society is constituted and reconstituted over time through the reciprocal interaction of doctrines and practice. Recognizing the connections among the conception, constitution, composition, and confrontation of territorially and politically organized groups of individuals can provide greater analytic clarity in examining and evaluating nation-based claims in contemporary world politics. It can also help us understand and explain failures in state-building efforts that do not take account of these processes and their implications, such as the protracted state-building effort in occupied Iraq.

Although a world of nation-states is only one of many possible worlds, the economic, political, and psychological factors that have contributed to the development of an international system based on the nation-state model suggest the likely persistence of such a system or something closely resembling it in the foreseeable future. The French Revolutionary experience indicates the limitations of a civic definition of nationhood as a panacea for exclusion and belligerence, and suggests a need for caution in adopting any political model based on the idea of a preexisting, internally cohesive group. Any viable polity must be able to generate cohesion, commitment, and compliance among members of the population. The challenge is to imagine and to implement forms of belonging and political association that provide the benefits associated with nation-statehood while avoiding exclusionary and belligerent outcomes. This challenge remains part of the French Revolution's enduring legacy—a legacy that, despite the intervening centuries, remains relevant and instructive for politics and international relations today.

Appendix

Grégoire's Déclaration du droit des gens, June 18, 1793

Art. 1. Les peuples sont entre eux dans l'état de nature; ils ont pour lien la morale universelle.

Art. 2. Les peuples sont respectivement indépendants et souverains, quel que soit le nombre d'individus qui les composent et l'étendue du territoire qu'ils occupent. Cette souveraineté est inaliénable.

Art. 3. Un peuple doit agir à l'égard des autres comme il désire qu'on agisse à son égard; ce qu'un homme doit à un homme, un peuple le doit aux autres.

Art. 4. Les peuples doivent en paix se faire le plus de bien, et en guerre le moins de mal possible.

Art. 5. L'intérêt particulier d'un peuple est subordonné à l'intérêt général de la famille humaine.

Art. 6. Chaque peuple a le droit d'organiser et de changer les formes de son gouvernement.

Art. 7. Un peuple n'a pas le droit de s'immiscer dans le gouvernement des autres.

Art. 8. Il n'y a de gouvernement conforme aux droits des peuples que ceux qui sont fondés sur l'égalité et la liberté.

Art. 9. Ce qui est d'un usage inépuisable ou innocent, comme la mer, appartient à tous, et ne peut être la propriété d'aucun peuple.

Art. 10. Chaque peuple est maître de son territoire.

Art. 11. La possession immémoriale établit le droit de prescription entre les peuples.

Art. 12. Un peuple a le droit de refuser l'entrée de son territoire, et de renvoyer les étrangers, quand sa sûreté l'exige.

Art. 13. Les étrangers sont soumis aux lois du pays et punissables par elles.

Art. 14. Le bannissement pour crime est une violation indirecte du territoire étranger.

Art. 15. Les entrepreises contre la liberté d'un peuple sont un attentat contre tous les autres.

Art. 16. Les ligues qui ont pour objet une guerre offensive, les traités qui peuvent nuire à l'intérêt d'un peuple, sont un attentat contre la famille humaine.

Art. 17. Un peuple peut entreprendre une guerre pour défendre sa souveraineté, sa liberté, sa propriété.

Art. 18. Les peuples qui sont en guerre doivent laisser un libre cours aux négociations propres à amener la paix.

Art. 19. Les agents publics que les peuples s'envoient sont indépendants des lois du pays où ils sont envoyés, dans tout ce qui concerne l'objet de leur mission.

Art. 20. Il n'y a pas de préséance entre les agents publics des nations.

Art. 21. Les traités entre les peuples sont sacrés et inviolables.

Volney's Proposed Declaration, May 18, 1790

L'Assemblée nationale, délibérant à l'occasion des armements extraordinaires de deux puissances voisines qui élèvent les alarmes de la guerre;

Dans cette circonstance, où pour la première fois elle porte des regards de surveillance au delà des limites de l'empire, désirant de manifester les principes qui la dirigeront dans ses relations extérieures, elle déclare solennellement:

1. Qu'elle regarde l'universalité du genre humain comme ne formant qu'une seule et même société, dont l'objet est la paix et le bonheur de tous et de chacun de ses membres;

2. Que, dans cette grande société générale, les peuples et les États, considérés comme individus, jouissent des mêmes droits naturels et sont soumis aux mêmes règles de justice que les individus des sociétés partielles et secondaires;

3. Que, par conséquent, nul peuple n'a le droit d'envahir la propriété d'un autre peuple, ni de le priver de sa liberté et de ses avantages naturels;

4. Que toute guerre entreprise par un autre motif et pour un autre objet que la défense d'un droit juste est un acte d'oppression qu'il importe à toute la grande société de réprimer, parce que l'invasion d'un État par un autre État tend à menacer la liberté et la sûreté de tous.

Par ces motifs, l'Assemblée nationale a décrété et décrète comme article de la Constitution française:

Que la nation française s'interdit de ce moment d'entreprendre aucune guerre tendant à accroître son territoire actuel.

Robespierre's Proposed Articles, April 24, 1793

1. Les hommes de tous les pays sont frères, et les différents peuples doivent s'entr'aider selon leur pouvoir, comme les citoyens du même État.

2. Celui qui opprime une nation se déclare l'ennemi de toutes.

3. Ceux qui font la guerre à un peuple pour arrêter les progrès de la liberté et anéantir les droits de l'homme devront être poursuivis par tous, non comme des ennemis ordinaires, mais comme des ennemis et des brigands rebelles.

4. Les rois, les aristocrates, les tyrans, quels qu'ils soient, sont des esclaves révoltés contre le souverain de la terre, qui est le genre humain, et contre le libérateur de l'univers, qui est la nature.

Notes

Prologue

1. *Gazette nationale ou le moniteur universel*, Réimpression de l'ancien moniteur [hereafter cited as *Moniteur*] 1, no. 9 (June 17, 1789): 82–83.

2. Ibid. 84 ("L'air pesant et pestilentiel exhalé du corps de plus de trois mille personnes concentrées dans la salle produira infailliblement un effet funeste sur tous les députés").

3. This definition is adapted from David Miller, *On Nationality* (Oxford: Clarendon, 1995), 19.

4. Ernest Gellner defines nationalism as "primarily a political principle, which holds that the political and the national unit should be congruent." Gellner, *Nations and Nationalism* (Oxford: Blackwell, 1983), 1.

5. See, for example, Alan James, *Sovereign Statehood: The Basis of International Society* (London: Allen and Unwin, 1986), 278; R. J. Johnston, David B. Knight, and Eleonore Kofman, "Nationalism, self-determination, and the world political map: An introduction," in *National Self-determination and Political Geography*, ed. Johnston, Knight, and Kofman, 8 (London: Croom Helm, 1988); and Hurst Hannum, *Autonomy, Sovereignty, and Self-Determination: The Accommodation of Conflicting Rights* (Philadelphia: University of Pennsylvania Press, 1990), 39.

6. Sir Ivor Jennings famously observed on the subject of decolonization debates: "On the surface it seemed reasonable: let the people decide. It was in fact ridiculous because the people cannot decide until someone decides who are the people." Jennings, *The Approach to Self-Government* (Cambridge: Cambridge University Press, 1956), 56.

7. See Ian Brownlie, *Principles of Public International Law*, 4th ed. (Oxford: Clarendon, 1990), 513, 515.

8. Exceptions to the paucity of analyses of the principles underlying international society include James Mayall, *Nationalism and International Society* (Cambridge: Cambridge University Press, 1990); and Charles Beitz, *Political Theory and International Relations* (Princeton, NJ: Princeton University Press, 1979).

9. To avoid this confusion, the Portuguese and Brazilian delegates in 1919 suggested that the League of Nations be termed instead the "League of States." See D. H. Miller, *The Drafting of the Covenant*, vol. 1 (New York and London: G. P. Putnam's Sons, 1928), 135, 141–42.

10. Michael Walzer writes: "The moral standing of any particular state depends upon the reality of the common life it protects and the extent to which the sacrifices required by that protection are willingly accepted and thought worthwhile. If no common life exists, or if the state doesn't defend the common life that does exist, its own defense may have no moral justification." Walzer, *Just and Unjust Wars: A Moral Argument With Historical Illustrations*, 2nd ed. (New York: Basic Books, 1992), 54. See also Walzer, "The Reform of the International System," in *Studies of War and Peace*, ed. Øyvind Østerud, 227–39 (Oslo: Norwegian University Press, 1986).

11. See Peter Alter, *Nationalism*, trans. Stuart McKinnon-Evans (London: Edward Arnold, 1989), 93; and Martti Koskenniemi, "National Self-Determination Today: Problems of Legal Theory and Practice," *International and Comparative Law Quarterly* 43 (April 1994): 245–46.

12. Alfred Cobban, *The Nation-State and National Self-Determination*, rev. ed. (New York: Thomas Crowell, New York, 1969), 107.

13. Hugh Seton-Watson writes in *Nations and States* (London: Methuen, 1977), 1: "A state is a legal and political organisation, with the power to require obedience and loyalty from its citizens [while a] nation is a community of people, whose members are bound together by a sense of solidarity, a common culture, a national consciousness."

14. Benedict Anderson's idea of imagined belonging in conditions of modernity may also help account for the phenomenon of identity not rooted in direct experience. See Anderson, *Imagined Communities: Reflections on the Origin and Spread of Nationalism* (London: Verso, 1983).

15. See, for example, accounts of nation-building in Anthony Smith, *National Identity* (London: Penguin, 1991); Ernest Gellner, *Nations and Nationalism* (Oxford: Blackwell, 1983); and comments by Cobban in *The Nation-State and National Self-Determination*, 26, 111. Charles Tilly's early work on *The Formation of National States in Western Europe* (Princeton, NJ: Princeton University Press, 1975) is often associated with this perspective.

16. U.N. General Assembly Resolution 1514 (XV), December 14, 1960; U.N. General Assembly Resolution 2625 (XXV), October 24, 1970; International Covenant on Civil and Political Rights, adopted December 16, 1966, entered into force March 23, 1976, 999 U.N.T.S. 171; International Covenant on Economic, Social and Cultural Rights, adopted December 16, 1966, entered into force January 3, 1976, 993 U.N.T.S. 3.

17. I am indebted to Adam Roberts for this observation.

18. See Robert Lansing, *The Peace Negotiations: A Personal Narrative* (London: Constable, 1921); and Cobban, *The Nation-State and National Self-Determination*, 129.

19. The conflation of national self-determination with self-government during later decolonization debates overlooked this premise, taking as a given arbitrarily imposed state boundaries, for example in Africa. See the 1963 Charter of the Organization of African Unity (OAU), art. 3, para. 3 ("respect for the sovereignty and territorial integrity of each State and for its inalienable right to independent existence"); and the OAU's Cairo Resolution of July 21, 1964, OAU Doc. AHG/Res. 16(1) ("Member States pledge themselves to respect the borders existing on their achievement of national independence."). See also Malcom Shaw, *Title to Territory in Africa: Legal Issues* (Oxford: Clarendon, 1986).

20. For another challenge to the "peaceful coexistence" argument, see Jack Snyder's view that national definitions of identity actually promote conflict in his "Nationalism and the Crisis of the Post-Soviet State," in *Ethnic Conflict and International Security*, ed. Michael Brown, 93 (Princeton, NJ: Princeton University Press, 1993).

21. Elie Kedourie, "A New International Disorder," in *The Expansion of International Society*, ed. Hedley Bull and Adam Watson, 347–56 (Oxford: Clarendon, 1984).

22. International Covenant on Civil and Political Rights, adopted December 16, 1966, entered into force March 23, 1976, 999 U.N.T.S. 171; International Covenant on Economic, Social and Cultural Rights, adopted December 16, 1966, entered into force January 3, 1976, 993 U.N.T.S. 3.

23. Boutros Boutros-Gali, "An Agenda for Peace: Preventive diplomacy, peacemaking and peace-keeping," Report of the Secretary-General pursuant to the statement adopted by the Summit meeting of the Security Council on January 31, 1992 (June 17, 1992), UN doc. A/47/277-S/24111.

24. See Albert Sorel, *L'Europe et la Révolution française. Première partie: Les moeurs politiques et les traditions*, 3rd ed. (Paris: Librairie Plon, 1893), 59; Sorel, *Deuxième partie: La Chute de la royauté* (Paris: Librairie Plon, 1895), 171; and Edgar Morin, *Penser l'Europe* (Paris: Gallimard, 1987), 53.

25. Examples include Peter Alter, *Nationalism*, trans. Stuart McKinnon-Evans (London: Edward Arnold, 1989), 56, 93; Malcom Anderson, *Frontiers: Territory and State Formation in the Modern World* (Cambridge: Polity, 1996) 2; Omar Dahbour, "Self-Determination in Political Philosophy and International Law," *History of European Ideas* 16 (1993): 881; G. P. Gooch, *Studies in Modern History* (London: Longmans, 1931), 217; Jürgen Habermas, "Citizenship and National Identity: Some Reflections on the Future of Europe," in *Theorizing Citizenship*, ed. Ronald Beiner, 257 (Albany: State University of New York Press, 1995); Eugene Kamenka, "Political Nationalism—The Evolution of the Idea," in *Nationalism: The Nature and Evolution of an Idea*, ed. Eugene Kamenka, 10 (London: Edward Arnold, 1976); Hans Kohn, *Prelude to Nation-States: The French and German Experience 1789–1815* (Princeton, NJ: D. van Nostrand, 1967), 82; and Anthony Smith, *National Identity* (London: Penguin, 1991), 18.

26. See Hedley Bull, "International Theory: The Case for a Classical Approach," *World Politics* 18 (April 1966): 361–77; and Herbert Butterfield and

Martin Wight, Preface, *Diplomatic Investigations: Essays in the Theory of International Politics* (London: George Allen and Unwin, 1966), 11–13.

27. For a historical survey, see Hagen Schulze, *States, Nations and Nationalism: From the Middle Ages to the Present*, trans. William Yuill (Oxford: Blackwell, 1996); for a theoretical approach, see Avishai Margalit and Joseph Raz, "Self-Determination," in Raz, *Ethics in the Public Domain: Essays in the Morality of Law and Politics* (Oxford: Clarendon, 1995), 125–45.

28. See Hedley Bull, *The Anarchical Society: A Study of Order in World Politics*, 2nd ed. (London: Macmillan, 1995), 33; and Martin Wight, *Power Politics*, 2nd ed., ed. Hedley Bull and Carsten Holbraad (London: Penguin, 1986), 85.

29. On the importance of the justification of power, see Istvan Bibó, *The Paralysis of International Institutions and the Remedies: A Study of Self-Determination, Concord Among the Major Powers, and Political Arbitration* (Sussex: Harvester, 1976), 11. On the enterprise of "conceptual history," see the Preface and first two chapters of Terence Ball, James Farr, and Russell Hanson, eds., *Political Innovation and Conceptual Change* (Cambridge: Cambridge University Press, 1989).

30. For insights into a specifically linguistic understanding of political culture, see Keith Michael Baker, *Inventing the French Revolution: Essays on French Political Culture in the Eighteenth Century* (Cambridge: Cambridge University Press, 1990), 4–5.

31. Alexis de Tocqueville, *The Old Régime and the French Revolution*, trans. Stuart Gilbert (Garden City, NY: Doubleday, 1955; orig. pub. 1856), 139.

32. Jennifer M. Welsh's *Edmund Burke and International Relations: The Commonwealth of Europe and the Crusade against the French Revolution* (London: Macmillan, 1995) incisively analyzes Burke's defense of traditional international society.

33. Robert Lansing recalls having foreseen these consequences in *The Peace Negotiations: A Personal Narrative* (Boston: Houghton Mifflin, 1921). Wilson admitted to the Committee of Foreign Relations of the Senate on August 19, 1919: "When I gave utterance to those words ('that all nations had a right to self-determination'), I said them without the knowledge that nationalities existed, which are coming to us day after day. . . . You do not know and cannot appreciate the anxieties that I have experienced as the result of many millions of people having their hopes raised by what I have said." *Hearings, Committee of Foreign Relations, US Senate, 66th Congress*, no. 106 (Washington: 1919), 838.

34. See V. I. Lenin, *The Right of Nations to Self-Determination: Selected Writings* (New York: International Publishers, 1951); and Joseph Stalin, *Marxism and the National and Colonial Question* (London: Martin Lawrence, 1936).

35. See, for example, Michael Freeden, "Is Nationalism a Distinct Ideology?" *Political Studies* 46 (September 1998): 748–65.

36. The fundamental importance of the territorial dimension of national self-determination is illustrated by a comment made about the first Palestinian autonomy plan put forward by Menachem Begin in December 1977, shared with

me by Avi Shlaim: "Yigal Allon, the late Labor party leader, remarked about this plan that it is only in Marc Chagall's paintings that people float in midair, free of the force of gravity, and that it is impossible to translate this artistic quirk into any meaningful political reality." Shlaim, "Prelude to the Accord: Likud, Labor, and the Palestinians," *Journal of Palestine Studies* 23 (Winter 1994): 7.

37. The Abbé Sieyès wrote in *Quelques idées de constitution, applicables à la ville de Paris* (A Versailles: chez Baudouin, Imprimeur de l'Assemblée Nationale, July 1789), 30: "Quoique la volonté nationale soit . . . indépendante de toute forme, encore faut-il qu'elle en prenne une pour se faire entendre."

38. Martin Wight observes in "International Legitimacy," *Systems of States* (Bristol: Leicester University Press, 1977), 165: "There is however a paradox about the principle of national self-determination: that the more passionately it has been asserted, the less it has led to impartial popular consultation."

39. Adam Roberts, "Communal conflict as a challenge to international organisation: the case of former Yugoslavia," *Review of International Studies* 21 (1995): 391.

Chapter One: Conception

1. See Christian Buzon and Chantal Girardin, "La Constitution du Concept de *Nation*: Analyse du Signe, Description de la Notion et Usage Socio-Politique dans le Traitement Lexicographique du Mot," in *Autour de Féraud: La léxicographie en France de 1762 à 1835* (Paris: Collections de l'École Normale Supérieure de Jeunes Filles, 1986), 185–91.

2. See P. Griffet, *Traité de la Connaissance des Hommes, Tome II des Mémoires pour servir à l'histoire du Dauphin* (Paris: 1758), 100–01.

3. Trans. in Boyd Schafer, "Bourgeois Nationalism in the Pamphlets on the Eve of the French Revolution," *Journal of Modern History* 10, no. 1 (1938): 32. See Marquis d'Argenson, entry of September 3, 1751, in *Journal et mémoires du marquis d'Argenson*, vol. 6, ed. J. B. Rathéry (Paris: Jules Renouard, 1864), 463–64; and Jacques Godechot, "Nation, patrie, nationalisme et patriotisme en France au XVIII siècle," *Annales historiques de la Révolution française* 43 (1971): 491, 493.

4. Kingsley Martin, *French Liberal Thought in the Eighteenth Century*, ed. J. P. Mayer (London: Phoenix House, 1962; orig. pub. 1929), 26.

5. H. F. Stewart and Paul Desjardins, Preface, *French Patriotism in the Nineteenth Century (1814–1833) Traced in Contemporary Texts* (Cambridge: Cambridge University Press, 1923), xi.

6. M***, *Dictionnaire raisonné de plusieurs mots qui sont dans la bouche de tout le monde, et ne présentent pas des idées bien nettes* (Paris: Palais-Royal, 1790), 153.

7. Nannerl O. Keohane, *Philosophy and the State in France: The Renaissance to the Enlightenment* (Princeton, NJ: Princeton University Press, 1980), 18. See also

Edme Champion, "L'Unité nationale et la Révolution," *La Révolution française* 19 (July–December 1890), 10.

8. Robert Darnton notes of the *Encyclopédie*: "Estimates put [distribution] at 15,000 copies between 1751 and 1789. The various editions ranged from 17 to 36 volumes of text and 3 to 11 volumes of plates. The *Encyclopédie* was sold all over France and its readers consisted not only of the literary elite, but of the lawyers, doctors, and other professionals in the provinces who later made their literary and revolutionary careers in Paris." See Reinhard Bendix, *Kings or People: Power and the Mandate to Rule* (Berkeley: University of California Press, 1978), 353 n. g.

9. De Jaucourt, "Etat," in *Encyclopédie* (1756), 6:19a.

10. *Encyclopédie* (1765), 11:36b.

11. See Jean-Yves Guiomar, *L'idéologie nationale: Nation, Représentation, Propriété* (Paris: Éditions Champ libre, 1974), 22.

12. Guiomar, *L'idéologie nationale*, 22.

13. Léon Duguit, *Traité de droit constitutionnel*, 2nd ed., vol. 1 (Paris: E. de Boccard, 1921), 607. The *Nouveau Petit Robert* (Paris: Dictionnaires Le Robert, 1993) cites the first sentence of this passage to illustrate the double sense of the term "originaire" as both "chronologically first" and "source of." A similar point is made in the *cahier* of the Négociants of Rouen, in *French Revolution Documents*, vol. 1, ed. J. M. Roberts and Richard Cobb (Oxford: Blackwell, 1966), 90.

14. *Catéchisme national* (1789; repr. Paris: Hachette, 1976), 7.

15. Pierre-Nicolas Chantreau, *Dictionnaire national et anecdotique pour servir à l'intelligence des mots dont notre langue s'est enrichie depuis la révolution, et à la nouvelle signification qu'ont reçue quelques anciens mots* (Paris: Politicopolis, 1790), 130–32.

16. Chantreau, *Dictionnaire national*, 132–33.

17. M***, *Dictionnaire raisonné*, 134–37.

18. André-Quentin Buée, *Nouveau dictionnaire pour servir à l'intelligence des termes mis en vogue par la Révolution* (Paris: 1792), 116–17.

19. See Godechot, "Nation, patrie, nationalisme," 495; Jean-Jacques Clere, "Etat-Nation-Citoyen au temps de la Révolution française," in *L'idée de nation*, ed. Marie-Françoise Conrad, Jean Ferrari, and Jean-Jacques Wunenburger (Dijon: Éditions universitaires de Dijon, 1986), 99.

20. See Jean-Claude Caron, *La nation, l'État et la démocratie en France de 1789 à 1914* (Paris: Armand Colin, 1995), 35, citing Louis XIV, *Mémoires de Louis XIV pour l'instruction du dauphin*, 2 vols. (Paris: Didier et Cie., 1860).

21. Jules Flammermont, ed., *Remontrances du parlement du Paris au XVIIIe siècle*, vol. 2 (Paris: Imprimerie Nationale, 1895), 557. Quotation translated in John Rothney, *The Brittany Affair and the Crisis of the Ancien Regime* (Oxford: Oxford University Press, 1969), 177.

22. Pasquale Pasquino notes that, ironically, it was probably the king who first articulated the idea of the nation as a separate body. Pasquino, "Le Concept de Nation et les Fondements Du Droit Public de la Révolution: Sieyès," in *L'héritage de la Révolution française*, ed. François Furet (Paris: Hachette, 1989), 313. See also Keith Michael Baker, *Inventing the French Revolution: Essays on French Political Culture in the Eighteenth Century* (Cambridge: Cambridge University Press, 1990), 232; and Guiomar, *L'idéologie nationale*, 40.

23. *Réponse du Roi à la déclaration des droits de l'homme*, read by the President of the National Assembly, Oct. 5, 1789, *Archives Parlementaires de 1787 à 1860*, première série (1787–1799) [hereafter cited as *AP*], vol. 9 (Paris: Paul Dupont, 1867–), 342.

24. See Albert Sorel, *L'Europe et la Révolution française. Deuxième partie: La Chute de la royauté*, 3rd ed. (Paris: Librairie Plon, 1895), 138.

25. Gérard Fritz, *L'Idée de peuple en France du XVIIe au XIXe siècle* (Strasbourg: Strasbourg University Press, 1988), 31. Internal citation from Paul-Henri Thiry, Baron d'Holbach, *Le Système social* (Paris: Librairie Arthème Fayard, 1994; orig. pub. 1773), 246.

26. Jacob Nicolas Moreau, *Exposition et défense de notre constitution monarchique française*, vol. 2 (Paris: Moutard, 1789), 105.

27. Henri Hauser, *Le principe des nationalités: Ses origines historiques* (1916); trans. in William F. Church, "France," in *National Consciousness, History, and Political Culture in Early-Modern Europe*, ed. Orest Ranum (Baltimore: John Hopkins, 1975), 44.

28. According to Alphonse Aulard, "Patrie, Patriotisme sous Louis XVI et dans les cahiers," *La Révolution Française: Revue d'histoire moderne et contemporaine* 68 (January–June 1915), 337, the word *patrie* was used by Claude Gruget in 1537, and the expression "mauvaise *patriote*" was used in a letter written by Mazarin on June 14, 1648. David Bell documents the rising frequency of use of the terms "nation" and "patrie" during the course of the eighteenth century. See David A. Bell, *The Cult of the Nation in France: Inventing Nationalism, 1680–1800* (Cambridge, MA: Harvard University Press, 2001), 225 n. 53.

29. Abbé Coyer, "Dissertation sur le vieux mot de patrie," in *Dissertations pour être lues: La première, sur le vieux mot de patrie: La seconde, sur la nature du peuple* (La Haye: Pierre Gosse junior, 1755), 10.

30. Coyer, "Dissertation sur le vieux mot de patrie," 15.

31. Jean de La Bruyère, "Du souverain ou de la république," *Les Caractères* (Paris: Librairie Générale Française, 1985; orig. pub. 1688), 239–40.

32. La Bruyère, "Du souverain ou de la république," 260.

33. De Jaucourt, "Patrie," in *Encyclopédie* (1765), 12:178b.

34. Buée, *Nouveau dictionnaire*, 95.

35. Beatrice Fry Hyslop, *French nationalism in 1789, according to the General Cahiers* (New York: Columbia University Press, 1934), 159.

36. Buée, *Nouveau dictionnaire*, 22.

37. See "Obéissance" and "Pouvoir," in Diderot's *Dictionnaire Encyclopédique*, vol. 4, ed. J. Assézat (Paris: Librairie Garnier Frères), 152, 385. See also de Jaucourt, "Souveraineté," in *Encyclopédie* (1765), 15:425a.

38. See François Furet, Introduction, *L'héritage de la Révolution française*, 18.

39. See Roger Bickart, *Les Parlements et la Notion de Souveraineté Nationale au XVIIIe siècle* (Paris: Librairie Félix Alcan, 1932), 260. More recently, Dale Van Kley has drawn attention to the important contribution of *pro*-ministerial propagandists to the development of nationalist rhetoric. See Dale Van Kley, "From the Lessons of French History to Truths for All Times and All People: The Historical Origins of an Anti-Historical Declaration," in *The French Idea of Freedom: The Old Regime and the Declaration of Rights of 1789*, ed. Dale Van Kley (Stanford, CA: Stanford University Press, 1994), 87–91.

40. Jean de Selve, *Lit de Justice* of December 1527, quoted in Sarah Hanley, "Constitutional discourse in France, 1527–1549," in *Politics and Culture in Early Modern Europe*, ed. Phyllis Mack and Margaret C. Jacob (Cambridge: Cambridge University Press, 1987), 160.

41. Joseph Saige, *Catéchisme du citoyen, ou Éléments du droit public français, par demandes et réponses, suivi de fragments politiques par le même auteur* (Paris: En France, 1788), 11, 14.

42. See Bernard Groethuysen, *Philosophie de la Révolution Française* (Paris: Gallimard, 1956), 130.

43. Thomas Hobbes, *Leviathan*, ed. C. B. MacPherson (London: Penguin, 1981; orig. pub. 1651).

44. See John Locke, *Two Treatises of Government*, ed. Mark Goldie (London: Dent, 1993; orig. pub. 1690).

45. For a classic comparison of the French and American Revolutions, see Friedrich von Gentz, *The origin and principles of the American Revolution, compared with the origin and principles of the French Revolution*, trans. John Quincy Adams (Philadelphia: Asbury Dickins, 1800). In an anonymous preface to the translation, Adams promoted Gentz's essay as "highly interesting to Americans" because "it rescues [the American] revolution from the disgraceful imputation of having proceeded from the same principles as that of France."

46. This point was central to the Canadian Supreme Court's 1998 decision that Québec does not have a right to secede under international law. *Reference re Secession of Quebec*, [1998] S.C.R. 217, paras. 126–38.

47. Pasquino in "Le Concept de Nation," 325 n. 10 notes that the *Social Contract* was in fact well-known on the eve of the Revolution, and cites F. Eppen-

steiner's findings in *Rousseaus Einfluss auf die vorrevolutionaren Flugschriften und den Ausbruch der Revolution* (PhD diss., Tübingen, 1914), 38, that 112 out of 460 brochures published between October 1788 and May 1789 show the influence of Rousseau.

48. See Pasquino, "Le Concept de Nation," 316–17.

49. See Maurice Cranston, "The Sovereignty of the Nation," in *The Political Culture of the French Revolution*, ed. Colin Lucas (Oxford: Pergamon, 1988), 101.

50. Jean-Jacques Rousseau, *Du Contrat Social ou Principes du Droit Politique*, ed. C. E. Vaughan (Manchester: Manchester University Press, 1947; orig. pub. 1762), 12 (hereafter cited as *CS*).

51. *CS*, 13.

52. *CS*, 13.

53. *CS*, 14.

54. See *CS*, 17, 80.

55. *CS*, 83, 45.

56. See *CS*, 46.

57. *CS*, 93.

58. *CS*, 12.

59. The *Encyclopédie* says of the term "Société civile": "s'entend du corps politique que les hommes d'une même nation, d'un même état, d'une même ville ou autre lieu, forment ensemble, & des liens politiques qui attachent les uns aux autres; c'est le commerce civil du monde, les liaisons que les hommes ont ensemble, comme sujets d'un même prince, comme concitoyens d'une même ville, & comme sujets aux mêmes lois, & participant aux droits & privileges qui sont communs à tous ceux qui composent cette même *société*." *Encyclopédie* (1765), 15:259a–259b.

60. Neera Chandhoke, *State and Civil Society: Explorations in Political Theory* (New Delhi: Sage, 1995), 98.

61. Alfred Cobban, *A History of Modern France. Volume 1: Old Régime and Revolution 1715–1799*, 3rd ed. (New York: Penguin, 1963), 179. John Hall notes that civil society is diametrically opposed to the republican tradition of civic virtue. Hall, "In Search of Civil Society," in *Civil Society: Theory, History, Comparison*, ed. John Hall (Cambridge: Polity, 1995), 10.

62. On the Revolution as a secular religion, see Connor Cruise O'Brien, "Religion, Nationalism, and Civil Society," in *The Idea of a Civil Society*, ed. Bronislaw Geremek, et al. (North Carolina: National Humanities Center, 1992), 23–28. For a comprehensive treatment of the relationship between religion and nationalism during the pre-Revolutionary and Revolutionary period, see Bell, *The Cult of the Nation in France*.

63. Ernest Gellner, "The Importance of Being Modular," in *Civil Society*, ed. John Hall, 46, drawing on German sociologist Ferdinand Tönnies's distinction between "society" and "community." See also Tönnies, Community and Society [*Gemeinschaft und Gesellschaft*], trans. Charles P. Loomis (New York: Harper and Row, 1957; orig. pub. 1887), 33–34.

64. For discussions of these competing allegiances and social structures, see works including Peter Sahlins, *Boundaries: The Making of France and Spain in the Pyrenees* (Berkeley and Los Angeles: University of California Press, 1989), and the rich historical narrative in Colin Jones, *The Great Nation: France from Louis XV to Napoleon* (New York: Columbia University Press, 2002).

Chapter Two: Constitution

1. This chapter draws largely on primary sources found in the French National Archives and cited in older works by Elie Carcassonne, Jean Egret, and Roger Bickart. Important recent research on the development of nationalist arguments in the eighteenth century can be found in works including David A. Bell, *The Cult of the Nation in France: Inventing Nationalism, 1680–1800* (Cambridge, MA: Harvard University Press, 2001); Peter Sahlins, *Boundaries: The Making of France and Spain in the Pyrenees* (Berkeley and Los Angeles: University of California Press, 1989); Colin Jones, *The Great Nation: France from Louis XV to Napoleon* (New York: Columbia University Press, 2002); and Dale Van Kley, ed., *The French Idea of Freedom: The Old Regime and the Declaration of Rights of 1789* (Stanford, CA: Stanford University Press, 1994).

2. For arguments that the *parlements* were primarily concerned with promoting their own privileges and influence, see Elie Carcassonne, *Montesquieu et le problème de la constitution française au XVIIIe siècle* (Paris: Presses Universitaires de France, 1927), 393; and H. Sée, "Doctrine politique des Parlements," *Revue historique de droit français et étranger* (April-June 1924), 294–96. Alfred Cobban notes in *A History of Modern France. Volume 1: Old Régime and Revolution 1715–1799*, 3rd ed. (New York: Penguin, 1963), 134: "By 'the nation' [the *parlements*] had all along meant themselves."

3. Paul Gilbert, "Criteria of Nationality and the Ethics of Self-determination," *History of European Ideas* 16, nos. 4–6 (1993): 516.

4. Mlada Bukovansky in "The altered state and the state of nature—the French Revolution and international politics," *Review of International Studies* 25 (1999): 209 dubs this phenomenon the "holistic turn": that is, the preclusion of legitimate political opposition based on the premise that the authentic national will is necessarily monolithic.

5. On the simultaneously tense and symbiotic relationship between the *parlements* and the king, see William Doyle, "The *Parlements* of France and the Breakdown of the Old Régime 1771–1788," *French Historical Studies* 6, no. 4 (Fall 1970): 435, 454; and Jean Egret, *Louis XV et l'opposition parlementaire 1715–1774* (Paris: Armand Colin, 1970), 217. R. R. Palmer highlights the crucial role of the

parlements in paving the way for the nation to challenge the king in "The national idea in France before the Revolution," *Journal of the History of Ideas* 1 (1940): 103.

6. See especially the reply of Louis XV to the *parlement* of Paris on March 3, 1766 in the so-called *séance de la flagellation*, in Jules Flammermont, ed., *Remontrances du Parlement de Paris au XVIIIe siècle*, vol. 2 (Paris: Imprimerie Nationale, 1895), 556–57.

7. The 1771 "Maupeou compromise" (named for the king's chancellor) allowed the *parlements* to make preliminary remonstrances on the condition that these remained secret. See Egret, *Louis XV*, 186. As noted above, this secrecy was honored more in the breach. For more on Maupeou's "revolution," see Colin Jones, *The Great Nation: France from Louis XV to Napoleon* (New York: Columbia University Press, 2002), 280–92.

8. See Simon Schama, *Citizens: A Chronicle of the French Revolution* (New York: Viking, 1989), 103, 106.

9. See Roger Bickart, *Les Parlements et la notion de souveraineté nationale* (Paris: Félix Alcan, 1932), 47–48; Carcassonne, *Montesquieu*, 429; and Kingsley Martin, *French Liberal Thought in the Eighteenth Century*, ed. J. P. Mayer (London: Phoenix House, 1962; orig. pub. 1929), 187–88.

10. "Souverains," *Encyclopédie* (1765), 15:423b.

11. See Carcassonne, *Montesquieu*, 392.

12. See, for example, Jean-Yves Guiomar, *L'idéologie nationale* (Paris: Éditions Champ libre, 1974), 52.

13. H. F. Stewart and Paul Desjardins, Preface, *French Patriotism in the Nineteenth Century (1814–1833) Traced in Contemporary Texts* (Cambridge: Cambridge University Press, 1923), xxii. It had been suggested as early as the sixteenth century that "Le Royaume est au Roi, et le Roi est aussi au Royaume." Register of the *Parlement*, December 20, 1527, in Bickart, *Les Parlements*, 49.

14. "Autorité," *Encyclopédie* (1751), 1:898b–899a.

15. See Pasquale Pasquino, "Le Concept de Nation et les Fondements Du Droit Public de la Révolution: Sieyès," in *L'héritage de la Révolution française*, ed. François Furet (Paris: Hachette, 1989), 329 n. 50; and Bickart, *Les Parlements*, 43.

16. On this distinction, see the Remonstrances of the *Parlement* of Toulouse, January 12, 1788, and the Arrêté of the *Parlement* of Grenoble, January 24, 1788, in Bickart, *Les Parlements*, 17, 32. As early as 1574, François Hotman wrote that "ceux qui estoyent appellez à la couronne de France, estoyent eleus pour estre Rois sous certaines loix et conditions qui leur estoyent limitées: et non point comme tyrans avec une puissance absolue, excessive et infinie." Hotman, *La Gaule Françoise* (Cologne: Hierome Bertulphe, 1574, repr. Paris: Fayard, 1991), 68–69. However, it was not until late in the eighteenth century that the *parlements* were able to use this observation as a basis for reasserting their political power. See Flammermont, Introduction, *Remontrances du parlement de Paris au XVIIIe siècle*, vol. 1 (Paris: Imprimerie Nationale, 1888), p. xliii.

17. Mably, *Des Droits et des Devoirs du Citoyen*, letter 3 (written in 1758, first published in 1789), xxv. See also the Grand Remonstrances of the *Parlement* of Paris, 1753, in Cobban, *A History of Modern France*, vol. 1, 130.

18. Remonstrances of February 18, 1771, written by Chrétien Guillaume de Lamoignon de Malesherbes, magistrate of the Paris Cour des Aides, in Carcassonne, *Montesquieu*, 408.

19. On public opinion and the *parlements*, see Doyle, "The *Parlements* of France," 453; and Malteste de Villey's unpublished remonstrances of 1771 for the *Parlement* of Dijon, in Carcassonne, *Montesquieu*, 410.

20. *Remontrances d'un citoyen aux Parlemens de France*, in Carcassonne, *Montesquieu*, 441–42.

21. Jean Denis Lanjuinais, *Préservatif contre l'avis à mes compatriotes* (Oct. 1788), *Oeuvres de Lanjuinais*, vol. 1, 139, cited in Jean Egret, *La Pré-Révolution Française 1787–1788* (Paris: Presse Universitaires de France, 1962), 337.

22. See Bickart, *Les Parlements*, 260.

23. Appeals to this Edict can be found, for example, in the Remonstrances of the *Parlement* of Rennes, July 24, 1771, in Bickart, *Les Parlements*, 82.

24. See Cobban, *A History of Modern France*, vol. 1, 130; and Bickart, *Les Parlements*, 106. The idea of the people was associated with the masses, with whose welfare the *parlements* were not particularly concerned. See Jacques Godechot, "Nation, patrie, nationalisme et patriotisme en France au XVIIIe siècle," *Annales historiques de la Révolution française* 43 (1971), 494.

25. See Godechot, "Nation, patrie, nationalisme," 486; and Gérard Fritz, *L'Idée de peuple en France du XVIIe au XIXe siècle* (Strasbourg: Presses Universitaires de Strasbourg, 1988), 2, 5, 60.

26. Remonstrances of the *Parlement* of Bordeaux, February 25, 1771, in Bickart, *Les Parlements*, 79.

27. See the Arrêté of the *Parlement* of Rennes, April 16, 1771, in Bickart, *Les Parlements*, 54.

28. See the Arrêté of the *Parlement* of Rennes, March 16, 1771; the Remonstrances of the *Parlement* of Toulouse, April 6, 1771; and the Objects of Remonstrances of the *Parlement* of Rennes, December 6, 1787; in Bickart, *Les Parlements*, 66–67.

29. Interestingly, at the time of Louis XIV, Colbert had remarked to Pomponne with regard to French soldiers who had crossed into Holland: "You are well aware that the obligation towards his sovereign that every subject contracts at birth can be annulled only with the sovereign's consent." This statement shows the early appearance of a contractualist paradigm, but one in which the sovereign retained exclusive control over the exit option. See Marie-Madeleine Martin, *The Making of France: The Origins and Development of the Idea of National Unity*, trans. Barbara and Robert North (London: Eyre and Spottiswoode, 1951), 173.

30. Carcassonne, *Montesquieu*, 397.

31. See the following Remonstrances: *Parlement* of Rennes, February 16, 1788, in Egret, *La Pré-Révolution Française*, 204–5; *Parlement* of Dijon, April 16, 1771, in Bickart, *Les Parlements*, 95; *Parlement* of Bordeaux, February 25, 1771, in Egret, *Louis XV*, 193–94. For stronger claims on behalf of the nation against the king, see the Remonstrances of April 11, 1788, in J. M. Roberts and Richard Cobb, eds., *French Revolution Documents* (Oxford: Basil Blackwell, 1966), 24–25, and the Arrêté of the *Parlement* of Brittany, March 1, 1788, in Egret, *Louis XV*, 243.

32. The *parlement* of Rouen invoked the "constitutive unity" of the *parlement* in its remonstrances of August 6, 1757, in Bickart, *Les Parlements*, 157. See also Keith Michael Baker, *Inventing the French Revolution: Essays on French Political Culture in the Eighteenth Century* (Cambridge: Cambridge University Press, 1990), 232.

33. Remonstrances of the *Parlement* of Paris, August 4, 1756, in Egret, *La Pré-Révolution Française*, 236; see also Egret, *Louis XV*, 47, 65. The *théorie des classes* helps explain why the *parlement* is referred to in both the singular and the plural.

34. See Bickart, *Les Parlements*, 99; Guiomar, *L'idéologie nationale*, 53; and the Remonstrances of the *Parlement* of Rennes, August 12, 1757, in Egret, *Louis XV*, 84.

35. Arrêt of the Council of State, March 27, 1766, responding to the claim that ties of obedience may be broken, made by Arrêtés of the *Parlement* of Grenoble, March 22 and July 30, 1765, in Bickart, *Les Parlements*, 69. See also the *séance royale* of November 19, 1787, in Bickart, *Les Parlements*, 69–70.

36. Remonstrances of the *Parlement* of Rennes, February 16, 1788, in Bickart, *Les Parlements*, 70.

37. *Oxford Encyclopedic English Dictionary*, 2d ed., ed. Judy Pearsall and Bill Trumble (New York: Oxford University Press, 1995), 1024.

38. *Le Nouveau Petit Robert* (Paris: Dictionnaires Le Robert, 1993), 1546.

39. Remonstrances of the *Parlement* of Rennes, February 16, 1788, in Bickart, *Les Parlements*, 106. See also Egret, *Louis XV*, 91.

40. See Bickart, *Les Parlements*, 111, 113; and Cobban, *A History of Modern France*, vol. 1, 130.

41. See *Mémoires au sujet d'un nouvel Écrit contre le Parlement, intitulé: Observations sur le refus que fait le Châtelet de reconnoître la Chambre royale, etc.* (1755); the statement by playwright Charles Collé (1771); and *Tableau des différents âges* (1772); all cited in Carcassonne, *Montesquieu*, 397, 421, 462.

42. Statement of December 8, 1788, in Egret, *La Pré-Révolution Française*, 350.

43. See Cobban, *A History of Modern France*, vol. 1, 132–41.

44. See Gabriel Ardant, "Financial Policy and Economic Infrastructure of Modern States and Nations," in *The Formation of National States in Western Europe*, ed. Charles Tilly (Princeton, NJ: Princeton University Press, 1975), 214. See also Palmer, "The national idea in France," 105. On August 8, 1788, the king summoned the Estates-General to meet on May 1, 1789; the *parlement* registered this declaration on September 25.

45. See the *Lettre du roi pour la convocation des États généraux à Versailles le 27 avril 1789*, issued on January 24, 1789, *AP*, vol. 1, 543–44.

46. Martin, *French Liberal Thought*, 89.

47. Edme Champion, *La France d'après les Cahiers de 1789*, 5th ed. (Paris: A. Colin, 1921), 236–37. See also Schama, *Citizens*, 314.

48. See Schama, *Citizens*, 859.

49. Beatrice Fry Hyslop, *French nationalism in 1789, according to the General Cahiers* (New York: Columbia University Press, 1934), 65.

50. The call for "une charte" between king and nation was pervasive in the *cahiers*. See Alphonse Aulard, *Le Patriotisme français de la Renaissance à la Révolution* (Paris: Étienne Chiron, 1921), 92; Hyslop, *French nationalism in 1789*, 66; Lucien Jaume, *Le discours jacobin et la démocratie* (Paris: Fayard, 1989), 299; and Bernard Groethuysen, *Philosophie de la Révolution Française* (Paris: Gallimard, 1956), 268. An interesting exception to the endorsement of the Estates-General came from French colonies in the Caribbean whose representatives feared that a metropolitan declaration of freedom would threaten their economic interest in preserving slavery. See the March 13, 1790, submission of the Assemblée coloniale de Guadeloupe, and the March 19, 1790, Instructions de l'Isle Martinique à ses députés à l'Assemblée nationale, in Monique Pouliquen and Jean Favier, eds., *Doléances des Peuples Coloniaux à l'Assemblée Nationale Constituante, 1789–1790* (Paris: Archives Nationales, 1989), 42, 59.

51. See the *Catéchisme national*, (Paris: En France, 1789; repr. Paris: Hachette, 1976), 15, 17; Léonard Snetlage, *Nouveau dictionnaire français contenant les expressions de nouvelle Création du Peuple Français. Ouvrage additionnel au Dictionnaire de l'Academie Française et à tout autre Vocabulaire* (Gottingue: chez Jean Chrêtien Dieterich Librairie, 1795), 48; Philippe-Antoine Grouvelle, *De l'Autorité de Montesquieu dans la révolution présente* (February 1789), 61; and Pierre-Louis de Lacretelle, *De la Convocation de la prochaine tenue des États généraux en France* (1788), 3, 20–22.

52. See Guillaume-Joseph Saige, *Catéchisme du citoyen, ou Éléments du droit public français, par demandes et réponses, suivi de fragments politiques par le même auteur* (En France, 1788), 25, 54, 115 n. 4, 179.

53. See Groethuysen, *Philosophie de la Révolution française*, 256. See also Claude Nicolet, *L'idée républicaine en France (1789–1924), Essai d'histoire critique* (Paris: Gallimard, 1982), 21.

54. See Patrice Higonnet, *Sister Republics: The Origins of French and American Republicanism* (Cambridge, MA: Harvard University Press, 1988), 222; see also Higonnet, *Sister Republics*, 158; and Maurice Cranston, "The Sovereignty of the Nation," in *The Political Culture of the French Revolution*, ed. Colin Lucas (Oxford: Pergamon, 1988), 94.

55. André Chénier, article in the *Journal de Paris*, February 26, 1792, in *Oeuvres en prose de André Chénier*, ed. Louis Moland (Paris: Garnier Frères, 1879), 126. Jean-Pierre Gallais wrote anonymously in *Extrait d'un dictionnaire inutile, Composé par une Société en commandite, & rédigé par un homme seul* (A 500 lieues de l'Assemblée nationale, 1790), 179 n. 1 on "Legislation": "Dans chaque ville, dans chaque village, on retrouve la nation exerçant tous les droits de la souveraineté, ce qui nous procure par fois des souverains assez féroces."

56. André-Quentin Buée, *Nouveau dictionnaire pour servir à l'intelligence des termes mis en vogue par la Révolution* (Paris: January 1792), 96–97.

57. Arrêt du Conseil, July 5, 1788, in Egret, *La Pré-Révolution Française*, 325.

58. See the anonymous *Credo du Tiers-État, ou symbole politico-moral. A l'usage de tous les amis de l'État & de l'Humanité* (1789), xx.

59. Lacretelle, *De la Convocation*, 6.

60. Lacretelle, *De La Convocation*, 7.

61. See Chantreau, *Dictionnaire national*, 49.

62. M***, *Dictionnaire raisonné de plusieurs mots qui sont dans la bouche de tout le monde, et ne présentent pas des idées bien nettes* (Paris: Au Palais-Royal, 1790), 44.

63. M***, *Dictionnaire raisonné*, 175.

64. M***, *Dictionnaire raisonné*, 144 (emphasis added).

65. See Georges Lefebvre, *The Coming of the French Revolution*, trans. R. R. Palmer (Princeton, NJ: Princeton University Press, 1947; orig. pub. 1939), 52.

66. Carcassonne, *Montesquieu*, 665.

67. Desmoulins, *La France Libre* (Paris, 1789), 2, trans. in Hyslop, *French nationalism in 1789*, 17.

68. *Moniteur* 1, no. 9 (June 17, 1789): 82–83.

69. *AP*, vol. 8, 137–39. The deputies vowed: "de ne jamais nous séparer . . . et de nous réunir partout où les circonstances l'exigent, jusqu'à ce que la Constitution du royaume soit établie et affermie sur des fondements solides."

70. On the self-perception of the delegates as representatives of the entire nation, see the cahier of the Nobles of Montargis, in Hyslop, *French nationalism in 1789*, 76l. See also Roland Debbasch, *Le Principe Révolutionnaire d'Unité et d'Indivisibilité de la République* (France: Economica, 1988), 44.

71. See Lynn Hunt, "The National Assembly," in *The French Revolution and the Creation of Modern Political Culture, Vol. 1, The Political Culture of the Old Régime*, ed. Keith Michael Baker (Oxford: Pergamon, 1987), 413.

72. This development was foretold in a remarkably prescient *note de lecture* by the Marquis d'Argenson in 1753: "si jamais la Nation allait rentrer dans sa volonté et dans ses droits, elle ne manquerait pas d'établir une Assemblée nationale universelle bien autrement dangereuse à l'autorité royale. . . . La Nation se réserverait la législation et ne donnerait au Roi qu'une exécution provisoire." *Mémoires et Journal inédit du Marquis d'Argenson*, vol. 5 (Paris: Jannet, 1858), 128–29.

73. See Pasquino, "Le Concept de Nation," 314.

74. *AP*, vol. 8, 611. See also Istvan Hont, "The Permanent Crisis of a Divided Mankind: 'Contemporary Crisis of the Nation State' in Historical Perspective," *Political Studies* 42, (1994): 200.

75. In the eyes of many contemporaries, the French polity was being fundamentally "regenerated" and transformed. See *Confédération nationale, ou récit exact et circonstancié de tout ce qui s'est passé à Paris, le 14 juillet 1790, à la Fédération* (Paris: Garnery, L'an second de la liberté, 1790), 2; and Comte Antoine de Rivarol, *Petit dictionnaire des grands hommes de la Révolution; Par un Citoyen actif, ci-devant* Rien (Paris: Au Palais Royal, Imprimerie nationale, 1790), vi–vii.

76. Jean Tulard, "Les Événements," in *Histoire et dictionnaire de la Révolution française*, ed. Jean Tulard, Jean-François Fayard, and Alfred Fierro (Paris: Robert Laffont, 1987), 62. For an incisive critique of this view of the king, see *Catéchisme national, par demandes et par réponses, à l'usage des patriotes démocrates. Par un Citoyen Monarchicrate* (Paris: De l'Imprimerie du Club de 1789, 1790), 7–8, 12–13, 24.

77. Debbasch, *Le Principe Révolutionnaire*, 49, referring to the decrees of August 4 abolishing feudal privileges. See also Martin Wight, "International Legitimacy," *Systems of States* (Bristol and Swansea: Leicester University Press, 1977), 153.

78. *Catalogue de la Bibliothèque nationale sur la Révolution française*, item 298, "Constitution du 3 septembre 1791. En marge du premier feuillet, est écrite l'acceptation du roi."

79. *Déclaration du roi adressée à tous les Français à sa sortie de Paris*, June 20, 1791, *AP*, vol. 27, 379.

80. Alfred Cobban, *In Search of Humanity: The Role of the Enlightenment in Modern History* (London: Johnathan Cape, 1960), 211.

81. The classic work on Sieyès remains Paul Bastid, *Sieyès et sa pensée* (Paris: Hachette, 1939). See also Murray Forsyth, *Reason and Revolution: the political thought of the Abbé Sieyès* (Leicester: Leicester University Press, 1987). Pasquale Pasquino has sought to resurrect Sieyès as a foundational French constitutional theorist, most extensively in his *Sieyes et l'invention de la constitution en France* (Paris: Éditions Odile Jacob, 1998), which also includes a useful selection of

Sieyès's unpublished texts. Arguments persist about the correct spelling of Sieyès's name; the most widespread version is employed here.

82. Pasquino, *Sieyes et l'invention de la constitution en France*, 54.

83. Sieyès, *Quelques idées de constitution, applicables à la ville de Paris* (A Versailles: chez Baudouin, Imprimeur de l'Assemblée Nationale, July 1789), 30.

84. *Discours sur le véto royal*, September 7, 1789, in *AP*, vol. 8, 595. See Jean-Jacques Clere, "Etat-Nation-Citoyen au temps de la Révolution française," in *L'idée de nation*, ed. Marie-Françoise Conrad, Jean Ferrari, and Jean-Jacques Wunenburger (Dijon: Éditions universitaires de Dijon, 1986), 107.

85. While Rousseau posited the top-down formulation of the national will by an omniscient legislator, Sieyès seems to have envisioned a process akin to what today would be called "deliberative democracy." Sieyès writes: "Quand on se réunit, c'est pour délibérer, c'est pour connaître les avis les uns des autres, pour profiter des lumières réciproques, pour confronter les volontés particulières, pour les modifier, pour les concilier, enfin pour obtenir un résultat commun à la pluralité." *AP*, vol. 8, 595. However, at times, he speaks of the people's representatives in terms more reminiscent of Rousseau: the people wants deputies "qui soient habiles à être *les interprètes de son voeu* et les défenseurs de ses intérêts" (emphasis added). Sieyès, *Qu'est-ce que le Tiers État?*, ed. Roberto Zapperi (Geneva: Librairie Droz, 1970; orig. pub. 1789), 134 [hereafter cited as *TE*].

86. Sieyès, *Bases de l'ordre social ou série raisonnée de quelques idées fondamentales de l'état social et politique* (An III), in Pasquino, *Sieyes et l'invention*, 185.

87. Sieyès, *Bases de l'ordre social*, 185.

88. Pasquino, *Sieyes et l'invention*, 127. See also Sieyès, *Quelques idées de constitution*, 30–31.

89. Pasquino, *Sieyes et l'invention*, 67.

90. Paul Bastid, "Sieyès et la pensée politique de la Révolution," *La révolution française: revue d'histoire moderne et contemporaine*, no. 18 (1938): 147–48; see also Bastid, "Sieyès et la pensée," 164. Pasquino also addresses this issue in "Emmanuel Sieyes, Benjamin Constant et le 'Gouvernement des Modernes.' Contribution à l'histoire du concept de représentation politique," *Revue française de science politique* 37, no. 2 (April 1987): 227.

91. Sieyès, *Contre la ré-totale* (unpublished, 1792), reprinted in Pasquino, *Sieyes et l'invention*, 175–76. Other sources date this text to 1795, after the Reign of Terror.

92. Sieyès, *Limites de la souveraineté* (An III), in Pasquino, *Sieyes et l'invention*, 177, 179.

93. Clere, "Etat-Nation-Citoyen," 107. See also Jacques Dehaussy, "La Révolution Française et le Droit des Gens," in *Révolution et Droit International* (Paris: A. Pedone, 1989), 60–62 nn. 20–21.

94. See Clere, "Etat-Nation-Citoyen," 108; and Bastid, "Sieyès et la pensée," 149.

95. See Bastid, "Sieyès et la pensée," 154, 161: "Unité toute seule est despotisme. Division toute seule est anarchie. Division avec unité, voilà la formule."

96. Sieyès writes in *Quelques idées de constitution*, 2: "Sous ce nouveau rapport . . . sont de vraies parties intégrantes & essentielles *d'un même tout*. Cette observation est importante, pour qu'on ne nous compare jamais aux *États-Unis* de l'Amérique." See Clere, "Etat-Nation-Citoyen," 112; and Bastid, "Sieyès et la pensée," 150–52, 163. From a Breton perspective, the slippage between the expression of social unity and the imperative of territorial integrity in Sieyès's vision and in the 1791 Constitution had oppressive implications. See Wolfgang Geiger, "L'Etat-Nation: concept révolutionnaire," *Dalc'homp song* 25 (1989): 23. The epithet "fédéraliste" came to be attached to the Girondin party, which argued for administrative decentralization in the face of Parisian preeminence. This is different from the "federalism" of the 1790 "Fête de la Fédération," in which brigades from all parts of France came together and vowed to form an indissoluble whole.

97. See the discussion in Pasquino, *Sieyes et l'invention*, 62–72.

98. See Bastid, "Sieyès et la pensée," 146; see also ibid. 147. Mitchell Garrett writes in *The Estates General of 1789: The Problems of Composition and Organization* (NY: D. Appleton-Century Co. Inc., 1935), 221: "When the Estates General met on May 5, 1789, the deputies of the third estate did not know each other by sight, but they already knew themselves to be of one mind and spirit." This description anticipates Benedict Anderson's idea of the nation in *Imagined Communities: Reflections on the Origin and Spread of Nationalism* (London: Verso, 1983).

99. Sieyès writes in *TE*, 157 n. 1: "La nation ne contracte point avec ses mandataires, elle *commet* à l'exercice de ses pouvoirs."

100. See Pasquino, "Le Concept de Nation," 327 n. 33. Sieyès's idea of the nation as the constituent power, rather than a contracting party, reinforces the view that the nation (identified by, but not reducible to, state institutions) may change its constitutional form regardless of violations by the existing government, a highly permissive view of national self-determination. The marquis de Condorcet also distinguished these two conceptions: the absolute (in which the people can change its governmental forms at will) and the contractual (in which the contract between governors and governed may not legitimately be dissolved in the absence of governmental violations). See Condorcet, *Réflexions sur la révolution de 1688 et sur celle du 10 août 1792*, in *Oeuvres*, vol. 12 (Paris: F. Didot frères, 1849), 209–10.

101. *TE*, 201.

102. *TE*, 121.

103. *TE*, 130.

104. *TE*, 126, 128, 149.

105. *TE*, 167 n. 1.

106. *TE*, 203. As an order and as a nation, the Third Estate is defined in four ways: by profession, by usefulness, by social participation, and by lack of privilege.

107. *TE*, 154, 157. When Sieyès invokes "la plus importante des loix, celle qui convertira les ordres en *une* nation," he has in mind the fourth criterion for nationhood, the absence of privilege, enshrined in the August 1789 decrees. *TE*, 131 n. 2.

108. *TE*, 178; see *TE* 182 for the claim that the only legitimate association is one that is "volontaire et libre."

109. *TE*, 178.

110. *TE*, 188.

111. *TE*, 172, 177. See also Pasquino, *Sieyes et l'invention*, 62, 64.

112. Sieyès, Compte Rendu de *Qu'est-ce que le tiers état?* (1789), in Pasquino, *Sieyes et l'invention*, 168.

113. *TE*, 126.

114. *TE*, 180. See also *TE*, 128; and Baker, *Inventing the French Revolution*, 257.

115. *TE*, 189.

116. *TE*, 160; see also *TE* 134, 198, 217, 218. To be "disposed of" in this sense means to be governed, but it also has connotations of being treated as chattel or property.

117. Pasquino, *Sieyes et l'invention*, 27, 113. See also ibid. 68; and Sieyès's 1791 *Représentation et élections*, reproduced in Pasquino, *Sieyes et l'invention*, 171–73.

118. Charles-Frédéric Reinhard, *Le néologiste français ou Vocabulaire portatif des mots les plus nouveaux de la langue Française* (Nurnberg: Grattenaver, 1796), 99–100.

119. These documents are reproduced in Jacques Godechot, *Les Constitutions de la France Depuis 1789*, rev. ed. (Paris: Garnier Flammarion, 1995; orig. pub. 1979).

120. *Principes sur l'exercice de la puissance législative et de la puissance exécutrice* (Paris: Bibliotheque Royale, April 1789), 45.

121. *Parliamentary History*, vol. 30, 901–02 (May 6–7, 1792).

Chapter Three: Composition

1. The language of "regeneration" was pervasive in characterizing the Revolutionaries' project and mandate. See, for example, *Moniteur* 1, no. 7 (June 15, 1789): 70; and *Moniteur* 1, no. 25 (July 25–27, 1789): 214.

2. *Déclaration des droits de l'homme et du Citoyen du 26 août 1789*, reprinted in Jacques Godechot, *Les Constitutions de la France Depuis 1789*, updated ed. (Paris: Garnier Flammarion, 1995; orig. pub. 1979), 33–35.

3. Despite its importance in Revolutionary rhetoric, widespread literacy and linguistic homogeneity were not achieved in France until the late nineteenth century. See Eugen Weber, *Peasants into Frenchmen: The modernization of rural France 1870–1914* (Stanford, CA: Stanford University Press, 1976).

4. See Suzanne Citron, *Le mythe national: L'histoire de France en question*, 2nd ed. (Paris: Éditions Ouvrières, 1991), 199.

5. See Gérard Noiriel, "L'identification des citoyens. Naissance de l'état civil républicain," *Genèses* 13 (Autumn 1993): 2.

6. See Jean-Yves Guiomar, *L'idéologie nationale* (Paris: Éditions Champ libre, 1974), 45, 47.

7. See Jacques LeGoff, *Histoire de la France: L'Etat et les pouvoirs* (Paris: Seuil, 1989), 286; and Bernard Groethuysen, *Philosophie de la Révolution Française* (Paris: Gallimard, 1956), 257.

8. The exclusionary aspects of Revolutionary ideology emphasized in this chapter do not negate the Revolutionaries' attempts at inclusion. For a corrective to the sweeping denunciation of Jacobinism, see Patrice Higonnet, *Goodness Beyond Virtue: Jacobins During the French Revolution* (Cambridge, MA: Harvard University Press, 1998). For more critical views of some of the Revolutionaires' attempts at inclusion, see, for example, Ronald Schechter, *Obstinate Hebrews: Representations of Jews in France, 1715–1815* (Berkeley and Los Angeles: University of California Press, 2003), 150–93 (discussing the puzzle of why the Revolutionaries spent so much time debating the "Jewish question" when their September 1791 emancipation of the Jews, in fact, had little practical impact), and Colin Jones, *The Great Nation: France from Louis XV to Napoleon* (New York: Columbia University Press, 2002), 563 (suggesting that the 1791 abolition of slavery in France was a "token gesture," and that its 1794 abolition in the colonies was also a "rhetorical gesture" because France's contact with its Caribbean colonies "had long been severed by England's naval blockade"). At no time was the French nation considered all-inclusive, although it remained unclear whether national membership was confined to "active citizens" or encompassed all the nonreactionary inhabitants of France. Despite women's participation in the Revolutionary movement, notably in a 1789 march on Versailles, their claims for political participation and recognition (encapsulated in Olympe de Gouges's 1791 *Déclaration des Droits de la Femme et de la Citoyenne*) went unheeded until 1944, when they were given the right to vote. See Joan Landes, *Women and the Public Sphere in the Age of the French Revolution* (Ithaca: Cornell University Press, 1988).

9. Internal revolt and external military defeat bred insecurity and triggered violent repression. For example, an insurrection on August 10, 1792, led to the arrest of thousands of supposed partisans of the king. The capture of Verdun by Prussian troops on September 2, 1792, sparked a panic that led to the officially

sanctioned and indiscriminate butchery of prisoners (the "September massacres"). This first wave of repression subsided after the September 20 victory against the Prussians at Valmy. The second wave was sparked by the fall of the Girondin Party on June 2, 1793. The victorious Montagnards organized a terror to discourage support for a Girondin return: two thousand executions took place in Paris in June 1794 alone.

10. *Oeuvres de Turgot*, vol. 4, ed. G. Schelle (Paris, 1913–23), 576. See Keith Baker, "French Political Thought at the Accession of Louis XVI," *The Journal of Modern History* 50, no. 2 (June 1978): 295. Mirabeau called France "une agrégation inconstituée de peuples désunis." See Edme Champion, *La France d'après les Cahiers de 1789*, 5th ed. (Paris: A. Colin, 1921), 45.

11. See, for example, "Lettre du roi pour la convocation des États-Généraux à Versailles le 27 avril, 1789," in J. M. Thompson, ed., *French Revolution Documents 1789–94* (Oxford: Basil Blackwell, 1933), 1–2.

12. The clergy of the district of Haut-Limousin declared explicitly that "la résistance d'une province particulière deviendrait un crime de lèse-patrie." *AP*, vol. 3, 562; see Roland Debbasch, *Le Principe Révolutionnaire d'Unité et d'Indivisibilité de la République* (France: Economica, 1988), 41. This statement stands in tension with a purely voluntarist ideal of national self-determination.

13. These include: Title III, Article 1 of the 1791 Constitution; Article XXV of the "Table of the Rights of Man" preceding the 1793 Constitution; and Article VII of the Constitutional Act of June 24, 1793. Documents reprinted in Godechot, *Les Constitutions de la France*, 38, 82, 83.

14. Just as the *parlements* had borrowed language from Rousseau, so did Marie Joseph de Lafayette (who strongly influenced the wording of this Article) draw in turn on the vocabulary of the *parlements*, particularly in his use of the term "nation" rather than "people." Louis Gottschalk and Margaret Maddox note in *Lafayette in the French Revolution, through the October Days* (Chicago: University of Chicago Press, 1969), 223 that Article III came almost verbatim from Lafayette's draft. This draft shows that Lafayette was looking for a strong, not a weak or limiting, adverb when he chose the word "essentiellement"; it can be found in Antoine De Baecque, Wolfgang Schmale, and Michel Vovelle, *L'an 1 des droits de l'homme* (Paris: Presses du CNRS, 1988), 66. This evidence tends to contradict Roland Debbasch's construction of the wording of Article III as restrained and cautious in Debbasch, *Le Principe Révolutionnaire d'Unité*, 50 and n. 79; and Charles Vaughan's similar interpretation in his Introduction to *Du Contrat Social ou Principes Du Droit Politique*, by J. J. Rousseau (Manchester: Manchester University Press, 1947), lxvii.

15. This role, consecrated by Article III, was announced by the Abbé Sieyès on June 15; see *Moniteur* 1, no. 7 (June 15, 1789): 71. See also Istvan Hont, "The Permanent Crisis of a Divided Mankind: 'Contemporary Crisis of the Nation State' in Historical Perspective," *Political Studies* 42 (1994): 196 n. 55; Halvdan Koht, "L'esprit national et l'idée de la souveraineté du peuple," *Bulletin of the International Committee of Historical Sciences*, no. 7 (October 1929): 223; and Gilbert

Chinard, *The Letters of Lafayette and Jefferson* (Baltimore, MD: Johns Hopkins and Paris: Les Belles Lettres, 1929), 136.

16. See Bronislaw Baczko, "Le contrat social des Français: Sieyès et Rousseau," in *The French Revolution and the Creation of Modern Political Culture*, vol. 1, ed. Keith Michael Baker (Oxford: Pergamon, 1987), 499. See also Hans Kohn, *The Idea of Nationalism: A study in its origins and background* (New York: MacMillan, 1944), 237; and Claude Nicolet, *L'idée républicaine en France (1789–1924), Essai d'histoire critique* (Paris: Gallimard, 1982), 445.

17. See Patrice Higonnet, *Sister Republics: The Origins of French and American Republicanism* (Cambridge, MA: Harvard University Press, 1988), 261; and, more generally, Carol Blum, *Rousseau and the Republic of Virtue: The Language of Politics in the French Revolution* (Ithaca: Cornell, 1986).

18. See Dominique Schnapper, *La Communauté des Citoyens: sur l'idée moderne de nation* (Paris: Gallimard, 1994), 47–48; and Jean-Claude Caron, *La nation, l'État, et la démocratie en France de 1789 à 1914* (Paris: Armand Colin, 1995), 23.

19. See Hedley Bull, *Justice in International Relations*, 1983–84 Hagey Lectures, University of Waterloo, 7; and Morton J. Frisch, "The Emergence of Nationalism as a Political Philosophy," *History of European Ideas* 16, no. 4–6 (1993): 888.

20. Political cartoon reproduced in Simon Schama, *Citizens: A Chronicle of the French Revolution* (New York: Viking, 1989), 850.

21. Lucien Jaume, *Le discours jacobin et la démocratie* (Paris: Fayard, 1989), 399. See also ibid. 12; and Caron, *La nation, l'Etat, et la démocratie en France*, 43.

22. See Pierre-Nicolas Chantreau, *Dictionnaire national et anecdotique pour servir à l'intelligence des mots dont notre langue s'est enrichie depuis la révolution, et à la nouvelle signification qu'ont reçue quelques anciens mots* (Paris: A Politicopolis, 1790), 115, 117.

23. Maurice Cranston, "The Sovereignty of the Nation," in *The Political Culture of the French Revolution*, ed. Colin Lucas (Oxford: Pergamon, 1988), 95 (emphasis added).

24. Rousseau insists that only a national character can generate sufficient attachment to ensure the survival of a nation-state: "tout peuple a, ou doit avoir, un caractère national; s'il en manquait, il faudrait commencer par le lui donner." Rousseau, "Project pour la Corse," *The Political Writings of Jean-Jacques Rousseau*, ed. C. E. Vaughan, vol. 2 (Oxford: Basil Blackwell, 1962), 319. This idea of creating a national identity stands in tension with the fiction of its automaticity.

25. Edme Champion, "L'Unité nationale et la Révolution," *La Révolution française* 19 (July–December 1890), 21–22; the first citation is from Mirabeau, the second from Rabaut Saint-Étienne.

26. Reinhard Bendix elaborates in *Kings or People: Power and the Mandate to Rule* (Berkeley, CA: University of California Press, 1978), 373: "Frenchmen were

born as citizens before they became Catholics, Protestants, or Jews. . . . A petition of the Jews from Avignon stated, 'There are no more Jews in France. There are no more Catholics, Protestants, Jews, sectarians of any kind, there are only Frenchmen.'" Citation from Zosa Szajkowski, *Jews and the French Revolutions of 1789, 1830, and 1848* (New York: KATV Publishing House, 1970), 584–85. Wolfgang Geiger, "L'Etat-Nation: concept révolutionnaire," *Dalc'homp song* 25 (1989): 20 cites the oath taken at the ceremony of federation at Pontivy in 1789: "Nous déclarons solennellement que, n'étant ni Bretons ni Angevins, mais Français et citoyens du même Empire (synonyme pour 'royaume' à l'époque, W. G.), nous renonçons à tous nos privilèges locaux et que nous les abjurons comme anti-constitutionnels."

27. Doléances des habitants du Sénégal, April 15, 1789, in Monique Pouliquen and Jean Favier, ed., *Doléances des Peuples Coloniaux à l'Assemblée Nationale Constituante, 1789–1790* (Paris: Archives Nationales, 1989), 99. The inclusiveness of this conception was not representative. Despite the emergence of abolitionist societies, the *Citoyens libres de couleur de Paris* (Free citizens of color of Paris) were quick to point out the hypocritical disjunction between egalitarian rhetoric and exclusionary reality that made them feel like "étrangers dans leur propre pays." *Doléances des Peuples Coloniaux*, 147–60.

28. Adresse des gardes nationaux de l'île de France, July 30, 1790, in *Doléances des Peuples Coloniaux*, 129.

29. Mémoire des Malabars de Pondichéry, March 11, 1790, in *Doléances des Peuples Coloniaux*, 143. The idea of colonized peoples as themselves French became a staple of French colonial policy, with children in the colonies famously being taught about "nos ancêtres les Gaulois."

30. Mona Ozouf, *La fête révolutionnaire* (Paris: Gallimard, 1976), 71. André-Quentin Buée presciently observed in *Nouveau dictionnaire pour servir à l'intelligence des termes mis en vogue par la Révolution* (Paris: January 1792), 128: "L'unité! l'unité! crie-t-on de toutes parts. Mais n'est-ce pas la *similitude* que l'on prend pour l'unité?"

31. The "Civil Constitution of the Clergy" of July 12, 1790, suppressed religious orders and required all priests to swear an oath of allegiance to the nation, the king, and the Constitution. The refusal of many to do this created a profound division within the clergy, and within the French population.

32. Abbé Grégoire, speech of September 29, 1789, in Jean Tulard, "Les Événements," in *Histoire et dictionnaire de la Révolution française*, ed. Jean Tulard, Jean-François Fayard, and Alfred Fierro (Paris: Robert Laffont, 1987), 61.

33. Grégoire, *Rapport sur la nécessité et les moyens d'anéantir les patois et d'universaliser l'usage de la langue française*, 16 prairial, year II of the Republic (1793), reprinted in H. de Certeau, D. Julia and J. Revel, *Une politique de la langue. La République française et les patois: L'enquête de l'Abbé Grégoire* (Paris: Gallimard, 1975), 300–17.

34. Grégoire, *Rapport*, 302.

35. Grégoire, *Rapport*, 304.

36. Grégoire, *Rapport*, 306.

37. Grégoire, *Rapport*, 309.

38. Grégoire, *Rapport*, 308 (emphasis added).

39. Bertrand de Barère, *Rapport du Comité de Salut Publique sur les Idiomes*, 8 pluviôse, year II (1793), reprinted in de Certeau et. al., *Une politique de la langue*, 291–99.

40. Barère, *Rapport*, 292.

41. Barère, *Rapport*, 292.

42. Barère, *Rapport*, 292, 293.

43. Barère, *Rapport*, 293.

44. Barère, *Rapport*, 293.

45. See Jean-Yves Lartichaux, "Linguistic Politics during the French Revolution," trans. Paul Mankin, *Diogenes* 97 (Spring 1977): 65–84.

46. Barère, *Rapport*, 294, 296.

47. Barère, *Rapport*, 296.

48. Barère, *Rapport*, 292.

49. Barère, *Rapport*, 297.

50. See Lartichaux, "Linguistic Politics," 74, 79.

51. Eric Hobsbawm, *Nations and Nationalism since 1780: Programme, myth, reality* (Cambridge: Cambridge University Press, 1990), 21.

52. Will Kymlicka, *Multicultural Citizenship: A liberal theory of minority rights* (Oxford: Clarendon, 1995), 217 n. 26.

53. See Elie Kedourie, *Nationalism* (London: Hutchinson, 1961), 62, 71; and Liah Greenfeld, *Nationalism: Five Roads to Modernity* (Cambridge, MA: Harvard University Press, 1992), 99.

54. *AP*, vol. 8, 350. See Alphonse Aulard, *Le Patriotisme français de la Renaissance à la Révolution* (Paris: Étienne Chiron, 1921), 130–31; Aulard refers to the night of August 4 as "l'abdication volontaire des divers particularismes." Ibid. 120.

55. Enjubault de la Roche, Report of September 27, 1791, in Champion, "L'Unité nationale et la Révolution," 23 n. 1.

56. Guy Jean-Baptiste Target, *Les états-généraux convoqués par Louis XVI* (Paris, 1789), 20, cited in Boyd Schafer, "Bourgeois Nationalism in the Pamphlets on the Eve of the French Revolution," *Journal of Modern History* 10, no. 1 (1938): 34.

57. *Crédo du tiers-état, ou symbole politico-moral. À l'usage de tous les amis de l'État & de l'Humanité* (1789), titre XX. See also Lucien Jaume, "Citoyenneté et souveraineté: le poids de l'absolutisme," in *The French Revolution and the Creation of Modern Political Culture*, vol. 1, 523. The imperative of national unity led to the outlawry of subnational groups and associations, made official in the 1791 Le Chapelier Law suppressing guilds.

58. Patrick Riley, "Rousseau's General Will: Freedom of a Particular Kind," *Political Studies* 39 (1991): 55 (emphasis added).

59. Buée, *Nouveau dictionnaire*, 18.

60. Pasquale Pasquino, *Sieyes et l'invention de la constitution en France* (Paris: Editions Odile Jacob, 1998), 104; see also ibid. 56.

61. Jean-Jacques Clere, "Etat-Nation-Citoyen au temps de la Révolution française," in *L'idée de nation*, ed. Marie-Françoise Conrad, Jean Ferrari, and Jean-Jacques Wunenburger (Dijon: Éditions universitaires de Dijon, 1986), 103, referring to Arthur Young's *Voyages en France*, trans. H. Sée, 3 vols. (Paris: A. Colin, 1931).

62. Clere, "Etat-Nation-Citoyen," 104.

63. See André Blum, "Les fêtes républicaines et la tradition révolutionnaire," *La Révolution Française: revue d'histoire moderne et contemporaine* 72 (January–December 1919), 199. Festivals included the *Fête de la Fédération* (July 14, 1790), the *Fête de la Liberté* (April 15, 1792), the *Fête de l'unité et de l'indivisibilité de la République ou fête de la Régénération* (August 10, 1793), the *Fêtes de la Raison* (20 brumaire year II), the *Fête de l'Etre suprême* (20 prairial year II), and the *Fête de J.-J. Rousseau* (20 vendémiaire year II). The Republican calendar was a symbolic way of reconstituting national reality, marking a rupture with the monarchical past. It consisted of twelve renamed months per year and three "décades" (ten-day weeks) per month; the first year of the Republic dated from September 22, 1792.

64. For a first-hand account of this Festival, see *Confédération nationale, ou récit exact et circonstancié de tout ce qui s'est passé à Paris, le 14 juillet 1790, à la Fédération* (Paris: Garnery, L'an second de la liberté, 1790). See also the second part of Aulard's *Le Patriotisme français*.

65. Jean Sylvain Bailly, "Adresse des citoyens de Paris au peuple français," delivered to the National Assembly on June 5, 1790, in *Confédération nationale*, 2.

66. *Confédération nationale*, 47–48; the double meaning of "demeurer" as to "stay" and to "live" reinforces the idea of Revolutionary fraternity as a new basis for social cohesion and solidarity in daily life.

67. "Poème séculaire par M. de Fontanes," *Confédération nationale*, 187.

68. See the argument in Ann Cohler, *Rousseau and Nationalism* (New York: Basic Books, 1970).

69. For example, Ernest Renan's often-cited arguments against ethnic determinism in his 1882 lecture *Qu'est-ce qu'une nation?* (Paris: Calmann-Levy,

1882) were elaborated in response to the North German Confederation's claims to Alsace-Lorraine, a culturally German area seen by the French as falling within France's "natural" frontiers. The French argument was largely nonvoluntarist, relying on the weight of history rather than the individual choice of Alsace's current inhabitants.

70. Ferdinand Baldensperger found the word "nationalisme" printed in *Mémoires pour servir à l'histoire du Jacobinisme* (1798) by the exiled French priest Jacques Barruel and noted this in *La Révolution française* 59 (July–December 1905), 262–63. The original passage begins: "A l'instant où les hommes se réunirent en nations . . . ils cessèrent de se reconnaître sous un nom commun. Le *Nationalisme*, ou l'amour national prit la place de l'amour général." See also G. Bertier de Sauvigny, "Liberalism, Nationalism, and Socialism: The Birth of Three Words," *The Review of Politics* 32 (April 1970): 155.

71. F. M. Barnard, *Self-Direction and Political Legitimacy in Rousseau and Herder* (Oxford: Clarendon, 1988), 299 n. 31.

72. Schnapper, *La Communauté des Citoyens*, 109.

73. Sieyès stated in 1795: "En fait de gouvernement, et plus généralement en fait de constitution politique, unité toute seule est despotisme, division toute seule est anarchie: division avec unité donne la garantie sociale, sans laquelle toute liberté n'est que précaire." *Moniteur* 25 (Conv. Nat. 12), no. 307 (July 20, 1795): 291.

74. Cited in Boyd Schafer, Letter of rebuttal to Jacques Godechot, April 9, 1974, *Annales historiques de la Révolution française* 47 (1975): 30.

75. Rousseau, *Lettres Écrites de la Montagne*, letter 1 (Neuchâtel: Editions Ides & Calendes, 1962), 77 n. 2.

76. Rousseau, letter to Leonhard Usteri, April 30, 1763, *Correspondance complète de Jean-Jacques Rousseau*, ed. R. A. Leigh (Switzerland: Theodore Besterman, 1972), 127.

Chapter Four: Confrontation

1. See Jacques Dehaussy, "La Révolution Française et le Droit des Gens," in *Révolution et Droit International* (Paris: A. Pedone, 1989), 96. By the turn of the century, French influence extended through areas of what is now Belgium, Holland, Switzerland, Germany, and even Italy.

2. For a comprehensive synthesis of recent scholarship on the Revolutionary period and an interpretation of the Revolution that focuses more on traditional power-political imperatives, see Bailey Stone, *Reinterpreting the French Revolution: A Global-Historical Perspective* (Cambridge: Cambridge University Press, 2002).

3. Jennifer M. Welsh, *Edmund Burke and International Relations: The Commonwealth of Europe and the Crusade against the French Revolution* (London: Macmillan, 1995), 3.

4. Ibid.

5. See Keith Michael Baker, *The Old Regime and the French Revolution* (Chicago: University of Chicago Press, 1997), 459; and Alfred Cobban, *In Search of Humanity: The Role of the Enlightenment in Modern History* (London: Jonathan Cape, 1960), 207, 210.

6. James Mayall argues in "1789 and the liberal theory of international society," *Review of International Studies* 15, no. 4 (October 1989): 305 that "the combination of universalism and nationalism allowed the French, unlike the Russian, revolution to establish a foundation myth for contemporary international society rather than merely an alternative vision and dissident tradition within western international thought."

7. See Théodore Ruyssen, *Les sources doctrinales de l'Internationalisme. Tome 3e: De la Révolution française au milieu du XIXe siècle* (Paris: Presses Universitaires de France, 1961), 13.

8. See Martin Wight's discussion of "Revolutionism" in *International Theory: The Three Traditions*, ed. Gabrielle Wight and Brian Porter (London: Leicester University Press, 1991), 8–12. See also the chapters on the French Revolution in David Armstrong, *Revolution and World Order: The Revolutionary State in International Society* (Oxford: Clarendon, 1993) and in Stephen Walt, *Revolution and War* (Ithaca and London: Cornell University Press, 1996).

9. See Martin Wight, "Western Values in International Relations," in *Diplomatic Investigations: Essays in the Theory of International Politics*, ed. Herbert Butterfield and Martin Wight (London: George Allen & Unwin Ltd., 1966), 96 n. 2; and Andrew Linklater, *Men and Citizens in the Theory of International Relations*, 2nd ed. (London: Macmillan, 1990), 231 n. 18.

10. Montesquieu, *Oeuvres complètes*, vol. 1, ed. Roger Callois (Paris: Pléiade, 1949), 980. See Michael A. Mosher, "Nationalism and the Idea of Europe: How Nationalists Betray the Nation-State," *History of European Ideas* 16, nos. 4–6 (1993): 891.

11. According to Simone Goyard-Fabre, Présentation, *Abbé de Saint-Pierre, Projet pour rendre la paix perpétuelle en Europe* (Paris: Garnier, 1981), 120 n. 119, the expression "world citizen" first appeared in French in 1750 in De Monbron, *Le Cosmopolite ou Le Citoyen du Monde*.

12. See Dominique Schnapper, *La Communauté des Citoyens: sur l'idée moderne de nation* (Paris: Gallimard, 1994), 68.

13. On the unprecedented scope of French ideological ambitions, see Eugene Kamenka, "Revolutionary Ideology and 'The Great French Revolution of 1789–?,'" 81; and Geoffrey Best, "The French Revolution and Human Rights," 102; both in *The Permanent Revolution: The French Revolution and its Legacy*, ed. Geoffrey Best (London: Fontana, 1988).

14. De Jaucourt, "Patriotisme," *Encyclopédie* (1765), 12:181b.

15. For similar language in the *cahiers* and its implications, see Beatrice Hyslop, *French nationalism in 1789, according to the General Cahiers* (New York: Columbia University Press, 1934), 172–73.

16. See, for example, Cloots's speech in *Moniteur* 18 (Conv. Nat. 5), no. 59 (Nov. 25, 1793): 454.

17. Tzvetan Todorov, *On Human Diversity* (Cambridge, MA: Harvard, 1993), 188. When asked in what country he was born, Cloots replied (on December 12, 1793): "Je suis de la Prusse, département futur de la République française." See Albert Soboul, "Anacharsis Cloots: 'l'Orateur du genre humain,'" *Annales Historiques de la Révolution Française* 52 (1980): 31. Cloots was subsequently executed by the Jacobin government as a foreign agent.

18. Louis Gabriel Ambroise de Bonald, as recounted by Sainte-Beuve in *Causeries du Lundi*, vol. 4, Aug. 18, 1851 (Paris: Garnier Frères), 443. Antoine Rivarol wrote in *Discours sur l'universalité de la langue française*, ed. Hubert Juin (Paris: Pierre Belfond, 1966), first published in 1784, p. 75: "Le temps semble être venu de dire le *monde français*."

19. Saint-Just, "Essai de Constitution pour la France," ch. 9, art. 9, *AP*, vol. 63, 215.

20. See Dehaussy, "La Révolution Française," 55; and Simon Schama, *Citizens: A Chronicle of the French Revolution* (New York: Viking, 1989), 594.

21. See Suzanne Citron, *Le mythe national: L'histoire de France en question*, 2nd ed. (Paris: Éditions Ouvrières, 1991), 282.

22. See Alphonse Aulard, "La Société des Nations et la Révolution Française," Conférence faite au collège libre des sciences sociales le 17 mars 1918, *La Révolution Française: Revue d'histoire moderne et contemporaine* 71 (January–December 1918): 110.

23. Aulard, "La Société des Nations," 112, describing a banquet at the Société du jeu de paume of June 20, 1790; episode recounted in *Procès-verbal de l'Assemblée*, vol. 22, 21–22.

24. Martin Wight, "Why is there no International Theory?," in *Diplomatic Investigations*, 24.

25. For the full text of this Declaration, see the Appendix.

26. Ruyssen, *Les sources doctrinales*, vol. 3, 57.

27. René-Jean Dupuy, "La Révolution française et le droit international actuel," *Recueil des Cours* 1989–II, 20; Dehaussy, "La Révolution française," 80.

28. *AP*, vol. 56, 676.

29. *Moniteur* 24 (Conv. Nat. 11), no. 217 (April 23, 1795): 294.

30. *AP*, vol. 56, 676.

31. These precepts show the clear imprint of Enlightenment thinking. On Voltaire's and Montesquieu's perspectives, see Ernest Nys, "La Révolution française et le droit international," in *Études de droit international et de droit politique* (Brussels: Alfred Castaigne, 1896), 330–31.

32. See Linklater, *Men and Citizens*, 4 (citing Butterfield and Wight, *Diplomatic Investigations*, 33).

33. Article 2(1) of the UN Charter states: "The Organization is based on the principle of the sovereign equality of all its members."

34. See Jean-René Suratteau, "La Nation de 1789 à 1799. Sens, idéologie, évolution de l'emploi du mot," in *Région-Nation-Europe: unité et diversité des processus sociaux et culturels de la Révolution française*, ed. Marita Gilli (Paris: Diffusion Les Belles Lettres, 1988), 688.

35. Constantin François de Chasseboeuf, comte de Volney, cited in Dupuy, "La Révolution française," 20.

36. *AP*, vol. 15, 576. The text is reproduced in the Appendix.

37. Aulard, "La Société des Nations," 116.

38. See Aulard, "La Société des Nations," 117–18. The text is reproduced in the Appendix.

39. See Wight, *International Theory*, 8–12.

40. See *Moniteur* 4, no. 136 (May 15, 1790): 371–72; *Moniteur* 4, no. 137 (May 16, 1790): 383–84; *Moniteur* 4, no. 138 (May 16, 1790): 385–86; *Moniteur* 4, no. 139 (May 18, 1790): 397–98; and *Moniteur* 4, no. 142 (May 20, 1790): 417–19. The debates over whether the Assembly or the King had the right to declare war and peace culminated in the following compromise: "Le droit de la paix et de la guerre appartient à la nation. La guerre ne pourra être décidée que par un décret de l'Assemblée nationale, qui sera rendu sur la proposition formelle et nécessiare du roi, et qui sera sanctionné par lui," and "Toute déclaration de guerre sera faite en ces termes: DE LA PART DU ROI ET AU NOM DE LA NATION." *Moniteur* 4, no.143 (May 22, 1790): 432. This compromise was enshrined in Chapter 4, Section III of the 1791 Constitution.

41. T. C. W. Blanning, *The French Revolutionary Wars 1787–1802* (London: Arnold, 1996), 48.

42. Godechot, *Les Constitutions de la France*, 65.

43. Cobban, *A History of Modern France*, vol. 1, 187.

44. Speech by M. le curé Jallet, *Moniteur* 4, no. 138, 386. See also the speech of Jacques Claude Beugnot in *AP*, vol. 37, 539.

45. Ruyssen, *Les sources doctrinales*, 37 notes: "En vain Mirabeau . . . rappelat-il que l'histoire a connu des républiques guerrières, des dictatures populaires plus agressives que des monarchies héréditaires; qu'aucun peuple n'est à l'abri des pas-

sions conquérantes." See Mirabeau's speech in *Moniteur* 4, no. 142 (May 20, 1790): 417–19. See also T. C. W. Blanning, *The Origins of the French Revolutionary Wars* (London: Longman, 1986), 76.

46. Dupuy, "La Révolution française," 21. See also François Furet, "Introduction," *L'héritage de la Révolution française*, ed. François Furet (Paris: Hachette, 1989), 28.

47. *AP*, vol. 53, 132. The record notes that Vergniaud's speech was followed by "*vifs applaudissements.*"

48. Dehaussy, "La Révolution française," 85. Anacharsis Cloots predicted: "if the Legislative Assembly were to launch an attack on 20 January, then by 20 February the revolutionary cockade would be sported by *20* liberated nations." *AP*, vol. 36, 79, trans. in Blanning, *The French Revolutionary Wars*, 61.

49. Nys, "La Révolution française," 380 (emphasis added).

50. *AP*, vol. 58, 102. Marita Gilli in "L'Allemagne et la Révolution française," *L'Europe et la Révolution française* (Paris: Les Belles Lettres, 1988), 25 claims that Georg Forster in his November 15, 1792 speech on *Les rapports des Mayençais avec les Francs* was in fact the first to introduce the idea of natural frontiers for France, with the boundary of the Rhine.

51. Dehaussy, "La Révolution française," 65 n. 25 presents an oversimplified view of the monarchy as taking advantage of opportunities for conquest whenever possible. Guy Hermet suggests the accuracy of a more balanced assessment in *Histoire des nations et du nationalisme en Europe* (Paris: Éditions du Seuil, 1996).

52. Quoted in Hermet, *Histoire des nations*, 105.

53. Pierre Victor Malouet, deputy to the Constituent Assembly, observed as early as 1791 in the context of debates over Avignon: "Il y a eu dans cette révolution un caractère qui n'appartient à aucune autre: c'est d'en généraliser les principes, de les rendre applicables à tous les peuples, à tous les pays, à tous les gouvernements; c'est un véritable esprit de conquête, ou plutôt d'apostolat, qui a saisi les esprits les plus ardents et qui cherche à se répandre au dehors." *Moniteur* 8, no. 123 (May 2, 1791): 280. See also a similar argument by the deputy Antoine Pierre Joseph Marie Barnave in *Moniteur* 8, no. 125 (May 5, 1791): 297.

54. See Jacques Godechot, "Les Variations de la politique française à l'égard des pays occupés 1792–1815," *Occupants/Occupés 1792–1815* (Brussels: University of Brussels, 1969), 18.

55. Dehaussy, "La Révolution française," 72. On the Girondins, see Mathiez, *La révolution et les étrangers*, 60.

56. See Dehaussy, "La Révolution française," p. 74 n. 55.

57. Speech in the Jacobin club on December 30, 1791, in Albert Mathiez, *La révolution et les étrangers: cosmopolitisme et défense nationale* (Paris: La Renaissance du livre, 1918), 61.

58. See Dehaussy, "La Révolution française," 62.

59. Jacques Godechot, *La Grande Nation: L'expansion révolutionnaire de la France dans le monde de 1789 à 1799*, 2nd ed. (Paris: Aubier Montaigne, 1983), 67.

60. For an overview of the key issues, see the report of Jacques François Menou "in the name of the diplomatic committee and of Avignon," in *Moniteur* 8, no. 121 (April 30, 1791): 264–65.

61. See *Moniteur* 8, no. 122 (April 30, 1791): 271; and *Moniteur* 8, no. 123 (May 2, 1791): 277. These debates underscore the perception of a fundamental division between the old system of international relations based on monarchical possession and the new system based on national sovereignty. Pierre Victor Malouet argued: "Tout le système du comité [diplomatique], les moyens, les raisonnements, les conclusions du rapport [sur l'Avignon], portent cumulativement sur des principes entre lesquels il faut opter, car ils se détruisent l'un l'autre. Ces deux principes sont le droit de propriété et suzeraineté du territoire qu'on attribue par transmission et hérédité au roi des Français . . . [et] le droit qu'a chaque peuple de se déclarer libre, indépendant de la domination du prince auquel il a obéi jusqu'au moment où il lui plaît de changer la forme de son gouvernement. . . . Avant de passer outre, je demande à M. le rapporteur: *Dans quel système raisonnez-vous?*" *Moniteur* 8, no. 123, 279 (emphasis added).

62. Dehaussy, "La Révolution française," 66.

63. Dehaussy, "La Révolution française," 67 n. 33.

64. Speech by Robespierre, *Moniteur* 6, no. 324 (Nov. 18, 1790): 419; complete version in *AP*, vol. 20, 525–30. See also the debates over Avignon in *AP*, vol. 20, 474–81.

65. Dehaussy, "La Révolution française," 68 n. 35.

66. The self-determination argument did have a historical precedent. When the States of Bourgogne, a French province, refused to be separated from France in accordance with the treaty of Madrid in the sixteenth century, the French King François I stated: "Il est fondé en droit qu'on ne peut nulles villes ou provinces contre la volonté des habitants et sujets transférer en autre, sinon par leur consentement exprès." François I's affirmation is cited proudly by historian Alphonse Aulard as an early example of voluntarist "Revolutionary patriotism." See Alphonse Aulard, *Le Patriotisme français de la Renaissance à la Révolution* (Paris: Étienne Chiron, 1921), 22. In fact François I's position, like that of the later Revolutionaries, only supported national self-determination insofar as it reinforced the territorial integrity of his own definition of France.

67. Florimond Claude, comte de Mercy, in Blanning, *The Origins of the French Revolutionary Wars*, 75.

68. *AP*, vol. 30, 631.

69. Clive Emsley, "Nationalist Rhetoric and Nationalist Sentiment in Revolutionary France," in *Nationalism in the Age of the French Revolution*, eds. Otto Dann and John Dinwiddy (London: Hambledon, 1988), 41.

70. Despite their emphasis on popular will, the French were wary of creating a precedent that could be used against them: Merlin de Douai in a report of October 28, 1790, made it clear that the bonds thenceforth established between Corsica and Alsace and the rest of France were "indissoluble," precluding the "slippery slope of secession." See "Comité de féodalité, rapport sur les droits seigneuriaux des princes d'Allemagne en Alsace," *AP*, vol. 20, 81. Title XIII, Article 2 of the Draft Constitution of 1793 struck a delicate balance between the goal of "reunion" and the danger of fragmentation based on France's own constitutional principles: "[La France] renonce solennellement à réunir à son territoire des contrées étrangères, sinon d'après le voeu librement émis de la majorité des habitants, et dans le cas seulement où les contrées qui solliciteront cette réunion, ne seront pas incorporées et unies à une autre nation, en vertu d'un pacte social, exprimé dans une Constitution antérieure et librement consentie." *AP*, vol. 58, 624.

71. These measures included the acts of August 4, 1789 (abolishing feudal rights); November 2, 1789 (appropriating the possessions of the clergy); and December 22, 1789 and February 26, 1790 (suppressing the provinces and creating departments in their place).

72. Merlin de Douai, quoted in Dehaussy, "La Révolution française," 69 n. 39. See also Nys, "La Révolution française," 360. In the end, the Assembly reaffirmed the sovereignty of the French nation (not the French king) over the territories, but it compromised by authorizing negotiations between the King and the Emperor to arrange indemnities for the princes. The Emperor's legal advisers rejected this offer, and their complaint contributed to the outbreak of war.

73. Ruyssen, *Les sources doctrinales*, 46. The same expression was used by a deputation of the National Assembly to the King on January 30, 1792. See Dehaussy, "La Révolution française," 73 n. 51.

74. Merlin de Thionville, speech of April 20, 1792, in Jean Tulard, "Les Événements," in *Histoire et dictionnaire de la Révolution française 1789–1799*, ed. Jean Tulard, Jean-François Fayard, and Alfred Fierro (Paris: Robert Laffont, 1987), 91. See also General Montesquiou's 1792 declaration upon occupying the Savoy, in the *Catalogue de la Bibliothèque nationale sur la Révolution française* (Paris: Éditions de la gazette des beaux-arts, January–March 1928), item 196.

75. Albert Soboul adds a useful footnote in Jaurès's *Histoire socialiste de la Révolution française, Tome IV: La Révolution et l'Europe*, ed. Soboul (Paris: Éditions Socialistes, 1971), 163 n. 3: "Selon A. Mathiez, cette formule se trouve pour la première fois dans le journal du banquier Proli, *Le Cosmopolite*, du 15 décembre 1791." It is also in the decree of November 15, 1792, permitting the legitimation of war, and in a speech by Pierre Joseph Cambon, *AP*, vol. 55, 70.

76. Citation from May 19 in Ruyssen, *Les sources doctrinales*, 37. See also M. Fauchet's speech to the Legislative Assembly in *AP*, vol. 37, 540–41. On the Revolutionaries' attempts to disregard established diplomatic practices that ran counter to their republican ideals, see Linda Frey and Marsha Frey, "'The Reign of the Charlatans Is Over': The French Revolutionary Attack on Diplomatic Practice," *The Journal of Modern History* 65, no. 4 (December 1993): 706–44.

77. "Suite d'un rapport de [Pierre Joseph] Cambon sur la conduite à tenir par les généraux français dans les pays occupés par les armées de la République," in *French Revolution Documents 1789–94*, ed. J. M. Thomson (Oxford: Basil Blackwell, 1933), 216; full report in *AP*, vol. 55, 70–73. This report also emphasizes the duty of French army not to "abandon" the "timid and weak" peoples it has liberated, and to follow up words (declarations of popular sovereignty) with actions (by abolishing the privileges and institutions of the old regime). Antonio Cassese rightly notes that the Revolutionary self-determination principle did not apply to colonies or minorities, but he underestimates its "internal" dimension. For him, the French Revolutionaries were concerned only with state boundary changes. Cassese, *Self-determination of Peoples: A Legal Reappraisal* (Cambridge: Cambridge University Press, 1995), 12. This position fails to recognize the degree to which the Revolutionaries saw themselves as exemplifying and exporting a domestic constitutional principle.

78. Blanning makes the point in *The French Revolutionary Wars*, 89, that the annexation of Savoy on November 27, 1792, and of Nice on January 31, 1793, were made to appear legitimate by the enlistment of local supporters of French Revolution in both the armies and in the new administration.

79. Dehaussy, "La Révolution française," 56.

80. See Etienne Fournol, "Le caractère international de la Révolution française," *La Révolution Française: Revue d'histoire moderne et contemporaine*, no. 6, nouvelle série, 3e trimestre (1936): 217.

81. Johann Wolfgang von Goethe, quoted in Ruyssen, *Les sources doctrinales*, 51.

82. Ruyssen, *Les sources doctrinales*, 53.

83. See Sophie Wahnich, "Les Républiques-Soeurs, Débat Théorique et Réalité Historique, Conquêtes et Reconquêtes d'Identité Républicaine," *Annales Historiques de la Révolution Française*, no. 2 (1994): 167 (emphasis added).

84. Armstrong, *Revolution and World Order*, 97.

85. Hayes, *The Historical Evolution of Modern Nationalism*, 40.

86. Billaud-Varenne, "Rapport fait à la Convention nationale au nom du Comité de Salut public sur la guerre et les moyens de la soutenir," *AP*, vol. 89, 95.

87. Gilli, "L'Allemagne et la Révolution française," 27.

88. John Stuart Mill, "A Few Words on Non-Intervention," *Essays on Politics and Culture*, ed. Gertrude Himmelfarb (Gloucester, MA: Peter Smith, 1973), 381. Wahnich echoes this view in "Les Républiques-Soeurs," 169: "En effet la liberté est justement ce que l'on ne peut prendre que par soi-même."

89. Jaurès, *Histoire Socialiste*, 175. Mathiez comments in *La révolution et les étrangers*, 189: "[la France] organise le despotisme de la liberté pour vaincre le despotisme des rois."

90. On the threat posed by royalist priests both inside and outside of France, see the speech by M. Biron in *Moniteur* 9, no. 214 (Oct. 20, 1791): 281. On external threats, see Brissot in *Moniteur* 10, no. 294, 163–64.

91. See Geoffrey Best, Introduction, *The Permanent Revolution*, 11.

92. Dehaussy, "La Révolution française," 87. According to Nys, "La Révolution française," 385, Brissot later called this decree "absurde, impolitique et excitant à juste titre l'inquiétude des cabinets étrangers."

93. Mathiez, *La révolution et les étrangers*, 82, 84. The lack of an appropriate response from "liberated" peoples came as a surprise to the French. See Godechot, "Les Variations de la politique française," 22.

94. See Schama, *Citizens*, 859; and Aminata Diaw, "Rousseau et la Révolution française: à propos de la théorie de l'état," in *Etat et Nation. Actes du colloque de mai 1988*, Cahiers de philosophie politique et juridique, ed. Simone Goyard-Fabre, no. 14 (Caen: Université de Caen, 1988), 148. The French *levée en masse* had the additional internal juridical effect of making a military traitor out of anyone deemed hostile to the *patrie*. See Dehaussy, "La Révolution française," 84 n. 78.

95. See Robert Devleeshouwer, Conclusion, *Occupants/Occupés*, 314; and Godechot, *La Grande Nation*, 374.

96. Godechot, "Les Variations de la politique française," 23–24.

97. Rapport fait à la Convention nationale, au nom du comité de salut public, par le citoyen Robespierre, membre de ce comité, sur la situation politique de la république, *Moniteur* 18 (Conv. Nat. 5), no. 60 (Nov. 17, 1793): 458.

98. See Schama, *Citizens*, 584, 592. The security dilemma galvanized both sides: "As the future King Louis Philippe, in 1792 styled the duc de Chartres, observed: 'This manifesto of the Duke of Brunswick inspired more enthusiasm in France for the defense of the fatherland and national independence than all the patriotic appeals of the National Assembly and the revolutionary societies put together.'" *Mémoires de Louis Philippe duc d'Orléans écrits par lui-même*, 2 vols. (Paris: 1974), vol. 2, 98, quoted in Blanning, *The French Revolutionary Wars*, 71.

99. See Best, "The French Revolution and Human Rights," 106.

100. Burke, *Reflections on the Revolution in France*, cited in George Steiner, "Aspects of Counter-Revolution," in *The Permanent Revolution*, 136–37.

101. On the possibility of "cosmopolitan nationalism," see Hayes, *The Historical Evolution of Modern Nationalism*, 10, 37; and Hyslop, *French nationalism in 1789*, 169–70.

102. Ruyssen, *Les sources doctrinales*, 56. See also Nys, "La Révolution française," 381; and Blanning, *The French Revolutionary Wars*, 156.

103. Quoted in Nys, "La Révolution française," 382.

104. Blanning, *The French Revolutionary Wars*, 239, describes the "transfer of liberationist rhetoric from revolutionaries to counter-revolutionaries, as the rebels presented themselves as patriots fighting for liberty against the French barbarians and tyrants."

105. Wahnich, "Les Républiques-Soeurs," 177.

106. See Bertrand de Jouvenel, "Reflections on Colonialism," *Confluence* 4, no. 3 (October 1955): 263. James Mayall highlights the simultaneous (and enduring) contestability and popularity of the Revolutionary nationalist platform in "1789 and the liberal theory of international society," 306: "The leaders of many Third World countries may see themselves as heirs to the Revolution, but so do their opponents."

107. *AP*, vol. 15, 576. See also Dupuy, "La Révolution française," 25; and Dehaussy, "La Révolution française," 79–82.

108. See Dehaussy, "La Révolution française," 85.

109. Dehaussy, "La Révolution française," 86.

110. See Hans Kohn, *Prelude to Nation-States: The French and German Experience 1789–1815* (Princeton: D. van Nostrand, 1967), 119; and Wahnich, "Les Républiques-Soeurs," 177.

111. Speech of April 16, 1793, quoted in Nys, "La Révolution française," 393.

112. Hayes, *The Historical Evolution of Modern Nationalism*, 80.

113. Alexander Hamilton, "The Warning," No. 1, January 29, 1797, in *The Papers of Alexander Hamilton*, ed. H. C. Syrett and J. E. Cooke, vol. 20 (New York: Columbia University Press, 1961), 494.

114. Thugut, "the most influential minister in Vienna," wrote to the ambassador in St. Petersburg on May 29, 1794, describing Revolutionary agitation in Poland (blamed on Paris): "it is war to the death between sovereignty and anarchy, between legitimate government and the destruction of all order"; quoted in Karl A. Roider, *Baron Thugut and Austria's Response to the French Revolution* (Princeton, NJ: Princeton University Press, 1987), 150. See also the reference to a 1791 letter from Chancellor Kaunitz to the Emperor's diplomatic agents, in Ruyssen, *Les sources doctrinales*, 49; and Dehaussy, "La Révolution française," 71.

115. Martin Wight, *Power Politics*, 2nd ed., ed. Hedley Bull and Carsten Holbraad (London: Penguin, 1986), 91.

116. Revolutionary innovations covered a wide range of issues. For example, the French opened the Escaut river after their victory at Jemappes in accordance with the principle of the freedom of international rivers, even though the Fontainebleau treaty of 1785 guaranteed Dutch sovereignty over the Escaut. As in Nootka Sound and in Alsace, Revolutionary principles trumped treaty law (conveniently threatening English commerce, which depended on exclusive navigation

rights). See the deliberations of the provisional executive council "sur la conduite des armées françaises dans le pays qu'elles occupent, spécialement dans la Belgique" of November 16, 1792, in *AP*, vol. 53, 512. The council relies on Revolutionary principles of domestic constitution as a basis for international confrontation in justifying freedom of navigation and commerce: "la nature ne reconnaît pas plus de peuples que d'individus privilégiés."

117. Albert Sorel, *L'Europe et la Révolution française. Deuxième partie: La Chute de la royauté*, 3rd ed. (Paris: Librairie Plon, 1895), 520.

118. Dehaussy, "La Révolution française," 88.

119. Dehaussy, "La Révolution française," 94.

120. Recounted by Thomas Raikes in *A Portion of the Journal*, 2nd ed., vol. 1 (London: Longmans, 1856), entry of November 18, 1832.

121. See Blanning, *The French Revolutionary Wars*, 179.

122. Wight, *Power Politics*, 85.

123. See Best, Introduction, *The Permanent Revolution*, 9.

124. Blanning, *The Origins of the French Revolutionary Wars*, 211.

125. Sorel, *L'Europe et la Révolution française, 2e partie*, 7.

126. Welsh, *Edmund Burke and International Relations*, 3.

Chapter Five: Synthesis

1. See, for example, Maxim Silverman, *Deconstructing the nation: immigration, racism, and citizenship in modern France* (London: Routledge and Kegan Paul, 1992).

2. See, for example, Hurst Hannum, *Autonomy, Sovereignty, and Self-Determination: The Accommodation of Conflicting Rights* (Philadelphia: University of Pennsylvania Press, 1990), 7.

3. Isaiah Berlin, "Two Concepts of Nationalism," *New York Review of Books* 38, no. 19 (November 21, 1992): 19–23. See also Kai Nielsen, "Liberal Nationalism and Secession," in *National Self-Determination and Secession*, ed. Margaret Moore (Oxford: Oxford University Press, 1998), 109.

4. Anthony Smith describes the "one overall striving—to be part of a recognized political and cultural unit, a 'nation'; if necessary, to invent one, for the protection and sustenance of a threatened identity." Smith, *Theories of Nationalism*, 2nd ed. (NY: Holmes and Meier, 1983), 192.

5. See Charles Tilly, *The Formation of National States in Western Europe* (Princeton, NJ: Princeton University Press, 1975); and Linda Colley, *Britons: Forging the Nation 1707–1837* (New Haven, CT: Yale University Press, 1992).

6. See, for example, Will Kymlicka and Wayne Norman, "Return of the Citizen," *Theorizing Citizenship*, ed. Ronald Beiner (Albany: State University of New York Press, 1995), 315 n. 34, and Charles Taylor, "Quel principle d'identité collective," in *L'Europe au soir du siècle: Identité et démocratie*, ed. Jacques Lenoble and Nicole Dewandre (Paris: Éditions Esprit, 1992), 61.

7. Eric Hobsbawm, *Nations and Nationalism Since 1870* (Cambridge: Cambridge University Press, 1990), 123–24.

8. *Report of the International Committee of Jurists by the Council of the League of Nations with the task of giving an advisory opinion upon the legal aspects of the Aaland Islands question*, L.N.O.J. Spec. Supp. No. 3 (1920), 5.

9. *The Aaland Islands Question, Report presented to the Council of the League by the Commission of Rapporteurs*, League of Nations Doc. B.7.21/68/106 (1921), 28.

10. See Hannum, *Autonomy, Sovereignty, and Self-Determination*, 32.

11. See UN Charter, art. 1, para. 2, and art. 55; General Assembly Resolution 1514 (XV) (Dec. 14, 1960); General Assembly Resolution 2625 (XXV) (Oct. 24, 1970); International Covenant on Civil and Political Rights (Dec. 16, 1966); International Covenant on Economic, Social, and Cultural Rights (Dec. 16, 1966).

12. See Thomas Franck, "The Emerging Right to Democratic Governance," *American Journal of International Law* 86 (1992): 46–91.

13. Martti Koskenniemi, "National Self-Determination Today: Problems of Legal Theory and Practice," *International and Comparative Law Quarterly* 43 (April 1994): 249–50.

14. Koskenniemi, "National Self-Determination Today," 250–51.

15. See the discussion of this distinction in Anthony Smith, *National Identity* (London: Penguin, 1991), 9–13.

16. See Johann Gottfried von Herder, "Yet Another Philosophy of History" (1774) and "Ideas for a Philosophy of the History of Mankind" (1784–91), in *J. G. Herder on Social and Political Culture*, ed. F. M. Barnard (Cambridge: Cambridge University Press, 1969), 181–223 and 255–326.

17. See, for example, Johan Gottlieb Fichte, "What is a People in the Higher Meaning of the Word, and what is love of Fatherland?" (1808), in *Addresses to the German Nation*, trans. R. F. Jones and Gil Turnbull (London: Open Court, 1922), 130–52; and Adolf Hitler, *Mein Kampf*, English ed. (New York: Stackpole, 1939).

18. See, for example, Portugal (First Oral Round of Pleadings): CR 95/4 (Feb. 1, 1995), morning, Mr. J. M. Servulo Correia: "Portugal expressed in its written pleadings that the character 'separate and distinct' of the non-self-governing territory [of East Timor] and of its people makes that people the holder of the sovereignty inherent in the capacity to decide for itself its future international legal status. But if the non-self-governing people possesses national sovereignty, it

is *still lacking* the exercise thereof" (emphasis added). The I.C.J. ultimately declined to exercise jurisdiction in this dispute between Portugal and Australia since it would have required ruling on the lawfulness of Indonesia's conduct in the absence of Indonesia's consent. Nevertheless, the Court affirmed that the "right of peoples to self-determination, as it evolved from the Charter and from United Nations practice, is irreproachable," and that for the two Parties, the UN General Assembly, and the Security Council, "the Territory of East Timor remains a non-self-governing territory and its people has the right to self-determination." *International Court of Justice: Case Concerning East Timor*, 34 I.L.M. 1581 (1995), 1590.

19. John Stuart Mill, *On Liberty and Considerations on Representative Government*, ed. R. B. McCallum (Oxford: Basil Blackwell, 1946; orig. pub. 1861), 292.

20. While Ernest Renan's 1882 essay *Qu'est-ce qu'une nation?* (Paris: Calmann-Levy, 1882) is often upheld as a classic statement of voluntarist nationalism, it is also important to recall the particular political motivations underlying his conception: namely, the desire to establish grounds for a claim to the largely ethnically German territories of Alsace-Lorraine which had been taken by the North German Confederation a decade earlier in the Franco-Prussian war, but which the French persisted in seeing as an integral part of France. Renan's insistence on the value of historical ties in his essay also belies a strictly voluntarist emphasis.

21. Michael Ignatieff, *Blood and Belonging: Journeys into the New Nationalism* (London: Vintage, 1994), 76.

22. Rousseau made this complaint in the context of an essay on the need to cultivate an exclusive definition of patriotic virtue in Poland, printed in *The Political Writings of J.-J. Rousseau*, vol. 1, ed. C. E. Vaughan (Oxford: Basil Blackwell, 1962), 432.

23. Maurizio Viroli, *For Love of Country: Essays on Patriotism and Nationalism* (Oxford: Clarendon, 1995).

24. Viroli, *For Love of Country*, 7.

25. Viroli, *For Love of Country*, 8.

26. See Viroli, *For Love of Country*, 13. Similar statements include: "we have to appeal to feelings of compassion and solidarity that are—when they are—rooted in bonds of language, culture, and history"; and "civic virtue has to be particularistic to be possible." Ibid., 10, 12.

27. Viroli, *For Love of Country*, 10.

28. Jürgen Habermas, "Citizenship and National Identity: Some Reflections on the Future of Europe," in *Theorizing Citizenship*, ed. Ronald Beiner (Albany: State University of New York Press, 1995), 255–81. In his later work, Habermas reveals a deeper appreciation of the need for "thicker" ties among members of a political community. Still, he believes that this function can be filled by a shared political culture that is strictly separate from "subcultures" and "pre-political identities (including that of the majority)." See Jürgen Habermas, "The European Nation-State—Its Achievements and Its Limits. On the Past and Future

of Sovereignty and Citizenship," in *Mapping the Nation*, ed. Gopal Balakrishnan (London: Verso, 1996), 281–94. The question of what such a political culture might look like remains unresolved; Habermas indicates elsewhere a belief in the possibility of a pan-European political culture forged through democracy as a "juridically mediated form of political integration" and through the discovery of "interests that transcend borders." See Jürgen Habermas, "The European Nation-State and the Pressures of Globalization," in *Global Justice and Transnational Politics*, ed. Pablo De Greiff and Ciaran Cronin (Cambridge, MA and London: The MIT Press, 2002), 217–34.

29. Habermas, "Citizenship and National Identity," 258–59.

30. In a related criticism, Bernard Yack observes in "The Myth of the Civic Nation," in *Theorizing Nationalism*, ed. Ronald Beiner (Albany: State University of New York Press, 1999), 108 that "Habermas's argument . . . assumes the existence of the very prepolitical cultural community that he, like most defenders of the civic idea of the nation, rejects in the name of a community based on rational consent and political principle."

31. Dominique Schnapper, *La Communauté des Citoyens: sur l'idée moderne de nation* (Paris: Gallimard, 1994), 78.

32. Habermas, "Citizenship and National Identity," 261.

33. Michael Billig, *Banal Nationalism* (London: Sage, 1995).

34. Brian Singer points to the United States as evidence that mere procedural consensus is not enough for national allegiance: "Thus, for example, since the Depression the United States has tended to speak of an 'American way of life'—which provides, as it were, the cultural ersatz required for the 'melting pot.'" Brian Singer, "Cultural vs. Contractual Nations: Rethinking their Opposition," *History and Theory: Studies in the Philosophy of History* 35, no. 3 (1996): 313.

35. Habermas, "Citizenship and National Identity," 269. Interestingly, Singer's association of this "cultural" emphasis with the Depression highlights the increased importance of finding other kinds of social and political cement when the state's provision of goods, services, and security is compromised.

36. Habermas, "Citizenship and National Identity," 271. The cosmopolitan ethic is also elaborated by Joseph Carens in "Aliens and Citizens," in *Theorizing Citizenship*, 229–53. In contrast, Habermas cites Michael Walzer's *Spheres of Justice: A defence of pluralism and equality* (New York: Basic Books, 1983), 31–63 for a defense of particularist standards. The idea of decoupling power and identity recalls Hedley Bull's description of "new mediaevalism" in *The Anarchical Society: A Study of Order in World Politics*, 2nd ed. (London: Macmillan, 1995), 255.

37. Bhikhu Parekh, "A Commitment to Cultural Pluralism," prepared for the IGC on Cultural Policies for Development (Stockholm, March 30–April 2, 1998), also contributed to the UNESCO-Commonwealth Secretariat conference *Towards a Constructive Pluralism*, Paris, January 28–30, 1999, UNESCO ref. CLT-99/CONF.601/CPL [hereafter cited as *TCP*], 1.

38. Parekh, "A Commitment to Cultural Pluralism," 2.

39. Parekh, "A Commitment to Cultural Pluralism," 7.

40. Different configurations of plurality lead to different kinds of tensions and may require different solutions. These include: multicultural vs. multinational self-understandings, "deep diversity" vs. cross-cutting cleavages, territorially consolidated vs. territorially dispersed cultural communities, and so forth. On cross-cutting cleavages and their potential to mitigate intrastate fragmentation and conflict, see Arend Lijphart, *Democracies in plural societies: A comparative exploration* (New Haven, CT: Yale University Press, 1977). On "dual societies," see Ali Mazrui, "Towards a Constructive Plural Order: Four principles of Reform," contribution to *TCP*. Mazrui observes: "Paradoxically, the dual society endangers the state by having less sociological differentiation than is needed for the politics of compromise." Ibid. 3–4.

41. See Roland Rich, "Recognition of States: The Collapse of Yugoslavia and the Soviet Union," *European Journal of International Law* 4 (1993): 36–65.

42. See generally Chimène I. Keitner and W. Michael Reisman, "Free Association: The United States Experience," *Texas International Law Journal* 39 (Fall 2003): 1–64.

43. See *The Rights of Minorities in Europe: A Commentary on the European Framework Convention for the Protection of National Minorities*, ed. Marc Weller (Oxford: Oxford University Press, 2005).

Chapter Six: Epilogue—Confrontation Revisited

1. Alexander Hamilton, "The Warning," No. 1, January 19, 1797, *The Papers of Alexander Hamilton*, vol. 20, ed. H. C. Syrett and J. E. Cooke (New York: Columbia University Press, 1961), 494.

2. "President Bush's Inaugural Address," Jan. 21, 2005, available at http://www.washingtonpost.com/wp-dyn/articles/A23747-2005Jan20.html. See also *The National Security Strategy of the United States of America* (Sept. 2002), available at http://www.whitehouse.gov/nsc/nss.html [hereafter cited as *NSS*].

3. Condoleeza Rice, "Remarks at the American University in Cairo," June 20, 2005, available at http://www.state.gov/secretary/rm/2005/48328.htm.

4. *NSS*, 7.

5. *NSS*, 4.

6. George W. Bush, "Address to a Joint Session of Congress and the American People," September 20, 2001, available at http://www.whitehouse.gov/news/releases/2001/09/20010920-8.html.

7. "President: Iraqi Regime Danger to America is 'Grave and Growing,'" October 5, 2002, available at http://www.whitehouse.gov/news/releases/2002/10/20021005.html.

8. "International Campaign Against Terror Grows," September 25, 2001, available at http://www.whitehouse.gov/news/releases/2001/09/20010925-1.html.

9. "President Says Saddam Hussein Must Leave Iraq Within 48 Hours," March 17, 2003, available at http://www.whitehouse.gov/news/releases/2003/03/iraq/20030317-7.html.

10. "President Bush Addresses Nation on the Capture of Saddam Hussein," December 14, 2003, available at http://www.whitehouse.gov/news/releases/2003/12/20031214-3.html.

11. President Building Worldwide Campaign Against Terrorism, September 19, 2001, available at http://www.whitehouse.gov/news/releases/2001/09/20010919–1.html.

12. "Address to a Joint Session of Congress and the American People," September 20, 2001, available at http://www.whitehouse.gov/news/releases/2001/09/20010920-8.html.

13. "President Bush Delivers Graduation Speech at West Point," June 1, 2002, available at http://www.whitehouse.gov/news/releases/2002/06/20020601-3.html.

14. "President Bush Outlines Iraqi Threat," October 7, 2002, available at http://www.whitehouse.gov/news/releases/2002/10/20021007-8.html.

15. "President Discusses War on Terror at Fort Hood," April 12, 2005, available at http://www.whitehouse.gov/news/releases/2005/04/20050412.html.

16. William J. Clinton, "1994 State Of The Union Address," January 25, 1994, available at http://www.washingtonpost.com/wp-srv/politics/special/states/docs/sou94.htm#foreignpolicy.

17. "President Says Saddam Hussein Must Leave Iraq Within 48 Hours," March 17, 2003, available at http://www.whitehouse.gov/news/releases/2003/03/iraq/20030317-7.html.

18. "President Bush Discusses Freedom in Iraq and Middle East," November 6, 2003, available at http://www.whitehouse.gov/news/releases/2003/11/20031106-2.html.

19. Ibid.

20. "President Sworn-In to Second Term," January 20, 2005, available at http://www.whitehouse.gov/news/releases/2005/01/20050120-1.html; see also "There Is No Justice Without Freedom," January 21, 2005, available at http://www.washingtonpost.com/wp-dyn/articles/A23747-2005Jan20.html.

21. "President Discusses War on Terror at FBI Academy," July 11, 2005, available at http://www.whitehouse.gov/news/releases/2005/07/20050711-1.html.

22. "President Says Saddam Hussein Must Leave Iraq Within 48 Hours," March 17, 2003, available at http://www.whitehouse.gov/news/releases/2003/03/iraq/20030317-7.html.

23. "Address to a Joint Session of Congress and the American People," September 20, 2001, available at http://www.whitehouse.gov/news/releases/2001/09/20010920-8.html.

24. "President Outlines War Effort," October 17, 2001, available at http://www.whitehouse.gov/news/releases/2001/10/20011017-15.html.

25. "President Discusses War on Terror at FBI Academy," July 11, 2005, available at http://www.whitehouse.gov/news/releases/2005/07/20050711-1.html.

26. *NSS*, 6.

27. "President Bush Delivers Graduation Speech at West Point," June 1, 2002, available at http://www.whitehouse.gov/news/releases/2002/06/20020601-3.html.

28. Condoleeza Rice, "Remarks at the American University in Cairo," June 20, 2005, available at http://www.state.gov/secretary/rm/2005/48328.htm.

29. Charles-Frédéric Reinhard, *Le néologiste français ou Vocabulaire portatif des mots les plus nouveaux de la langue Française* (Nurnberg: Grattenaver, 1796), 99–100.

Conclusions

1. See generally Michael Walzer, "The Reform of the International System," in *Studies of War and Peace*, ed. Øyvind Østerud (Oslo: Norwegian University Press, 1986), 227; and Michael Walzer, "The Moral Standing of States: A Response to Four Critics," in *International Ethics*, ed. Charles Beitz (Princeton, NJ: Princeton University Press, 1985), 217–36.

2. Roger Scruton, "The First Person Plural," in *Theorizing Nationalism*, ed. Ronald Beiner (Albany: State University of New York Press, 1999), 292.

3. Charles Schmidt, "Le mot 'nationalisme' en 1813," *La Révolution Française: Revue d'histoire moderne et contemporaine* 46 (January–June 1904): 45, citing the use of the term "nationalism" to mean what "today" (1904) would be called "pan-germanism."

Selected Bibliography

Armstrong, David. *Revolution and World Order: The Revolutionary State in International Society*. Oxford: Clarendon, 1993.

Aulard, Alphonse. *Le Patriotisme français de la Renaissance à la Révolution*. Paris: Étienne Chiron, 1921.

Baczko, Bronislaw. "Le contrat social des Français: Sieyès et Rousseau." In *The French Revolution and the Creation of Modern Political Culture*. Vol. 1. *The Political Culture of the Old Regime*. Edited by Keith Michael Baker, 493–513. Oxford: Pergamon, 1987.

Baker, Keith Michael. "Defining the Public Sphere in Eighteenth-Century France." In *Habermas and the Public Sphere*. Edited by Craig Calhoun, 181–211. Cambridge, MA: MIT Press.

———. *Inventing the French Revolution: Essays on French Political Culture in the Eighteenth Century*. Cambridge: Cambridge University Press, 1990.

Barry, Brian. "The Limits of Cultural Politics." *Review of International Studies* 24, no. 3 (July 1998): 307–19.

Bastid, Paul. *Sieyès et sa pensée*. Paris: Hachette, 1939.

Beitz, Charles. *Political Theory and International Relations*. Princeton, NJ: Princeton University Press, 1979.

Bell, David A. *The Cult of the Nation in France: Inventing Nationalism, 1680–1800*. Cambridge, MA: Harvard University Press, 2001.

Berlin, Isaiah. "The Bent Twig: On the Rise of Nationalism." In *The Crooked Timber of Humanity: Chapters in the History of Ideas*. Edited by Henry Hardy, 238–61. London: John Murray, 1990.

Best, Geoffrey. "The French Revolution and Human Rights." In *The Permanent Revolution: The French Revolution and its Legacy*. Edited by Geoffrey Best, 100–27. London: Fontana, 1988.

Bickart, Roger. *Les Parlements et la Notion de Souveraineté Nationale au XVIIIe siècle*. Paris: Félix Alcan, 1932.

Blanning, T. C. W. "The French Revolution and Europe." In *Rewriting the French Revolution.* Edited by Colin Lucas, 183–206. Oxford: Oxford University Press, 1991.

———. *The French Revolutionary Wars 1787–1802.* London: Arnold, 1996.

———. *The Origins of the French Revolutionary Wars.* London: Longman, 1986.

Brubaker, Rogers. *Citizenship and Nationhood in France and Germany.* Cambridge, MA: Harvard University Press, 1992.

Buchanan, Allen. "Democracy and Secession." In *Self-Determination and Secession.* Edited by Margaret Moore, 14–33. Oxford: Oxford University Press, 1998.

Bull, Hedley. "Society and Anarchy in International Relations." In *Diplomatic Investigations: Essays in the Theory of International Politics.* Edited by Herbert Butterfield and Martin Wight, 35–50. London: George Allen and Unwin, 1966.

———. "International Theory: The Case for a Classical Approach." *World Politics* 18, no. 3 (April 1966): 361–77.

Butterfield, Herbert and Martin Wight. Preface to *Diplomatic Investigations: Essays in the Theory of International Politics.* Edited by Herbert Butterfield and Martin Wight, 1–13. London: George Allen and Unwin, 1966.

Canovan, Margaret. *Nationhood and Political Theory.* Cheltenham: Edward Elgar, 1996.

Carcassonne, Elie. *Montesquieu et le problème de la constitution française au XVIIIe siècle.* Paris: Presses Universitaires de France, 1927.

Carens, Joseph. "Aliens and Citizens." In *Theorizing Citizenship.* Edited by Ronald Beiner, 229–53. Albany: State University of New York Press, 1995.

Caron, Jean-Claude. *La nation, l'État et la démocratie en France de 1789 à 1914.* Paris: Armand Colin, 1995.

Cassese, Antonio. *Self-determination of Peoples: A Legal Reappraisal.* Cambridge: Cambridge University Press, 1995.

Champion, Edme. *La France d'après les Cahiers de 1789*, 5th ed. Paris: A. Colin, 1921.

Church, William F. "France." In *National Consciousness, History, and Political Culture in Early-Modern Europe.* Edited by Orest Ranum, 43–66. Baltimore, MD: John Hopkins, 1975.

Clere, Jean-Jacques. "Etat-Nation-Citoyen au temps de la Révolution française." In *L'idée de nation.* Edited by Marie-Françoise Conrad, Jean Ferrari, and Jean-Jacques Wunenburger. Dijon: Éditions universitaires de Dijon, 1986.

Cobban, Alfred. *In Search of Humanity: The Role of the Enlightenment in Modern History.* London: Jonathan Cape, 1960.

———. *Rousseau and the Modern State*, 2nd ed. London: George Allen and Unwin, 1964.

———. *The Nation-State and National Self-Determination*, rev. ed. New York: Thomas Crowell, 1969.

Cohler, Ann. *Rousseau and Nationalism*. New York: Basic Books, 1970.

Cranston, Maurice. "The Sovereignty of the Nation." In *The Political Culture of the French Revolution*. Edited by Colin Lucas, 97–104. Oxford: Pergamon, 1988.

Crawford, James. *The Creation of States in International Law*. Oxford: Clarendon, 1979.

Debbasch, Roland. *Le Principe Révolutionnaire d'Unité et d'Indivisibilité de la République*. Paris: Economica, 1988.

Dehaussy, Jacques. "La Révolution Française et le Droit des Gens." *Révolution et Droit International*, 49–98. Paris: A. Pedone, 1989.

Dérathé, Robert. "Patriotisme et Nationalisme au XVIIIe siècle." *Annales de Philosophie Politique*, no. 8, L'idée de nation, 69–84. Paris: Presses Universitaires de France, 1969.

Doyle, Michael. "Kant, Liberal Legacies, and Foreign Affairs." *Philosophy and Public Affairs* 12, nos. 3–4 (1983): 205–35, 323–53.

Doyle, William. "The Parlements of France and the Breakdown of the Old Régime 1771–1788." *French Historical Studies* 6, no. 4 (Fall 1970): 415–58.

Dunn, John. "Nationalism." In *Western Political Theory in the Face of the Future*. Canto ed., 57–81. Cambridge: Cambridge University Press, 1993.

Dupuy, René-Jean. "La Révolution française et le droit international actuel." *Recueil des Cours*, 1989-II: 17–29.

Egret, Jean. *La Pré-Révolution Française 1787–1788*. Paris: Presses Universitaires de France, 1962.

———. *Louis XV et l'opposition parlementaire 1715–1774*. Paris: Armand Colin, 1970.

Emerson, Rupert. "Self-Determination." *American Journal of International Law* 65, no. 3 (July 1971): 459–75.

Emsley, Clive. "Nationalist Rhetoric and Nationalist Sentiment in Revolutionary France." In *Nationalism in the Age of the French Revolution*. Edited by Otto Dann and John Dinwiddy, 39–52. London: Hambledon, 1988.

Ford, Caroline. "Which Nation? Language, identity, and republican politics in post-revolutionary France." *History of European Ideas* 17, no. 1 (1993): 31–46.

Forsyth, Murray. *Reason and Revolution: the political thought of the Abbé Sieyès*. Leicester: Leicester University Press, 1987.

Franck, Thomas. "The Emerging Right to Democratic Governance." *American Journal of International Law* 86 (1992): 46–91.

Frey, Linda and Marsha Frey. "'The Reign of the Charlatans Is Over': The French Revolutionary Attack on Diplomatic Practice." *The Journal of Modern History* 65, no. 4 (December 1993): 706–44.

Frisch, Morton J. "The Emergence of Nationalism as a Political Philosophy." *History of European Ideas* 16, no. 4–6 (1993): 885–90.

Fritz, Gérard. *L'Idée de peuple en France du XVIIe au XIXe siècle.* Strasbourg: Presses Universitaires de Strasbourg, 1988.

Furet, François. Introduction to *L'héritage de la Révolution française.* Edited by François Furet. Paris: Hachette, 1989, 13–31.

———. *Penser la Révolution française.* Paris: Gallimard, 1978.

Gauthier, Florence. "Universal Rights and National Interest in the French Revolution." In *Nationalism in the Age of the French Revolution.* Edited by Otto Dann and John Dinwiddy, 27–37. London: Hambledon, 1988.

Gellner, Ernest. "The Importance of Being Modular." In *Civil Society: Theory, History, Comparison.* Edited by John Hall, 32–55. Cambridge: Polity, 1995.

Godechot, Jacques. "Les Variations de la politique française à l'égard des pays occupés 1792–1815." *Occupants/Occupés 1792–1815*, 15–41. Brussels: University of Brussels, 1969.

———. "Nation, patrie, nationalisme et patriotisme en France au XVIII siècle," *Annales historiques de la Révolution française* 43 (1971): 481–501.

———. "The New Concept of the Nation and its Diffusion in Europe." In *Nationalism in the Age of the French Revolution.* Edited by Otto Dann and John Dinwiddy, 13–26. London: Hambledon, 1988.

———. *La Grande Nation: L'expansion révolutionnaire de la France dans le monde de 1789 à 1799.* 2nd ed. Paris: Aubier Montaigne, 1983.

Goyard-Fabre, Simone. Présentation to *Abbé de Saint-Pierre, Projet pour rendre la paix perpétuelle en Europe*, 39–122. Paris: Garnier, 1981.

Greenfeld, Liah. *Nationalism: Five Roads to Modernity.* Cambridge, MA: Harvard University Press, 1992.

Groethuysen, Bernard. *Philosophie de la Révolution Française.* Paris: Gallimard, 1956.

Guiomar, Jean-Yves Guiomar. *L'idéologie nationale: Nation, Représentation, Propriété.* Paris: Éditions Champ libre, 1974.

Habermas, Jürgen. "The European Nation-state—Its Achievements and Its Limits. On the Past and Future of Sovereignty and Citizenship." In *Mapping the Nation.* Edited by Gopal Balakrishnan, 281–94. London: Verso, 1996.

Hall, John. "In Search of Civil Society." In *Civil Society: Theory, History, Comparison*. Edited by John Hall, 1–31. Cambridge: Polity, 1995.

Hampson, Norman. "The Idea of the Nation in Revolutionary France." In *Reshaping France: Town, country and region during the French Revolution*. Edited by Alan Forrest and Peter Jones. Manchester: Manchester University Press, 1991.

———. *Will & Circumstance: Montesquieu, Rousseau, and the French Revolution*. London: Duckworth, 1983.

Hannum, Hurst. *Autonomy, Sovereignty, and Self-Determination: The Accommodation of Conflicting Rights*. Philadelphia: University of Pennsylvania Press, 1990.

Hayes, C. J. H. *France, a Nation of Patriots*. New York: Columbia University Press, 1930.

———. *The Historical Evolution of Modern Nationalism*. London: Macmillan, 1948.

Higonnet, Patrice. *Goodness Beyond Virtue: Jacobins During the French Revolution*. Cambridge, MA: Harvard University Press, 1998.

———. *Sister Republics: The Origins of French and American Republicanism*. Cambridge, MA: Harvard University Press, 1988.

Hinsley, F. H. *Sovereignty*. London: C. A. Watts & Co., 1966.

Hobsbawm, E. J. *Nations and Nationalism since 1780: Programme, myth, reality*. Cambridge: Cambridge University Press, 1990.

Hont, Istvan. "The Permanent Crisis of a Divided Mankind: 'Contemporary Crisis of the Nation State' in Historical Perspective." *Political Studies* 42 (1994): 166–231.

Hunt, Lynn. "The National Assembly." In *The French Revolution and the Creation of Modern Political Culture*. Vol. 1. Edited by Keith Michael Baker, 403–15. Oxford: Pergamon, 1987.

Hyslop, Beatrice Fry. *French nationalism in 1789, according to the General Cahiers*. New York: Columbia University Press, 1934.

James, Alan. *Sovereign Statehood: The Basis of International Society*. London: Allen & Unwin, 1986.

Jaume, Lucien. *Le discours jacobin et la démocratie*. Paris: Fayard, 1989.

Jones, Colin. *The Great Nation: France from Louis XV to Napoleon*. New York: Columbia University Press, 2002.

Kamenka, Eugene. "Political Nationalism—The Evolution of the Idea." In *Nationalism: The Nature and Evolution of an Idea*. Edited by Eugene Kamenka, 2–20. London: Edward Arnold, 1976.

———. "Revolutionary Ideology and 'The Great French Revolution of 1789–?.'" In *The Permanent Revolution: The French Revolution and its Legacy*. Edited by Geoffrey Best, 75–99. London: Fontana, 1988.

Kedourie, Elie. *Nationalism*. London: Hutchinson, 1961.

Keitner, Chimène I. "National Self-Determination in Historical Perspective: The Legacy of the French Revolution for Today's Debates." *International Studies Review* 2 (2000): 3–26.

———. "Nationalism and War in the French Revolution." *The ASEN Bulletin*, no. 17 (Summer 1999): 12–19.

———. "The 'False Promise' of Civic Nationalism." *Millennium: Journal of International Studies* 28 (1999): 341–51.

Keohan, Nannerl O. *Philosophy and the State in France: The Renaissance to the Enlightenment*. Princeton, NJ: Princeton University Press, 1980.

Kohn, Hans. *Prelude to Nation-States: The French and German Experience 1789–1815*. Princeton, NJ: D. van Nostrand, 1967.

———. *The Idea of Nationalism: A study in its origins and background*. New York: Macmillan, 1944.

Koht, Halvdan. "L'esprit national et l'idée de la souveraineté du peuple." *Bulletin of the International Committee of Historical Sciences* 7 (October 1929): 217–24.

Kymlicka, Will. "The Value of Cultural Membership." In *Liberalism, Community, and Culture*. By Will Kymlicka, 162–81. Oxford: Clarendon, 1991.

Linklater, Andrew. *Men and Citizens in the Theory of International Relations*. 2nd ed. London: Macmillan, 1990.

Margalit, Avishai, and Joseph Raz. "Self-Determination." In *Ethics in the Public Domain: Essays in the morality of law and politics*. By Joseph Raz, 125–45. Oxford: Clarendon, 1995.

Martin, Kingsley. *French Liberal Thought in the Eighteenth Century*. Edited by J. P. Mayer. London: Phoenix House, 1962. First published in 1929 by Little, Brown and Co.

Martin, Marie-Madeleine. *The Making of France: The Origins and Development of the Idea of National Unity*. Translated by Barbara and Robert North. London: Eyre and Spottiswoode, 1951.

Mason, John Hope. "Individuals in Society: Rousseau's Republican vision." *History of Political Thought* 10 (1989): 89–112.

Mathiez, Albert. "Pacifisme et Nationalisme au XVIIIe siècle." *Annales historiques de la Révolution française*, no. 73 (January–February 1936): 1–17.

———. *La révolution et les étrangers: cosmopolitisme et défense nationale*. Paris: La Renaissance du livre, 1918.

Mayall, James. "1789 and the liberal theory of international society." *Review of International Studies* 15, no. 4 (October 1989): 297–307.

———. *Nationalism and International Society*. Cambridge, Cambridge University Press, 1990.

Miller, David. *On Nationality.* Oxford: Clarendon, 1995.

Nicolet, Claude. *L'idée républicaine en France (1789–1924), Essai d'histoire critique.* Paris: Gallimard, 1982.

Nielsen, Kai. "Liberal Nationalism and Secession." In *National Self-Determination and Secession.* Edited by Margaret Moore, 103–33. Oxford: Oxford University Press, 1998.

Noiriel, Gérard. "L'identification des citoyens. Naissance de l'état civil républicain." *Genèses* 13 (Autumn 1993): 2–28.

Norman, Wayne. "Theorizing Nationalism (Normatively): The First Steps." In *Theorizing Nationalism.* Edited by Ronald Beiner, 51–65. Albany: State University of New York Press, 1999.

Nys, Ernest. "La Révolution française et le droit international." In *Études de droit international et de droit politique.* By Ernest Nys, 318–406. Brussels: Alfred Castaigne, 1896.

O'Brien, Connor Cruise. "Nationalism and the French Revolution." In *The Permanent Revolution: The French Revolution and its Legacy.* Edited by Geoffrey Best, 17–48. London: Fontana, 1988.

Ozouf, Mona. *La fête révolutionnaire.* Paris: Gallimard, 1976.

Palmer, R. R. "The national idea in France before the Revolution." *Journal of the History of Ideas* 1 (1940): 95–111.

Pasquino, Pasquale. "Le Concept de Nation et les Fondements Du Droit Public de la Révolution: Sieyès." In *L'héritage de la Révolution française.* Edited by François Furet, 309–33. Paris: Hachette, 1989.

———. *Sieyes et l'invention de la constitution en France.* Paris: Editions Odile Jacob, 1998.

Raz, Joseph. "Multiculturalism: A Liberal Perspective." *Dissent* (Winter 1994): 67–79.

Roberts, Adam. "Communal Conflict as a Challenge to International Organisation: The Case of Former Yugoslavia." *Review of International Studies* 21, no. 4 (October 1995): 389–410.

Ruyssen, Théodore. *Les sources doctrinales de l'Internationalisme. Tome 3e: De la Révolution française au milieu du XIXe siècle.* Paris: Presses Universitaires de France, 1961.

Sagnac, Philippe. "L'Idée de la Nation en France (1788–1789)." *Revue d'histoire politique et constitutionnelle* 1, no. 1 (1937): 158–63.

———. "Les grands courants d'idées et de sentiments en France vers 1789." *Revue d'histoire politique et constitutionnelle* 2, no. 3 (1938): 317–41.

Sahlins, Peter. *Boundaries: The Making of France and Spain in the Pyrenees.* Berkeley and Los Angeles, CA: University of California Press, 1989.

Sauvigny, G. Bertier de. "Liberalism, Nationalism and Socialism: The Birth of Three Words." *The Review of Politics* 32 (April 1970): 155–61.

Schafer, Boyd. "Bourgeois Nationalism in the Pamphlets on the Eve of the French Revolution." *Journal of Modern History* 10, no. 1 (1938): 31–50.

Schama, Simon. *Citizens: A Chronicle of the French Revolution.* New York: Viking, 1989.

Schnapper, Dominique. *La Communauté des Citoyens: sur l'idée moderne de nation.* Paris: Gallimard, 1994.

Scruton, Roger. "The First Person Plural." In *Theorizing Nationalism.* Edited by Ronald Beiner, 279–93. Albany: State University of New York Press, 1999.

Shklar, Judith. *Men and Citizens: A Study of Rousseau's Social Theory.* Cambridge: Cambridge University Press, 1969.

Singer, Brian. *Society, Theory, and the French Revolution: Studies in the Revolutionary Imaginary.* London: Macmillan, 1986.

Smith, Anthony. *National Identity.* London: Penguin, 1991.

Smith, Anthony, and John Hutchinson, eds. *Nationalism.* Oxford: Oxford University Press, 1994.

Sorel, Albert. *L'Europe et la Révolution française. Première partie: Les moeurs politiques et les traditions*, 3rd ed. Paris: Librairie Plon, 1893.

———. *L'Europe et la Révolution française. Deuxième partie: La Chute de la royauté*, 3rd ed. Paris: Librairie Plon, 1895.

Stone, Bailey. *Reinterpreting the French Revolution: A Global-Historical Perspective.* Cambridge: Cambridge University Press, 2002.

Suratteau, Jean-René. "La Nation de 1789 à 1799. Sens, idéologie, évolution de l'emploi du mot." In *Région-Nation-Europe: unité et diversité des processus sociaux et culturels de la Révolution française.* Edited by Marita Gilli, 687–92. Paris: Diffusion Les Belles Lettres, 1988.

———. *L'idée nationale de la révolution à nos jours.* Paris: Presses Universitaires de France, 1972.

Tamir, Yael. *Liberal Nationalism.* Princeton, NJ: Princeton University Press, 1993.

Taylor, Charles. "Quel principle d'identité collective." In *L'Europe au soir du siècle: Identité et démocratie.* Edited by Jacques Lenoble and Nicole Dewandre, 59–66. Paris: Éditions Esprit, 1992.

Van Kley, Dale. "From the Lessons of French History to Truths for All Times and All People: The Historical Origins of an Anti-Historical Declaration." In *The French Idea of Freedom: The Old Regime and the Declaration of Rights of 1789.* Edited by Dale Van Kley, 72–113. Stanford, CA: Stanford University Press, 1994.

Viroli, Maurizio. *For Love of Country: Essays on Patriotism and Nationalism*. Oxford: Clarendon, 1995.

Wahnich, Sophie. "Les Républiques-Soeurs, Débat Théorique et Réalité Historique, Conquêtes et Reconquêtes d'Identité Républicaine." *Annales Historiques de la Révolution Française*, no. 2 (1994): 165–77.

Waldron, Jeremy. "Minority Cultures and the Cosmopolitan Alternative." In *The Rights of Minority Cultures*. Edited by Will Kymlicka, 93–119. Oxford: Oxford University Press, 1995.

Walker, R. B. J. *Inside/Outside: International Relations as Political Theory*. Cambridge: Cambridge University Press, 1993.

Walt, Stephen. *Revolution and War*. Ithaca and London: Cornell, 1996.

Walzer, Michael. "Pluralism: A Political Perspective." In *The Rights of Minority Cultures*. Edited by Will Kymlicka, 139–54. Oxford: Oxford University Press, 1995.

———. "The Moral Standing of States: A Response to Four Critics." In *International Ethics*. Edited by Charles Beitz, Marshall Cohen, Thomas Scanlon, and A. John Simmons, 217–36. Princeton, NJ: Princeton University Press, 1985.

———. "The Reform of the International System." In *Studies of War and Peace*. Edited by Øyvind Østerud, 227–39. Oslo: Norwegian University Press, 1986.

Welsh, Jennifer M. *Edmund Burke and International Relations: The Commonwealth of Europe and the Crusade against the French Revolution*. London: Macmillan, 1995.

Wieviorka, Michel. "Is multinationalism the solution?" *Ethnic and Racial Studies* 21, no. 5 (September 1998): 881–910.

Wight, Martin. "International Legitimacy." In *Systems of States*. Edited by Hedley Bull, 153–73. Bristol and Swansea: Leicester University Press, 1977.

———. "Why is there no International Theory?" In *Diplomatic Investigations: Essays in the Theory of International Politics*. Edited by Herbert Butterfield and Martin Wight, 17–34. London: George Allen and Unwin, 1966.

———. *International Theory: The Three Traditions*. Edited by Gabrielle Wight and Brian Porter. London: Leicester University Press, 1991.

Yack, Bernard. "The Myth of the Civic Nation." In *Theorizing Nationalism*. Edited by Ronald Beiner, 103–18. Albany: State University of New York Press, 1999.

Young, Crawford. "The Dialectics of Cultural Pluralism: The Nation-State at Bay?" In *The Rising Tide of Cultural Pluralism*. Edited by Crawford Young, 3–35. Wisconsin and London: University of Wisconsin Press, 1993.

Index